The Occupation of Alcatraz Island

.\\.\\.\\.

The Occupation of Alcatraz Island

/.\.\.\

Indian Self-Determination
and the Rise of Indian Activism

TROY R. JOHNSON

FOREWORD BY DONALD L. FIXICO

University of Illinois Press
URBANA AND CHICAGO

Library of Congress Cataloging-in-Publication Data
Johnson, Troy R.
The occupation of Alcatraz Island :
Indian self-determination and the rise of Indian activism /
Troy R. Johnson ; foreword by Donald L. Fixico.
p.   cm.
Includes bibliographical references (p.) and index.
ISBN 0-252-02254-8 (cloth : acid-free paper) —
ISBN 0-252-06585-9 (pbk. : acid-free paper)
1. Alcatraz Island (Calif.)—History—Indian occupation,
1969–1971. 2. Indians of North America—Government
relations. 3. Indians of North America—Politics and
government. 4. Alcatraz Island (Calif.)—History. I. Title.
E78.C15J612   1996
979.4'61—dc20   96-4452
CIP

This book is dedicated to my wife, Lorene,
who patiently waited as I completed my Ph.D.
and the research and writing of this book.
Yes dear, it's finally done.

Contents

.\.\.\.\

Acknowledgments

/\\.\\/\\.\\/\\

I would like to express my appreciation to all of the people who participated in the process of bringing this book to completion. The Institute of American Cultures at the University of California at Los Angeles provided field research funding and a predoctoral fellowship. Special thanks is given to the archivists at the National Archives in Washington, D.C., and San Bruno, California; the Nixon Presidential Archives in Alexandria, Virginia; and the Pacifica Radio Archives in North Hollywood, California. Many librarians were especially helpful, particularly those at the various locations of the Doris Duke Oral History Project, the University Research Library at the University of California, and Vee Salabiye of the American Indian Studies Library at the University of California at Los Angeles. I would like to acknowledge Susan Lobo, who introduced me to the extensive files of the Community History Project at the Intertribal Friendship House in Oakland, California, and Duane Champagne, director of the American Indian Studies Center at the University of California at Los Angeles, my friend and mentor, who acted as sounding board and critic. I would also like to thank my photographer friend Ilka Hartmann for her assistance and constant encouragement.

Most of all I would like to thank all of the American Indian people who opened their homes, their hearts, and their personal archives and memories to relive the days of Alcatraz. Without exception I found the people who participated in the occupation to be enthusiastic and excited about the opportunity to share their experiences and memories of those exhilarating days. My fondest memory is of a cold snowy December day with LaNada Boyer in her home on the Fort Hall Indian Reservation in Idaho, where we shared moosemeat stew while she told the story of Alcatraz. Thank you, LaNada, and thank you everyone associated with this wonderful experience.

Foreword

/\\.\\.\\/\\

DONALD L. FIXICO

Although Native Americans have been a popular topic among journalists for many years, only recently have scholars turned to serious studies of their cultures since World War II. Troy Johnson's work is one of the first to address the Indian militancy of the late 1960s and early 1970s. In his focus upon the 1969 occupation of Alcatraz Island, he makes it clear that this was one of the cornerstone events in modern Indian history. By using policy history, social history, political history, ethnohistory, and oral history, Johnson places the occupation within both Native American culture and the societal upheavals of the period.

For American Indians, the 1950s and 1960s provided a pivotal shift in their societies as the government relocation program was established to clear out the reservations. Indians volunteered or were coaxed into moving to cities across the United States until two-thirds of them were living in urban environments. Bewildered by their new surroundings, many turned to the Bureau of Indian Affairs for help but were disappointed by broken promises. Cut off from their traditional cultures, Native Americans adapted by identifying themselves with American Indians as a whole instead of limiting themselves to tribal ties. As they began thinking of themselves in this new light, pan-Indian organizations developed and Native Americans started working together.

The occupation of Alcatraz was led by Indians in these organizations and grew out of the social movements and political turmoil of a troubled decade. Shattered dreams and recognition of continuing injustice with little hope for the future spurred protests, particularly by young people, against the "establishment." As other groups spoke out about their identities and their equal rights, the time was right for Native Americans to be heard. Years of anger and frustration at their endless struggle with the federal bureaucracy led to the occupation that would launch a new American Indian history of self-determination and identity that came directly from the Indians themselves.

In this sensitive treatment of the Alcatraz occupation, Johnson gives careful consideration to its complexity and analyzes its full scope. Rather than viewing the Alcatraz takeover from a single point of view, he lets us hear all sides of the story to enable us to fully understand and appreciate the actions of everyone involved. Johnson provides us with media portrayals of the occupiers and public opinion about the demonstration. We hear the planning of the takeover and how difficult it was to convince others of its importance and to execute it. As the occupation continues, we hear stories of discontent, hardship, dissension, and public relations. At the same time Johnson gives us insight into attitudes of government officials, the grinding of government bureaucracy, and domestic policy strategies through numerous documents and interviews.

More important is that Johnson has made sure that Native American voices are part of this study. Too often scholars write about American Indians without including their viewpoints or even consulting them. The many interviews with Indians breathe life into Alcatraz again and do not let us forget the frustration and anger felt by Native Americans during these difficult years. Unlike most books about them, Indians will see themselves in this one.

Troy Johnson's intricate and complete history of the occupation of Alcatraz takes us inside a turbulent time in America's history, inside Indian activism, and inside an Indian community. By offering us many perspectives, he shows us how natural was its outgrowth from the social protests of the 1960s, how vital the occupation was to the impetus of Indian activism and self-determination, and how important it remains as a symbol for Native Americans today.

Introduction

/\.\/\.\/\

In the early morning hours of November 20, 1969, eighty-nine American Indians landed on Alcatraz Island in San Francisco Bay. Identifying themselves as "Indians of All Tribes," these young urban college students claimed the island by "right of discovery," demanded clear title to Alcatraz Island, and called for the establishment of an American Indian university, an American Indian cultural center, and an American Indian museum. Their nineteen-month occupation, a culmination of two previous attempts at seizing the island, ushered in a new era of American Indian activism that continued well into the mid-1970s and kept national attention focused on Indian rights and grievances. For the Indians, Alcatraz Island would serve as a symbol of everything they had been promised but never received from the government, their lost land, and government waste. This symbolism proved strong because Native Americans remembered the importance of this island to their people.

Indigenous peoples had been traveling to Alcatraz Island for 10,000 to 20,000 years before Europeans ever entered the San Francisco Bay Area. Although much of the oral history of these peoples has been lost, it is clear that Alcatraz was at once used, feared, and revered. Jack Forbes asserts that "the Muwekma Indian people of San Francisco and the Hukueko of Marin County were, in the old days, frequent visitors to all of the islands in San Francisco Bay."[1] Forbes suggests that Alcatraz was most likely utilized by these peoples as a camping spot and an area for gathering bird eggs and sealife. In addition many of their neighbors, including the Coast Miwok, Pomo, Wintun, Wappo, Maidu, and Northern Yokut, may also have used the rocky, barren island as a way station when navigating the bay in their balsa canoes.

Fear perhaps contributed to the virtual shunning of the island by an indigenous people later named the Ohlone. They used the island as a place of isolation or ostracism for those who had violated laws or taboos and only under the most unusual circumstances, such as being caught in a boat on the bay waters in a sudden storm, did they voluntarily land on Alcatraz. Some Native Americans today are familiar with the formidable reputation of this island among their ancestors and still fear the "curse" of Alcatraz.[2] In contrast, the Pit River Indians, indigenous to Northern California, consider Alcatraz instead to be a holy place, calling it "Allisti Ti-Tanin-Wiji," meaning "Rock, Rainbow," or "Diamond Island."

This island that had played a significant role in the lives of the indigenous people of the area soon proved important to Europeans as well. The first recorded European sighting of the islands within San Francisco Bay came during the Spanish mission effort by Father Junípero Serra underway in the late eighteenth century. Lieutenant Manuel de Ayala may have been the first European to actually set foot on Alcatraz Island. In August 1775, Ayala sailed his ship *San Carlos* into San Francisco Bay to survey the area to better secure the Spanish claim to the land. On August 12 he set out in a small boat fashioned by his carpenters "in the manner learned from the Coast Indians."[3] Ayala named the the island Isla de los Alcatrazes (Island of the Pelicans) because of the large number of pelicans that covered the island.

Following Ayala's mapping of the Bay Area, Alcatraz remained undisturbed by Europeans until the 1850s. In 1850 President Millard Fillmore issued an order reserving Alcatraz and other selected parcels of land for federal use. The U.S. Army began plans to develop Alcatraz Island as a defense installation. International events soon turned Alcatraz into a strategic territory. In 1853, Commodore Matthew Calbraith Perry opened Japan to trade with the west, and both Britain and the United States were looking toward the Hawaiian Islands for future ownership; by 1854 it was considered likely that the Sandwich Islands would be annexed by the United States. War was being fought in the Crimea in 1853–54, and Spanish authorities seized the U.S. merchant vessel *Black Warrior* in Havana, Cuba. Because of the international tension, Congress passed an appropriation for coastal defenses in March 1855.

On December 30, 1859, Company H, Third Artillery, U.S. Army, under the command of Captain Joseph Stewart, occupied Alcatraz and began seventy-seven years of military administration. While additional batteries and fortifications were being planned, the onset of the Civil War stopped all construction on the island and the government turned to plans for housing arms and ammunition "for better safe-keeping against any secessionists' raids."[4] In addition to weapons between ten and twenty prisoners and deserters were housed at a time in a small military jail between 1864 and 1865. The Spanish-American War brought additional prisoners. The army used the facilities to hold the large number of court-martialed soldiers returning from the Philippines.

In addition to the general and military prisoners, civilians, among them many Native Americans, were also incarcerated on the island. The first known Indian prisoner was called Paiute Tom, who was sent to Alcatraz from Camp McDermit, Nebraska, arriving on June 5, 1873. He was fatally wounded two days later by an Alcatraz guard. Tom was followed by Guiwhatanava, a Muallpai Apache. Guiwhatanava arrived on May 18, 1873, and was released to his tribe on October 25, 1873.[5] Barancho and Sloluck, two Modoc, were imprisoned as a result of their participation in the murder of General Edward R. S. Canby during the California Modoc Wars in 1873. The *San Francisco Chronicle* claimed the men "appear[ed] to be well contented and to rather enjoy being fed and clothed and with a roof over their heads."[6] Barancho and Sloluck were joined by Natchez, a Paiute Indian and brother of Sarah Winnemucca, in early 1874. Little Captain and Pete, two other Paiute, followed Natchez in July 1881 and April 1882. Barancho died in the prison on May 18, 1875, while Sloluck served his sentence and was released in February 1878.[7]

In July 1884, General George Crook was involved in the attempt to subdue the Chiricahua Apaches in Arizona. Broken promises on the part of Crook and the confinement of reservation life led young Apache chief Ka-e-ten-na to escape from government control. Captured, tried, and sentenced, Ka-e-ten-na was sent to Alcatraz in July 1884, where he remained until March 1886.[8] Skolaskin, a Sanpoil from the Pacific Northwest, was placed on Alcatraz in November 1889 for safekeeping after having escaped from Fort Huachuca, Arizona, earlier in the year. Skolaskin remained on Alcatraz from 1889 to 1892.

The largest single group of Indian prisoners was sentenced to confinement on Alcatraz in January 1895. Nineteen Moqui Hopi had rejected a government-enforced policy requiring the abandonment of traditional religious and cultural practices and had opposed the U.S.

policy forcing Indian children to attend government schools. They remained on the island until September 1895.[9] Indian people continued to be confined in the disciplinary barracks through the 1800s and the early 1900s.

In 1907, Alcatraz Island was formally dropped as an army post and renamed Pacific Branch, United States Military Prison, under the authority of the adjutant general of the army. A building was erected in 1910 to hold approximately 400 prisoners until the new permanent facility was completed on February 6, 1912. In June 1915, the name was changed to Pacific Branch, United States Disciplinary Barracks.[10] The island remained under the control of the U.S. Army until 1934 when the attorney general took over and ordered the establishment of a federal penitentiary.

Once new security upgrades were installed and tighter regulations were instated, Alcatraz began to receive prisoners from Leavenworth, Leavenworth Annex, Atlanta, Northeastern, and McNeil Island penitentiaries. Its average population of 263 was complemented by additional prisoners from the Federal Hospital for Defective Delinquents in Springfield, Missouri, prison camps, and federal reformatories, correctional camps, and jails. In 1961, Attorney General Robert F. Kennedy announced plans to construct a new maximum security institution in Marion, Illinois. In light of the new construction and the expense of maintaining the facility on Alcatraz, the government elected to close Alcatraz's maximum security facility. On March 21, 1963, the U.S. penitentiary on Alcatraz Island ceased operations and was declared surplus property. The remaining prisoners were taken from the island and reassigned to other penal institutions.[11]

Following the closure of the penitentiary, only a lighthouse, the first on the Pacific Coast, and a fog signal remained functional. An acting warden, Richard J. Willard, and a caretaker, A. L. Aylworth, were assigned to care for the abandoned correctional facility. Aylworth was the only person present on the island when Indians first reclaimed the island on March 27, 1964. Alcatraz was occupied by American Indian activists again on November 9 and November 20, 1969. Although the occupations were carried out primarily by urban Indians and Indian college students who reflected the Bay Area ethos of unrest, only the November 20 occupation captured national attention and brought the concerns of Indian people into stark focus. This last occupation became the rallying point for Indian people who had been searching for the means to express their outrage at social injustices forced upon them by what they perceived as an uncaring society and an unyielding government.

Notes

1. Forbes, "Alcatraz: What Its Seizure Means," 44–45. For an extensive listing and mapping of the tribelets and village locations in the Bay Area, see Milliken, "An Ethnohistory," map 4, p. 139.

2. Costo, "Alcatraz," 7–8.

3. Ibid.

4. Quoted in Thompson, *The Rock*, 87.

5. Odier, *The Rock*, 227.

6. "The Rock Was for the Birds," *San Francisco Chronicle*, June 30, 1969.

7. Quoted in Thompson, *The Rock*, 296.

8. Alcatraz Post Returns; Alcatraz Register of Prisoners; Crook, *Resumé*, 15, quoted in Thompson, *The Rock*, 297; see also Bourke, *On the Border*, 459–60.

9. Whitley, *Bacavi*, 37–38, 49–51; see also Thompson, *The Rock*, 298–99.

10. Thompson, *The Rock*, 245, 260.

11. Twenty-seven convicts were incarcerated on the island at the time of closure. For a comprehensive description of prison life, see Thompson, *The Rock*, 351–452, which includes prisoners' offenses, riots, strikes, and escapes.

1

The Relocation Program, Urban Indians, and Alcatraz

⋀⋁⋀⋁⋀

Assimilation and relocation had long been the U.S. government's ways of dealing with Native Americans. In the nineteenth century, when the government was first intent upon western expansion, Indians were moved from their ancestral homelands and settled on reservations. By the 1950s, however, the government focused upon breaking up those reservations so that even more land would be available. Assimilation of Indians into mainstream society became the goal of both those bent on further westward expansion and those who considered themselves supporters of the Indian people. Each reasoned that assimilation would benefit Native Americans by eliminating reservations, thereby breaking up remaining tribal structures, beliefs, cultures, and religious practices that hampered success in mainstream society.

Education became a central issue for assimilationists because education was a way to break Indians and teach them white culture. As the first superintendent of the Carlisle Indian Boarding School in Pennsylvania, U.S. Army captain Richard H. Pratt held that "the only good Indian is a dead one. . . . All the Indian there is in the race should be dead. Kill the Indian in him and save the man."[1] By governing with this philosophy, whites made life at the boarding schools physically cruel and culturally destructive. Children were not allowed to speak their traditional languages, wear traditional clothing, practice traditional religions, or wear their hair in traditional manners. They were kept at boarding school for up to eight years, during which time they rarely, if ever, saw their parents, relatives, or friends. Anything Indian was uncompromisingly prohibited.[2]

The real Termination Era for Indian peoples was not begun by education, however, but was rather ushered in by House Concurrent Resolution 108 in August 1953. When introduced to Congress, the resolution was not considered controversial and was placed on the unanimous-consent calendar. No member of Congress spoke against it, and with only minor modification it was passed into law. As a result, approximately 109 tribes and bands were terminated. A minimum of 1,362,155 acres of land and 11,466 individuals were affected. The resolution was seen by many as a reasonable action even though the bulk of Indian testimony was overwhelmingly in opposition. Despite government promises of relocation to major urban areas, vocational training, financial assistance during training, job placement programs, and adequate housing, Indian people recognized House Concurrent Resolution 108 as an attempt to acquire what little Indian land remained and assimilate Indian peoples into mainstream culture. Their arguments against the resolution focused on financial concerns, loss of rights and privileges established by treaties or by federal law, concern about tribal preparedness for termination, procedural issues, and Indian relationships to traditional lands. Termination ended the special federal-tribal relationship almost completely and transferred responsibility and power for the majority of terminated tribes and people from the federal government to individual states.[3]

House Concurrent Resolution 108 was not the only, nor the first, legislative action to transfer responsibility for the maintenance of law and order on Indian reservations to state and local authorities. By 1952, such legislation already applied to all Indian reservations in Kansas and New York, the Devil's Lake Reservation in North Dakota, the Sac and Fox Reservation in Iowa, and the Agua Caliente Reservation in California. With the passage of Public Law 280 in 1953, nearly all Indian lands in California, Minnesota, Nebraska, Oregon, and Wisconsin were placed under state criminal jurisdiction.[4]

This was also not the first attempt by the government to relocate Indian peoples into urban areas. The first was a regional program restricted primarily to the southwestern United States known as the Labor Recruitment and Welfare program for the Navajo and Hopi Reservations. In 1946, the Bureau of Indian Affairs (BIA) began a five-year experimental vocational education program in which Navajo and Hopi youth were sent to Sherman Institute in Riverside, California, and other locations throughout the country for special education and training. The intent of the program was to relieve the pressure on reservation resources by relocating Indians to urban areas such as Denver, Los Angeles, Phoenix, and Salt Lake City.

The Navajo-Hopi work program was similar to another employment experiment in the early 1930s in which Acoma and Laguna pueblos in New Mexico agreed that the Sante Fe Railroad Company would be given right-of-way through tribal lands in return for jobs for the Pueblo peoples. The BIA and the Sante Fe Railroad Company placed Acoma and Laguna people all along the rail lines from New Mexico to the San Francisco Bay Area in worker's villages that became known as Indian railroad "colonies." The colonies were situated within railroad rights-of-way in towns such as Winslow, Arizona; Barstow, California; and Richmond, California. Following the example set by other employees, Indian workers often moved their families with them along the rail system. The success of these two work experiments influenced the BIA in the design of a program to encourage more Indian people to move away from reservations.[5]

In 1952 the BIA established a national relocation assistance program for family heads to seek employment off their reservations. The program was expanded in 1956 and given additional impetus by Public Law 84–959, which authorized the BIA to provide Native Americans between the ages of eighteen and thirty-five with vocational, on-the-job, and apprenticeship training. Renamed the Employment Assistance Program in 1962, its purview was expanded to include vocational training and placement on or near reservations, as well as in certain metropolitan areas. Those who chose to relocate under this program were provided with transportation to one of eight urban areas and promised vocational training, assistance in finding employment, and other services to adjust to city life.[6]

Clearly, attempts to urbanize American Indians had been occurring on a small scale for many years and for many different reasons. The institution of the official relocation program proved to be the beginning of the largest organized effort by the U.S. government to systematically relocate American Indian individuals and families to fast-growing metropolitan regions designated as relocation centers. In total more than 100,000 Native Americans were moved to Los Angeles, Phoenix, Denver, Dallas, Cleveland, and San Francisco.[7]

As a result of the government relocation program, the Indian population of the San Francisco Bay Area grew to between 15,000 and 20,000 in 1964. Because of ambiguous ethnic classification criteria used in census reporting, however, estimates for this Indian population run as high as 40,000, of which approximately two-thirds were federal government relocatees from some one hundred different tribal groups. Others settled as a result of Indian boarding school placements and Sante Fe Railroad employment.[8]

Another group of Indian people in the Bay Area had served in the military during World War II. These veterans often brought their families with them. During World War II, 25,000 Indians served in the armed forces. Most had left the reservation for the first time in their lives to serve in the military and soon became accustomed to living with electricity, modern appliances, and hot and cold running water. Although they were taken for granted in non-Indian homes, these basic conveniences were rare or nonexistent on reservations. It was only natural that, once exposed to the comforts of modern life, veterans would want to establish a similar lifestyle for themselves and their families. Some veterans returned to their reservations after the war and then chose to move to an urban area. Others fled the cities only to return after meeting with disappointment on the reservation. Some Indian people wanted to see what was available in the cities that relatives had visited during their military service. Many others relocated to join military relatives who had moved to such urban areas as New York, San Diego, Los Angeles, and San Francisco.

Hope of employment proved to be a major impetus for relocation. Most reservations throughout the United States have historically been economically depressed areas where employment opportunities are often nonexistent and problems of health, housing, and education are endemic. For many Native Americans, relocation provided an opportunity to escape a life of helplessness and hopelessness. A study conducted by Congress and the BIA revealed that a sizable percentage of Indians wanted to leave their reservations and engage in employment other than traditional farming or raising livestock. Especially among younger Indians, particularly those with military backgrounds, there was a normal and growing urge to seek alternate employment.[9] Many of these people migrated to the Bay Area during the war to work in defense industries. A 1957 joint congressional and BIA study found that Indians were recruited as industrial workers in both government and private industries and were willing and capable employees.[10]

Once in urban areas Indians were employed in a wide range of unskilled, semiskilled, and skilled positions in both large and small industries and in service-related fields. The largest number of Indians worked at unskilled or semiskilled jobs but found steady employment difficult to obtain and maintain. Layoffs were common and hit unskilled workers particularly hard. Despite economic promises urban living often led to severe hardships and unemployment. Most relocated families lived in typical working-class housing, although many took advantage of low-rent housing developments. Most families moved at least three or four times after their arrival.

Because of their lifestyle and their frequent moves, Native Americans who relocated to the Bay Area were unable to form what would be recognized as an "Indian community."[11] No serious attempt was made by relocation officials to settle tribal members near one another. Indian people connected with each other only through chance meetings in trade schools, at the BIA office, in apartment corridors, in "Indian bars," in Indian community centers, and through social organizations. While persons related through ties of kinship and tribal affiliation visited each other, informal gatherings of a number of families of one tribe occurred infrequently. Cultural destruction and alienation were inevitable. With their familiar culture lost to them, Indians thus found themselves caught between two conflicting impulses: the economic necessity that caused them to leave the reservation and the cultural and emotional ties that made them want to return to the reservation.[12]

Calling the massive relocation from the reservations to the cities the most significant crisis to face Native Americans since the Indian wars of the late 1800s, the final report of the Native American Research Group issued in 1975 highlighted the concerns felt by the first urban Indian generation. According to the report, relocation presented Indian people with a series of difficult problems: How could they retain their identity under the pressures of separation, assimilation, and urbanization? How could Indian families socialize young Indians in both traditional and non-Indian ways? Would the city environment accomplish what four hundred years of European attempts had failed to do—eliminate Native Americans as a distinct people?[13] LaNada Boyer, a Shoshone/Bannock student at the University of California at Berkeley, admitted, "It's hard for me to go to college and eventually be assimilated and never be able to relate to the American Indian and their problems. I feel they're trying to make me into a white person. . . . There is little opportunity to learn anything about my own history: I've tried to take courses in history at the University. I can't find out anything about my own people."[14]

The Native American Research Group also reported that American Indians found urban relocation depersonalizing, confusing, frightening, and cruel. While generally appreciating the conveniences and diversions of urban life, Indian people found it difficult to tolerate traffic, crowds, the many buildings pushed together, and the ever present white man's laws. Relocation restrained them in ways difficult to comprehend. The frustration generated by the relocation program, particularly among young people, created an angry generation. They were angry because they had no voice, angry because they lacked a clear identity, and angry because the urban world was trying to constrain and control them.

The Indian relocatees often found themselves caught between government promises and reality. Indians who had been promised job training, employment, and housing assistance soon found themselves without skills, unemployed, and living in poverty in rat- and roach-infested housing. Unfortunately, Indian culture and heritage frequently exacerbated this situation. Economic difficulties frequently stemmed from a cultural emphasis on sharing and hospitality as well as a mind-set of living in the present. Many new city dwellers were unable or unwilling to budget their finances and were inexperienced at paying for urban services or fees, such as rent, utilities, transportation, and city taxes. Many Native Americans had difficulty relating to community agencies because of their long-standing apprehension in dealing with government agencies and non-Indian people. Traditionally valued personality characteristics such as noncompetitiveness, passivity, and withdrawal in the face of unpleasant situations were often unfamiliar traits in mainstream culture. Other values turned Native Americans into outcasts. Speaking about mainstream culture's attraction to wealth and disregard for natural resources, Al Elgin, director of the Intertribal Friendship House in Oakland, remarked, "If you don't measure up to these materialistic values, then you're nothing—you don't belong."[15] Excessive alcohol consumption also became a problem. Seen as a means to alleviate anxiety, drunkenness led to marital conflict, loss of jobs and money, and difficulties with law enforcement agencies.[16]

In a 1970 interview, John Trudell, a Sioux from Nebraska, characterized San Francisco as a typical urban relocation city. Trudell presented a desperate picture of Indian life punctuated by bars filled with drunk Indians. Relocation had done nothing for them. The *San Francisco Examiner* similarly documented the "uncounted and mostly unknown, who have been so wasted by the smashing of their culture and the crush of the city that they wander in alcoholic sleepwalks through the streets of San Francisco."[17] Trudell focused on the root cause of the problem: "You just can't take a people and keep them uneducated and give them nothing—for example most of their early life, and just send them to a city and say here, here is a job doing this and then cut you loose. I think I would just as soon stay on the reservation, and be poor as to move to a city on relocation and have to live in a ghetto area, and that is exactly where they put us."[18] Richard McKenzie, a Sioux instrumental in the 1964 occupation of Alcatraz and involved in the urban Indian unrest of 1969, remarked that many Indians, "because they have been sent from the reservation with lack of training, information, and money . . . would be victims of the hardships and loneliness of the disillusioned Indian in the city."[19]

Lehman Brightman, president of United Native Americans in 1968, vented the frustration felt by many urban Indians: "So the politicians don't have to give a damn about us. They can flood Indian land from now to doomsday and nobody's going to give a damn but American Indians." Brightman, a Sioux, listed the horrors of his people's condition: unemployment at 70 to 80 percent; average income in 1966 at $1,200 per year; death from tuberculosis at seven to eight times the non-Indian rate; infant mortality at double the rate for whites; one-fifth of Indian deaths the result of preventable diseases; life expectancy at fifteen to twenty years shorter than the national average; suicide rate at one hundred times the national average; 90 percent of housing on reservations was substandard; a tremendous rate of alcoholism stemming from the frustrations of their condition. What was needed, claimed Boyer, was "a university of our own with Indian teachers who understand the problems we're going through."[20]

Many relocatees, discouraged, disillusioned, and with no other place to turn, returned to their reservations. No exact number is available for those who abandoned urban life, but an anecdote captures their experience. In 1969 two Indian men in a Chicago bus station were overheard talking. One said to the other that the United States was planning to put a man on the moon. It seems that the United States had the technology to get the man on the moon, but lacked the technology to get him back. The other Indian man said that the solution was simple. All the government had to do was put an Indian in the rocket ship, tell him he was being relocated, and after he got to the moon, the Indian would find his own way home again.

Even despite the disadvantages, most Native Americans chose to remain in urban areas and hang onto their dream of a better life, a better future to pass on to their children, an easier life with running water, indoor toilets, automobiles, telephones, employment, educational opportunities, and material goods not obtainable on most reservations. Because they remained, the urbanization programs did not result in the elimination of Native Americans as a distinct people. Government officials had encouraged termination, assimilation, and relocation under the assumption that these programs would bring Native Americans into the mainstream of American society and thus destroy any remaining vestiges of Indian power.[21]

This strategy backfired, however, because it actually gave Native Americans an opportunity to meet each other and work together toward pan-Indianism. Pan-Indianism is a process whereby members of Indian cultures that had suffered collapse due to European pressures and tribal destruction formulated new survival techniques. Rather than becoming assimilated, Native Americans preserved their traditional cultural patterns through intertribal unity. Sometimes political, sometimes military, and sometimes religious, pan-Indian alliances allowed for a broader Indian identity and unity based on shared cultural beliefs and practices.[22]

In the Bay Area, a network of some forty active social, religious, and political Indian organizations emerged in 1964 to meet the needs of the new urban Indians. These social organizations became the means of expressing political and social concerns, including discrimination in employment, poor and crowded living conditions, failure of the federal government to live up to promises made during the relocation process, and an increase in police brutality toward Indian peoples.

Many of the groups formed by the Bay Area urban Indians, such as the Intertribal Friendship House, the Four Winds Club, the San Jose Dance Club, the American Indian Baptist Church, the Haskell Institute Alumni, the Navaho Club, the Chippewa Club, and the Tlingit-Haida Club, were both social and religious in nature. These clubs and service centers provided gathering places where urban Indians could come together to reinforce and maintain their traditional beliefs and teach their children to be proud of their Indian heritage and the Indian way of life. Social events and social clubs allowed individuals and groups to show their identities through traditional ceremonies and dress. Traditional dances were performed after dinners and on weekends and developed into regularly scheduled "powwows" in which all individuals gathered together. More importantly, these groups were extremely influential and served as the planning base for the 1969 occupation of Alcatraz Island. They also provided the Indian leadership with whom the U.S. government negotiated during the occupation period.

During this period the United Native Americans was formed as a way to awaken the Indian minority and promote and strengthen cultural pride in the Bay Area. The National Congress of American Indians, founded in 1944, represented a broad base of resistance among Indian leadership and fought strongly against House Concurrent Resolution 108.[23] In 1961, at the American Indian Chicago Conference, approximately five hundred Native Americans representing seventy tribes rejected termination and asserted the right of Indian communities to choose their own ways of life. The conference produced the first pan-Indian call for self-determination, a key element and driving force that would provide the staying power during the nineteen-month occupation of Alcatraz Island.

One of the most important elements in stimulating contemporary pan-Indianism was the expanding educational opportunities for Indian people. Among the new urban Indians, particularly those who enrolled in colleges and universities, a fierce loyalty to their individual tribes and to Indian people in general developed. As pride in ethnic and social identities increased during the fifties and sixties, these educated Indian people began to think in terms of civil rights generally, and Indian sovereign rights specifically. Hostility toward the U.S. government, as epitomized by the BIA, prompted a move toward Indian activism and a call for Indian self-determination.[24]

Notes

1. Albert and Albert, *The Sixties Papers*, 121.

2. Prucha, *Americanizing*, 260–66, quoted in Getches and Wilkinson, *Federal Indian Law*, 121.

3. Getches and Wilkinson, *Federal Indian Law*, 130–34. For an excellent analysis and discussion of the federal government programs of termination and relocation and the effect those programs had on Indian people see Fixico, *Termination and Relocation*, and Weibel-Orlando, *Indian Country, L.A.*

4. Washburn, *Red Man's Land*, 86–87.

5. Garcia, "'Home,'" 40–42.

6. Ibid., 45.

7. Ablon, "Relocated American Indians," 297.

8. Ibid.

9. U.S. Congress Subcommittee on Indian Affairs, *Indian Relocation*, 2. See also Neils, *Reservation to City*, 47.

10. Ibid.

11. Ablon, "Relocated American Indians," 297. Ablon defines an "Indian community" as an organized, visible body or persons who interrelate with regularity in socially meaningful ways (299).

12. Ibid. Ablon captured the essence of Indian relocation in the Bay Area in 1964, the year of the first occupation of Alcatraz Island. This article supplements material in her Ph.D. dissertation of 1963, which is an extensive study of two groups of relocatees: thirty-four persons or families brought to the Bay Area in the first years of the federal relocation program, nineteen families relocated through the federal relocation program in the years following 1955, and five families who were self-relocated.

13. Native American Research Group, *American Indian*, 4.

14. "Awakened Indians Battle the System," *San Francisco Examiner*, Sept. 26, 1968.

15. "He's Sick of Society Leaning on Indians," *San Francisco Examiner*, July 17, 1969.

16. Ablon, "Cultural Conflict," 200–205.

17. "City Life Baffles Reservation Indian," *San Francisco Examiner*, July 15, 1969.

18. Trudell interview by Ron J. Lujan, 13.

19. Steiner, *The New Indians*, 179.

20. "Awakened Indians Battle the System."

21. Bahr, "An End to Invisibility," 409.

22. Stephen Cornell identifies these shared traits as a new "supratribal consciousness and constituency" rather than as pan-Indianism. While the term is different, the meaning is essentially the same. See *The Return of the Native*, 72.

23. Senese, *Self-Determination*, 36.

24. Garcia, "'Home,'" 64.

2

Urban Indian Unrest and the 1964 Occupation of Alcatraz

/\.\/.\/\

"ALCATRAZ INVASION" and "Wacky Indian Raid, Alcatraz 'Invaded'" read the March 9, 1964, headlines of the *San Francisco Chronicle* and the *San Francisco Examiner.*[1] Carrying sleeping bags, tents, and food, five Bay Area Sioux—Garfield Spotted Elk, Walter Means, Richard McKenzie, Mark Martinez, and Allen Cottier—climbed aboard a chartered boat, landed, pounded sticks into the rocky soil, and laid claim to Alcatraz Island. The Sioux were met by prison warden Richard J. Willard and declared the landing a peaceful movement. Allan Cottier, president of the Bay Area branch of the American Indian Council, read from a typewritten declaration: "Under the U.S. Code we as Sioux Indians are settling on Federal land no longer appropriated. Because we are civilized human beings, and we realize that these acts give us land at no cost we are willing to pay the highest price for California land set by the Government—47 cents per acre. It is our intention to continue to allow the U.S. Government to operate the lighthouse, providing it does not interfere with our settlement."[2] After they signed a formal claim statement they would file with the Bureau of Land Claims in Sacramento, the Indians held a victory dance in the shadow of the lighthouse.[3] The dance was symbolic, perhaps, of a coup against a traditional foe. At their lawyer's urging, the occupiers then collected their food, sleeping bags, and tents and left the island.

The arrival of the occupation force need not have come as a surprise to the city or to the warden and his assistant on the island. The *San Francisco Examiner* had announced on March 8 that an occupation might well take place the following day. In a news article by Sam Blumenfeld, the planned occupation was described in detail:

An American Indian "rights" movement to invade and take possession of Alcatraz Island is planned here by members of the Sioux tribe, *The Examiner* learned yesterday. . . . Tribal leaders say they have the right to claim the island under provisions of old treaties and they plan to parcel the land into homesites. A boatload of claimants and their supporters will land on the bleak island and file claim to it "possibly" today, a spokesman said last night. The leader of the group is Richard Delaware Dion McKenzie. . . . The group will land on the island equipped with a tent and provisions for several days. . . . "This is no uprising or any such wild plot. We're entitled to the land free under the law. . . . We feel the rights given to the American Indian should and can be exercised."[4]

The invasion had begun as the brainchild not of one of the Sioux men involved in the occupation but rather of Belva Cottier, also a Sioux and the wife of Allen Cottier. In an interview conducted in 1979 Belva explained how she conceived of the idea of taking over Alcatraz and the evolution of the plan:

One morning I was reading the newspaper and there was this story that the government didn't know what to do with Alcatraz, which was surplus land after the federal prison was discontinued. So I thought about the old Sioux Treaty of 1868 which entitled us to claim surplus land. . . . We [she and a Sioux cousin] went to the Bancroft Library and searched under land and public domain. We did find a copy of the treaty. . . . Later we turned it over to a lawyer who had six students research it as a legal document for about six weeks. . . . A minister. . . got involved and got us a map of Alcatraz. We looked up all the history and found out that many Indians had been held prisoners there, so in a way it already was Indian land. We studied the tides, planned strategy and looked for someone to take us to the Island.[5]

She went on to explain that other pressures were beginning to build in the Bay Area at the same time and focused on anger about the federal relocation program. Although Native Americans had been promised jobs, housing, training, and medical care, they were dumped instead in city ghettos and forgotten, with little more than $500 to buy dishes and clothing and to get established. Whole families were left

stranded and young girls sat in bus depots as long as five days waiting for counselors. Many Indian men who participated in the relocation program in the hope of building a future ended up on skid row
with broken spirits.[6]

With so many Native Americans filled with such anger and unrest,
preparations for the landing of Alcatraz Island began. Speaking as
though she had been there, Belva described the events:

> We told the young Indians from the center [the San Francisco
> American Indian Center] that we were going to do something and
> to meet us in costume. There were five of us Sioux, and we ac-
> tually had claims sticks to do it like Lewis and Clark did. . . . The
> committee had scrounged up a boat for early Sunday morning and
> supplies enough for 30 days. We had notified Washington of our
> plans but they didn't respond and after we gathered on Pier 41,
> half on shore and half in the boats, we called the news media and
> said, "We're going to claim Alcatraz." Only about 10 people from
> the newspapers showed up. They didn't believe us. For a signal
> we had a round mirror—three flashes for clear and four for dan-
> ger. We went to the island's west side . . . but there was a guard
> there with a police dog telling us, "Don't you know that you
> aren't allowed within 200 feet of the island?" We went around
> to the east side . . . and jumped off. Each of the Sioux men with a
> claim stick dashed off to put it on different parts of the 12 1/2
> acres. The rest started singing victory songs. . . .
>
> The officials [A. L. Aylworth, acting warden] were still on the
> island, so the Sioux leader read them the proclamation claiming
> the island as Indian land for all tribes. The official telephoned the
> Federal Marshal . . . "There are Indians on the island, feathers,
> bells and all." In the meantime the officials notified Washington
> and Sacramento and . . . we were advised to stay until we could
> meet with the U.S. marshal, but somehow this was never accom-
> plished. But we felt that we had completed our mission by test-
> ing the 1868 treaty. . . . We loaded up and went back to shore.[7]

Elliott Leighton, the San Francisco attorney for the five Sioux men,
filed a petition with the General Services Administration (GSA) on
April 10, 1964, citing 25 USC 474, 334 and the 1868 treaty, particularly Article 6, paragraph 6, as their authority.[8] The Indian occupiers
also offered to purchase the island at a price of 47 cents per acre, the

price the government had recently offered for the 65,000,000 net acres taken from California Native Americans under the Indian Claims Commission Act of 1946.[9]

The question then became who had the responsibility for Alcatraz Island and ruling on the Sioux claim. On April 12, 1963, the GSA had taken control of Alcatraz Island as excess federal property and on April 17 screening began to determine if a use for the island could be found within any other federal governmental agency. One month later, the Bureau of Prisons estimated that protection and maintenance cost for Alcatraz Island would be $100,000 annually. On May 27 the screening of federal agencies was completed with negative results; Alcatraz Island remained the property and responsibility of GSA.[10]

A presidential commission was created by Public Law 88–138, approved on October 16, 1963, and was charged with conducting an investigation, studying its possible future, and recommending the most appropriate use for the island. In the interim, the San Francisco regional administrator of the GSA was authorized to assume custody on or before July 1, 1964, and was instructed, "prior to assuming custody and accountability, you shall determine the property to be surplus."[11]

Following the invasion, the commission, headed by Senator Edward V. Long of Missouri and Lieutenant Governor Glenn M. Anderson of California, met at Fort Mason and was transported to Alcatraz Island aboard a Justice Department launch to take stock of the property. The commission's mandate was to hold public hearings to allow interested parties to present proposals for the development of Alcatraz Island. Following the hearings, the commission would meet again in executive session for a review of the various proposals and other considerations relative to the disposition of the island. Various protocols for public announcement, screening, and review were established, and public hearings for the disposal of Alcatraz Island began on April 24, 1965.

Recommendations regarding development or disposition of Alcatraz Island were not new. On at least two occasions, while Alcatraz was an active prison, it was suggested that the island be used as a platform for a large statue—perhaps a West Coast version of the Statue of Liberty or a statue of peace. The United Nations Association proposed raising $3,000,000 to erect the statue, and a bill was introduced in Congress; however, the U.S. State Department opposed placing a statue for peace on the site of a maximum security prison.

By May 15, when the commission met again in Washington, D.C., approximately 500 letters containing proposals and suggestions for the future use of the island had been presented to the GSA, Mayor Joseph Alioto of San Francisco, and members of the commission. Proposals for monuments ranging from a fountain to Saint Francis accounted for 134 suggestions; 84 others felt that the island should be opened to the public as a prison museum; 34 asked that the land be made private property; 28 wanted a playland and marina; 1 requested an American Indian university; and other suggestions included a candy store, a nudist metropolis, a park with only vegetation, an international cultural center, and an elaborate apartment development.[12]

Because of the tremendous public interest in the island, the presidential commission believed that public hearings should be held in San Francisco so that legitimate groups could present their proposals. The commission emphasized that every legitimate person or group should be given the opportunity to present proposals and the GSA would screen interested organizations and individuals. The offices of California member of Congress Jeffery Cohelan and California state senator J. Eugene McCarthy were designated to collect the proposals. Proposals were then forwarded to Richard F. Laws, regional director of the GSA's Property Management and Disposal Service (PMDS), who would prepare a brochure outlining each proposal for final presentation to the commission. A deadline of April 10, 1964, was established for receipt of proposals.[13]

A total of thirty-three proposals were presented to the commission on April 24 and April 25. Elliott Leighton appeared on behalf of the American Indian Foundation and submitted one of the proposals for Native Americans. Leighton's proposal called for Alcatraz to be conveyed to the Indian people for operation as a "Tourist Monument."[14] In addition, the foundation proposed that an Indian cultural center and university, estimated to cost between $15 and $50 million, be built on Alcatraz. An Indian university was needed, according to Richard McKenzie, who also attended the hearings, because the average reservation-educated Indian could not cope with the high standards at mainstream schools.[15] Although Leighton made the actual proposal presentation other Indian leaders from the Bay Area attended the commission hearing, including Bob Zohn, Richard McKenzie, George Woodard, Nolan Smith, Virgil Standing Eagle, and Wilford Cadood. According to a *San Francisco Examiner* article commission members were unresponsive to the Indian proposal, mainly because of its connection with increasingly unpopular segregated education.[16] Following the presentations, the commission returned to Washington for its final evaluation meeting.

Senator Edward V. Long, the commission chair, was aware of the invasion on March 8, the claim filed under the Sioux treaty of 1868, and the effect that such a claim might have on the outcome of the commission's decision. Accordingly, on May 6, he wrote an inquiry to the Department of Justice to see if a legal basis existed for Native American claims made on Alcatraz. On May 15 Attorney General Ramsey Clark replied that although "some discussion" of the situation was merited, the Department of Justice was "satisfied that there is no way in which the American Indian Foundation or similar groups can assert rights which can inhibit the Presidential Commission on the Disposal of Alcatraz or the General Services Administration's freedom in planning what to do with the Island."[17]

The commission's final report issued on June 15 explained why a special commission for the disposition of Alcatraz Island was necessitated and reported the results of the hearings:

> Alcatraz Island is not a usual piece of property. Many of its characteristics make it unique and militate against its disposal through normal procedures. The Island occupies a predominant position in San Francisco Bay. Due to its use over the past thirty years as a penitentiary, *the Island has become well known throughout the world and is highly susceptible to improper exploitation.* It is clear that the use to which Alcatraz Island is put will have a significant impact on the San Francisco Bay Area and will affect the State of California as well as the entire nation. *Under no circumstance should anyone be allowed to use the Island to glorify the criminal acts which brought men to Alcatraz or to exploit the human misery associated with crime.*[18]

After reviewing the proposals presented, the commission recommended that the island be the site for a monument, selected through an international architectural competition, commemorating the founding of the United Nations in San Francisco in 1945 and standing as a symbol of peace. The remainder of the island should be retained in its natural state.[19]

Unhappy with the findings and recommendations of the presidential commission, Elliott Leighton filed a suit on September 13, in the U.S. District Court for the Northern District of California, Southern

Division, San Francisco, California, on behalf of Richard Delaware Dion McKenzie, one of the occupiers. McKenzie's suit sought an injunction against the sale of Alcatraz, title to the property, and, as an alternative, demanded that McKenzie receive a money judgment for the value of the property in the sum of $2,500,000 or the sum of its assessment.[20]

On June 3, 1968, attorneys for the federal government filed a request for dismissal of the case, stating in part:

> From plaintiff's allegations and answers to interrogatories, it is apparent that he believes his attempted "occupation" of Alcatraz Island in the spring of 1964 gave him a right to an allotment of the Island under appropriate provisions of Title 25, U.S.C. The Government feels that plaintiff does not sincerely believe that he has a meritorious case; and that the attempted occupation of Alcatraz was designed to attract attention and publicity to plaintiff and other American Indians. The defendants feel that this case may properly be dismissed for lack of prosecution.[21]

McKenzie's suit was dismissed for lack of prosecution on June 5, 1968.

Despite the efforts of the presidential commission and the recommendations that came out of the formal hearings, development on the island did not occur. The presidential commission introduced bills in both the House and the Senate on January 18, 1965, to implement the commission recommendations; however, the bills went without action.

Between January 1967 and June 1968, congressional bills for the disposal of Alcatraz Island met with opposition from both the GSA administrator and the Bureau of the Budget. Finally, on June 17, 1968, the city of San Francisco advised the GSA of the city's interest in acquiring the island. The GSA responded by advising the city that a plan for acquisition and development must be received within sixty days. The city had no plan for acquisition or development and was granted five ninety-day extensions while it attempted to determine the best use of the Island.[22]

On July 28, 1969, Lamar Hunt presented his proposal for the development of the island to a meeting of the Surplus Property Commission, city of San Francisco, a plan opposed by both the Indian and non-Indian Bay Area communities. Hunt, the son of a Texas oil millionaire, offered to develop part of the island as a park commemorating the U.S. space program, complete with illuminated gardens and an underground museum. He also proposed restoring the prison for tours and constructing a shopping center that would recreate San Francisco of the 1890s. *Newsweek* magazine reported that Hunt wanted to give San Francisco $2,600,000 to purchase Alcatraz from the federal government. Hunt would then rent the island back for 1 percent of its revenue each year.[23]

The Surplus Property Commission accepted Hunt's plan for redevelopment. Alvin Duskin, a local citizen, was outraged at the idea of private development for profit by the Hunt family fortune and mounted a campaign to "save Alcatraz," which included two full-page ads in two San Francisco newspapers. Calling the proposal "as big a steal as Manhattan Island," Duskin intimated that Hunt wanted Alcatraz as a deep-water dock for oil tankers from Alaska.[24]

Duskin's "save Alcatraz" campaign included clip-out coupons from his newspaper ad, which were filled out and returned to the newspapers. The response from the public was overwhelming. Within four days, 8,000 readers mailed protest letters or coupons. Additionally, Secretary of the Interior Walter Hickel became personally involved in the island's future, and in October 1969 the GSA agreed to allow the Department of Interior until December 1, 1969, to explore the potential of a federal recreation use of Alcatraz.[25]

Although urban Indians learned during this battle that they could be heard and understood by a large audience, the failure of the presidential commission to adopt their proposals remained one of a number of growing concerns in the Bay Area Indian community. According to the *Oakland Tribune*, Native Americans were increasingly troubled by their economic situation. Because Indian people relocating to urban areas often lacked training, they had to settle for menial jobs that were not satisfying and did not pay well. As a result, they were relegated to living in the very oldest, most poverty-stricken areas of town, collecting unemployment or living on welfare. They often had to rely upon the BIA, which many distrusted, at least in part because "it was formed as a department of war to deal with people conquered by military force." According to Native Americans, the failure of the BIA to recognize their independence tended to generate feelings of paternalism and dependency, which damaged Indian culture and its strengths. The BIA asserted, however, that the Indians wanted the support and aid offered by the BIA, but resented needing it.[26]

These frustrations were compounded by suddenly being thrust into an unfamiliar society. Ordinary tasks such as riding the bus to the grocery store were frightening and confusing for people who had never even seen a bus and had limited knowledge of the language. Self-reliance and forcefulness, traits unfamiliar in societies that placed little value on the acquisition of material goods and where the willingness to share, prompted by strong feelings of kinship among family and friends, was nearly universal, became necessary for survival.[27]

Some coped by regularly traveling back to their reservations to mark religious occasions such as births, marriages, puberty ceremonies, and deaths. Events such as powwows were well attended because families traveled many miles to take their children and thus continue their tribal traditions. Parents felt this helped their children hold onto and understand their heritage. Among some Native Americans, especially young people, "a fierce cultural pride" developed.[28]

Cultural pride and education could not keep mainstream culture at bay, however. Although Indians wanted to maintain their cultural heritage many found it increasingly difficult to do so in an urban environment. One mother reported that her children did not know they were Indian, even though they were told every day. In a game of "cowboys and Indians" they were "as likely to take the role of the cowboy as the Indian." Most urban Indians would "go back in a minute" if they could find a well-paying job on the reservation, but instead most turned for support to tribal clubs or Indian organizations, which provided a place to meet friends and relatives, but more importantly, offered an arena to overcome traditional intertribal hostilities. Urban Indians found that these were "not too apparent in the city, for many families would find they're standing alone against the world."[29]

Although intertribal hostility may have decreased, hostility from non-Indians was prevalent. According to Stella Leach, an Oakland nurse, her Sioux ancestry caused her and her six children to be the targets of constant harassment by non-Indian neighbors. The family's trouble began shortly after she rented a modest, two-bedroom home. The neighbors, resentful of her Indian ancestry, began making threats, including obscene telephone calls and messages scrawled on the house. When these threats did not force the Leach family to move, the front door of the house was ripped off its hinges, the family possessions were ransacked, and many acts of violence were committed, according to Leach. Despite Leach's determination to stay (she was "sick of moving once a year") the situation "just got to be too much."

On May 28, 1968, with the help of students from the University of California, Mills College, and volunteer organizations, Leach and her children departed Oakland and relocated to San Leandro, where she hoped to find a new home.[30]

Discrimination was prevalent in schools, housing, employment, health care, and among the police, who would wait outside of "Indian bars" at closing time to harass, beat, and arrest Indians.[31] Native Americans daily had to fight stereotypes of paint, headdresses, military battles, inability to handle "fire water" and dependence on federal assistance. Many Americans still believed that all Indians lived on reservations, carried tomahawks, and lived in teepees.

To protest their countrywide mistreatment one dozen Indian protesters took to the San Francisco streets in March 1969 and picketed the federal office building at 100 McAllister Street. Its organizer, Lehman Brightman, told reporters that although the protest was taking place in San Francisco, it was aimed at those in Washington, D.C., particularly the BIA. Concentrating his protest on the failed education of relocated Indians, Brightman carried a sign that read "BIA is a flop."[32]

On April 18, 1969, Brightman and Earl Livermore, director of the San Francisco Indian Center and a member of the San Francisco Human Rights Commission, called a press conference to protest racial slurs by police officers who referred to Indians as "a pack of wild Indians."[33] Younger Indians at the press conference complained also that police frequently mistreated Native Americans while making arrests and inevitably used words such as *chief, warpath,* and *firewater,* words painfully offensive to Indian people. Although the police officers may not have understood the racism inherent in such derogatory epithets, Indian people were acutely aware of the pejorative meanings. With growing anger and frustration, Native Americans demanded increased understanding and respect.

The March 9, 1964, landing on Alcatraz Island grew out of this anger and frustration. Spurred on by press conferences, protests, and their growing power, five Sioux men, supported by their wives and other Bay Area Indian people, occupied Alcatraz Island because they had been ignored. They had been ignored by their communities, the police, mainstream culture, and the government. Their peaceful invasion was the first step in a more public and more radical attempt at self-determination and self-respect for Indian people.

Notes

1. *San Francisco Chronicle*, Mar. 9, 1964; *San Francisco Examiner*, Mar. 9, 1964.

2. "Indians Stake Alcatraz Claim," *San Francisco Chronicle*, Mar. 9, 1964.

3. "War Dance on Alcatraz: Sioux Stake a Claim on the Rock," *Oakland Tribune*, Mar. 9, 1964.

4. "Sioux on the Warpath," *San Francisco Examiner*, Mar. 8, 1964.

5. "Indian in the City," *Catholic Voice*, Mar. 15, 1973.

6. Ibid.

7. Ibid.

8. GSA Chronology, 1. Title 25 U.S. Code embodies the rules and regulations that control the destiny and the lives of American Indians and regulates land use, leasing, heirship, land control, and, in certain cases, civil matters. The Sioux treaty of 1868 ended the Red Cloud War, which was the result of the United States having illegally built military forts on Indian land and having granted rights of way to railroads through Sioux lands.

9. California Indian Legal Services, "How California Was Taken," 84–85. Land claim issues are considered central to the development of American Indian activism in the 1960s, as I will explicate throughout this book. The Indian people who occupied Alcatraz Island in March 1964 were aware of the pending California settlement as well as the proposed land claims settlements on the part of the Western Shoshone in Nevada, the United Paiutes in western Nevada, and the Pit Rivers in northern California. Forbes, "Alcatraz: Symbol and Reality," 24.

10. GSA Chronology, 1.

11. Moreland to San Francisco Regional Administrator, GSA.

12. For a complete breakdown of suggestions see President's Commission on the Disposition of Alcatraz Island, "Alcatraz Island Explanatory Statement, Addendum no. 1," and "Report."

13. Scott, memorandum for the file, Mar. 24, 1964.

14. President's Commission on the Disposition of Alcatraz Island, minutes.

15. "The Indians' New School of Thought on Alcatraz," *San Francisco Examiner*, Apr. 26, 1964.

16. Ibid.

17. Clark, letter to Long.

18. President's Commission on the Disposition of Alcatraz Island, "Report," emphasis in original.

19. Ibid.

20. *McKenzie, Richard Delaware Dion*.

21. Costo, "Alcatraz," 9.

22. GSA Chronology.

23. "Siege of 'The Rock,'" *Newsweek*, Oct. 27, 1969, 81.

24. Ibid. Lamar Hunt was the son of H. L. Hunt, a Texas oil millionaire.

25. Thompson, *The Rock*, 467.

26. "City Indians a Neglected Minority," *Oakland Tribune*, Dec. 17, 1967.

27. Ibid.

28. Ibid.

29. Ibid.

30. "Just Too Much: Harassed Indian Woman Gives Up, Departs Oakland," *Alameda Times Star*, May 29, 1968.

31. Ablon, "Relocated American Indians."

32. "'Indian Power' Protest in S.F.," *San Francisco Chronicle*, Mar. 29, 1969.

33. Brightman and Livermore, press conference, 1.

3

Social Movements of the 1960s and Indian Leadership

∧∨∧

The unrest and frustration experienced by Bay Area Indians were not isolated or specific to Californians. The American Indian occupation of Alcatraz Island was part of the much larger movement for social change rooted in the 1950s. During that period the San Francisco Bay Area became home to bohemian artists and writers calling themselves the "Beat Generation." Influenced by jazz, drugs, and Eastern philosophy, the black-garbed artists proposed withdrawing from conventional society and seeking personal illumination. The Bay Area population often cast a tolerant eye on the bohemian followers of eccentric artists, poets, and writers such as Allen Ginsberg and Jack Kerouac. In the easygoing San Francisco environment the "beatniks" were ridiculed, but considered harmless.

By the sixties any aspiring radical, nonconformist, or renegade knew the way to San Francisco. The Bay Area, especially the Haight-Ashbury district, became a magnet for political and social ferment and apprehension. The Beat Generation was soon joined by college students, who turned to radical political activity and forms of sexual behavior, music, and dress designed to shock their parents. They became part of a larger social movement, generated mainly by African Americans, Hispanics, and women, intended to challenge the comfortable, established lifestyle of the older generation and to cultivate individual participation in the future of America.

Political awareness and activity surged during the sixties, especially in the civil rights arena. The Student Non-Violent Coordinating Committee (SNCC) was founded in April 1960 at a conference held in Raleigh, North Carolina, by nonviolent Black activists. Within a year, however, SNCC members determined that a new "in-your-face" approach was needed to bring their agenda before the American pubic. They decided to begin deliberately provoking confrontations with segregationists, local police, the southern power structure, and eventually the federal government. SNCC would provide a powerful paradigm, which combined with Students for a Democratic Society (SDS) formed a new movement that came to be called the "new left." SDS, founded in 1962, became the largest and most broadly based origination of Black radical protest in the sixties.

Both SDS and SNCC originally shared an egalitarian image of government that came to be termed "participatory democracy." This idea would become a linchpin for new left thought and protest activity. New leftists took for their gurus Bob Dylan, Mao Tse-tung, Che Guevara, and Emma Goldman. As envisioned by SNCC and SDS, the new participatory democracy meant that all members would be involved in formulating the political decisions that would shape their private lives.

By the fall of 1964 the influence of SNCC and SDS was evident on the national scene, particularly on college campuses. In 1964 a confrontation erupted between the administrators of the University of California at Berkeley and the student body. Administrators became concerned when veterans of the southern freedom rides and students who had been influenced by SNCC and SDS publicly began raising money for the civil rights movement on the campus. The confrontation was called the Free Speech Movement and ended in a massive sit-in and the arrest of over 800 demonstrators. A group called the "young new leftists" emerged from the sit-ins and forms of protest that had developed in the southern freedom struggle were effectively transplanted onto college campuses nationwide. The Berkeley campus was recognized as the home of this new nonviolent movement, which would continue through the late sixties. Demonstration against the escalating U.S. involvement in the Vietnam war became central to this movement.

The war divided the country in the second half of the sixties between supporter and protesters. The antiwar movement was extraordinary for its size and duration. Massive demonstrations, some with as many as 500,000 participants, took place in Washington, D.C., New York, and on major college campuses. These events were organized by the National Mobilization against the War, SDS members, young new leftists, and other counterculture revolutionary groups. University campuses became centers of antiwar protests and the sites of teach-ins, marches, sit-ins, moratoriums, and the occupation of official buildings. Young people who were angered at the widening Vietnam conflict began forming grass-roots antiwar organizing committees on many college campuses. In March 1965 an all-night teach-in was held at the University of Michigan to protest the major escalation in the bombing of North Vietnam. In May 1965 the Vietnam Day Committee of Berkeley held a thirty-six-hour marathon event. Over 12,000 people attended.[1] Black Americans returning from Vietnam were among those who participated in the growing antiwar movement.

Young Black Americans were hearing an angrier and more militant voice, a voice coming from former members of SNCC and participants in the civil rights movement. Malcolm X, their new cultural icon, advocated self-defense and the establishment in America of a separate Black nation. Between 1964 and 1967, over one hundred major racial riots and scores of minor disruptions occurred in cities across the country. By the end of 1968 racial upheavals had resulted in over two hundred deaths and property destruction valued at approximately $800 million. It was during this time that Stokely Carmichael popularized the slogan "Black Power." Within this new power and the rising tide of Black anger the Black Panther Party (BPP) was born.[2]

By 1970 the BPP was recognized as the leading voice of black militancy in America. The party produced a weekly newspaper and had thirty chapters and numerous community centers across the country. Following the teachings of Malcolm X, the BPP advocated the use of violence and supported revolution as a positive force to alter the circumstances of Black life. Revolution called for armed self-defense and urban guerrilla warfare wherever and whenever necessary. It was against the BPP that J. Edgar Hoover launched a full-scale counterintelligence program (COINTELPRO) aimed at disrupting and neutralizing the group. By 1972, as a direct result of FBI infiltration and disruption, the BPP had ceased to function as a national organization.

In 1968 new battle strategies were also being drawn by a small number of women liberationists who gathered in cities across the nation. Many of these women had participated in SNCC, SDS, and the BPP, although those organizations were dominated by men and patronizing at best toward women. In San Francisco many of these women met to discuss their experiences with sexual discrimination, the lack of employment opportunities, and ubiquitous male tyranny.

The outcome of the newly awakened consciousness was the growth of the women's movement, led by the National Organization for Women, which ushered in a new era of feminism in America.

In the late sixties an increasingly large number of young people became engaged in political protest and were attracted to a new form of lifestyle known as "The Movement." The new movement culture encapsulated SNCC's early idea of community, the new left's participatory democracy, the Black Panthers' anger, women's ideas about equality, and Haight-Ashbury's experimental attitude toward drugs and sexual freedom. The Movement crossed cultural and socioeconomic lines and brought together individuals who were usually separated from each other by class, age, race, or cultural differences. The Movement was dominated by young college students who were joined by Vietnam veterans, gay rights activists, women's liberation activists, urban American Indian people, Mexican-American farm workers, and members of the newly emerging Chicano/Chicana empowerment movement La Raza. These disparate groups began to work together for cultural change. Instead of waiting and relying on help from others, the oppressed rose up to fight their own battles.

Native Americans heard the lessons of the civil rights movement across the country and especially in the Bay Area. American Indian people, under the leadership of Richard Oakes, Dennis Banks, Clyde Bellecourt, and LaNada Boyer, formed such groups as Indians of All Tribes and the American Indian Movement to pursue their own rights aggressively. As civil rights issues and rhetoric dominated the headlines, some Indian groups adopted the vocabulary and techniques of African Americans in order to get Indian issues covered by the media and thus before the American public. The National Indian Youth Council (NIYC), a group of young college-educated Indians who had organized following the American Indian Charter Convention held in Chicago in 1961, held numerous fish-ins in the Pacific Northwest, where Washington State was attempting to use state laws to restrict Indian fishing rights guaranteed by federal treaties.[3] On the Berkeley campus of the University of California students and members of United Native Americans (UNA) located an unused bungalow, occupied it, and later received permission to develop a native cultural center.[4]

Of equal concern to Indian people was the Vietnam War, in which Indian men and women fought to defend a concept of freedom that they themselves had never experienced. Although Native Americans may have been forgotten by politicians and bureaucrats, they did not forget their duty in time of war or national emergency. American Indians were required to serve and did serve honorably: 1,000 in World War I, 44,500 in World War II, and 29,700 during the Korean conflict. The Vietnam war proved no exception. A total of 61,100 American Indians served.[5]

Beginning with the commitment of troops to Vietnam by President John F. Kennedy in 1963, American Indians either served voluntarily or were drafted into military service for this undeclared war against a people whom some considered to be oppressed in much the same manner they were. Indian military personnel returning from Vietnam often stated that they could identify and empathize with the Vietnamese people. Wallace "Mad Bear" Anderson, a Tuscarora Indian who visited Vietnam seven times, agreed, "When I walk down the streets of Saigon those people look like my brothers and sisters."[6] Robert Thomas, a Cherokee anthropologist, stated that Indian people understood the war in Vietnam better than his university colleagues did. The conflict in Vietnam was tribal in origin, and the Vietnamese were tired of the war machine flattening their crops. American Indians, according to Thomas, were tribal peasants in much the same way that the Vietnamese were.[7]

Native Americans returning from Vietnam were faced with difficult choices. Those who went to the reservations returned to high unemployment rates, poor health facilities, and substandard housing conditions just as Indian veterans who had returned from World War II did. Those who elected to relocate or settle in urban areas encountered what can best be described as double discrimination. First, they were discriminated against because they were Indian. Second, they were discriminated against because they were Vietnam veterans; rather than being hailed as heroes or shown some measure of respect for their sacrifices, they were considered third-rate citizens and treated as outcasts of society. In an attempt to retreat for a period of time, to adjust to a changing society, or perhaps simply to acquire skills for future employment, many of these returning veterans utilized their GI bill educational benefits and enrolled in colleges in the Bay Area. Indian students from these colleges, many of them Vietnam veterans, filled the ranks of the rising Indian activism movement now emerging as Red Power.

More disillusioned Indian youth from reservations, urban centers, and universities spoke out against the treatment they were receiving from their local, state, and federal governments, both in the cities and on the reservations.[8] Members of these Red Power groups strongly advocated the right to real self-government or autonomy. The NIYC emphasized the psychological impact of powerlessness on Indian youth in connection with the need for self-determination. This powerlessness and lack of self-determination was explained by Clyde Warrior, a Ponca Indian and co-founder of the NIYC, when he told government officials in Washington in 1967, "We are not allowed to make those basic human choices and decisions about our personal life and about the destiny of our communities which is the mark of free mature people. We sit on our front porch or in our yards, and the world and our lives in it pass us by without our desires or aspirations having any effect."[9] An article in *Warpath*, the first militant, pan-Indian newspaper in United States, established in 1968 by UNA, summed up the attitude of the Bay Area Indian community: "The 'Stoic, Silent Redman' of the past who turned the other cheek to white injustice is dead. (He died of frustration and heartbreak.) And in his place is an angry group of Indians who dare to speak up and voice their dissatisfaction at the world around them. Hate and despair have taken their toll and only action can quiet this smoldering anger that has fused this new Indian movement into being."[10]

The rhetoric of Indian self-determination can be traced to the early sixties, when Melvin Thom, a Paiute Indian from Walker River, Nevada, co-founder and president of the NIYC, recognized the need to alleviate the poverty, unemployment, and degrading lifestyles forced on both urban and reservation Indians. Thom realized that it was essential that Indian people, Indian tribes, and Indian sovereign rights not be compromised in the search for solutions to their many problems: "Our recognition as Indian people and Indian tribes is very dear to us. We cannot work to destroy our lives as Indian people."[11] Thom recognized that the strengths of family, tribalism, and sovereignty had sustained Indian people through the many U.S. government programs designed to destroy them as a people and nationalize Indian traditional lands. The official government policy, dating back to 1953, was termination of the relationship between the federal government and Indian communities, which meant that they would lose tax-exempt status of their lands; federal responsibility for their economic and social well-being would be terminated; and Indian tribes themselves would be effectively destroyed. Thom described the termination policy as a "cold war" that was being fought against Indian people: "The opposition to Indians is a monstrosity which cannot be beaten by any single action, unless we as Indian people could literally rise up, in unison, and take what is ours by force. . . . We know the odds are against us, but we also realize that we are fighting for the lives of future Indian generations. . . . We are convinced, more than ever, that this is a real war. No people in this world ever has been exterminated without putting up a last resistance. The Indians are gathering."[12]

Native Americans wanted self-determination rather than termination. This included the right to assume control of their own lives independent of federal control, the creation of conditions for a new era in which the Indian future would be determined by Indian acts and Indian decisions, and the assurance that Indian people would not be separated involuntarily from their tribal groups.

In March 1966, President Lyndon Johnson attempted to quiet the fears of Indian people. In a speech before the Senate he proposed a "new goal for our Indian programs; a goal that ends the old debate about termination of Indian programs and stresses self-determination; a goal that erases old attitudes of paternalism and promotes partnership and self-help."[13] In October 1966, Senator George McGovern from South Dakota introduced a Senate resolution highlighting the increased desire of Indian people to be allowed to participate in decisions concerning their development. The frustration resulting from years of BIA paternalism and new awareness of their powerlessness resulting from years of neglect, poverty, and discrimination had finally attracted the attention of the bureaucracy in Washington.

On April 11, 1969, the National Council on Indian Opportunity (NCIO), established by President Lyndon Johnson through Executive Order 11399, conducted a public forum before the Committee on Urban Indians in San Francisco. The purpose was to gain as much information as possible on the condition of the Native Americans living in the San Francisco area and thereby help find solutions to their problems and ease rising tensions. The cabinet members appointed by the president were impressive, an indication of the government's recognition that serious problems existed. Vice President Spiro Agnew chaired the committee and members included Secretary of the

Interior Walter J. Hickel, Secretary of Agriculture Clifford M. Harden, Secretary of Commerce Maurice H. Stans, Secretary of Labor George P. Schultz, Secretary of Health, Education, and Welfare Robert H. Finch, Secretary of Housing and Urban Development George W. Romney, and director of the Office of Economic Opportunity Donald Rumsfeld.

The hearings began with a scathing rebuke by the Reverend Tony Calaman, founder of Freedom for Adoptive Children. Reverend Calaman attacked the San Francisco Police Department, the California Department of Social Welfare, and the Indian child placement system, stating that the non-Indian system emasculated Indian people. When asked to explain, Reverend Calaman described the actions of the Social Welfare Department and the San Francisco Police Department: "It is a dirty, rotten, stinkin' term [emasculation], and the social workers are doing it and the police officers are doing it when they club you on the head. It is a racist institution, just pure racism—and you all know what racism is, and you all know what racists are. Look in the mirror, and you will see a racist."[14]

Earl Livermore, director of the San Francisco American Indian Center, appeared next and concentrated his testimony on problems Indian people face in adjusting to urban living, particularly Indian students faced with unfavorable conditions in the public school system. Those conditions ranged from the lack of understanding by school officials to false and misleading statements in school textbooks. Livermore pointed out that many of the textbooks in use damaged the Indian child's sense of identity and personal worth. His testimony included urban Indian health problems, which often were the result of not being properly oriented to urban living, and the consequent frustration and depression. Lack of education, according to Livermore, resulted in unemployment; unemployment led to depression; and depression led Native Americans deeper into the depths of despair. Alcoholism, poor nutrition, and inadequate housing were also highlighted as major problems. Livermore ended his testimony by pointing out the critical need for ethnic studies programs in local colleges.

A total of thirty-seven Indian people took advantage of the opportunity to appear at this public forum. Twenty-five of those would occupy Alcatraz Island seven months later. Richard Oakes, an important figure during the 1969 Alcatraz occupation, reiterated Livermore's call for college courses relevant to American Indians and called for new textbooks that accurately portrayed the role of American Indians in U.S. history. The need for culturally relevant courses for Indian students and Indian studies programs permeated the testimony as did the lack of opportunity for upward mobility for relocated Indian people. Dennis Turner, a Luiseño, testified before the committee about his personal frustrations resulting from the relocation program and about the inadequacy of the educational system to meet Indian needs. He also highlighted problems of inadequate housing and lack of counselors for Native Americans newly relocated to the urban areas. More directly, Turner addressed the problem of governmental agencies such as the NCIO conducting hearings and making promises and the frustration of seeing no change as a result. Addressing LaDonna Harris, a Comanche and chair of the Committee on Indian Affairs, Turner contended that after the hearing, "you're going to wonder what is going to happen? Is something going to come off or not? The Indian is still hoping. If he keeps on hoping, he's going to die of frustration. . . . This is really going to be a kind of test case, in my life, to see really what you're going to do here."[15]

Harris replied that she understood Turner's frustration, that he was right in being skeptical and frustrated. Harris insisted that, as a result of her own personal experiences, she understood Turner and the other Indian people who said, "I don't have any faith." She said, "I've been to a million more hearings than you have—because of our age difference. The point is, the non-Indian public does not know this [the problems faced by urban Indians], and it is not an Indian problem." "We have been studied to death, and we have been looked at, but still nobody knows. The message does not get across."[16]

Harris's next statement in reply to a press inquiry was in fact a look into the future, to plans not yet formalized but soon to capture the attention of Americans throughout the nation and to be played out as a nineteen-month drama on Alcatraz Island. A reporter asked, "Are you going to have some militant Indians?" Harris replied, "Heavens, I hope we will."[17]

Harris's hopes were soon realized. Richard McKenzie, one of the 1964 occupiers, recognized the uniqueness of the Native American situation. In a 1969 meeting at the San Francisco Indian Center, McKenzie contended, "Kneel-Ins, Sit-Ins, Sleep-Ins, Eat-Ins, Pray-Ins like the Negroes do, wouldn't help us. We would have to occupy the government buildings before things would change."[18] The rise of Indian activism was called for by Walter Wetzel, the leader of the Blackfeet of Montana and former president of the National Congress of American Indians: "We Indians have been struggling unsuccessfully with the problems of maintaining home and family and Indian ownership of the land. We must strike."[19] Finally, the beginning of the new Indian activism was announced by Wallace "Mad Bear" Anderson, the Tuscarora Indian who turned back the bulldozers when a dam was planned on Iroquois land. Anderson declared, "Our people were murdered in this country. And they are still being murdered. . . . There is an Indian nationalist movement in the country. I am one of the founders. We are not going to pull any punches from here on in."[20]

The call to action by Harris, Wetzel, and Anderson actually began to build in the fifties, when more than twenty major demonstrations or nonviolent protests by Indian people occurred. The demonstrations were aimed at ending further reductions of the Indian land base, stopping the termination of Indian tribes, and halting brutality and insensitivity toward Indian people. This rise in Indian activism was largely tribal in nature, however; very little, if any, pan-Indian or supratribal activity occurred. Typified by the participation of elders, healers, and entire communities, this militancy was primarily carried out by traditional people and was not the forging of alliances outside of tribal boundaries such as would later occur during the Alcatraz occupation.

In the fifties, the Six Nations people used passive resistance and militant protests to block various New York State projects.[21] Tuscaroras and Mohawks demonstrated in opposition to the building of power projects such as the Fort Randall Dam on the Missouri River and the Kinzua Dam in upstate New York, which required the displacement of Indians and the flooding of their land. In 1957, Mad Bear Anderson helped the Mohawk fend off a New York State income tax on the grounds of Indian sovereignty on Indian reservations. Anderson led a protest group of several hundred from the St. Regis Reservation to the Massena, New York, courthouse, where they tore up summonses for nonpayment of state taxes.[22]

In April 1958, Anderson led a stand against the tide of land seizures, a move that ultimately brought armed troops onto Indian land. The New York Power Authority, directed by Chair Robert Moses, planned to expropriate 1,383 acres of Tuscarora land to build a reservoir and back-flood. Anderson and others blocked surveyors' transits and deflated vehicle tires as harassment tactics. When Power Authority workers tapped the Indian leaders' telephones, Tuscaroras switched to speaking their tribal language. When the Tuscarora refused to accept the state's offer to purchase the land, 100 armed state troopers and police invaded their lands. The troops were met by a nonviolent front of 150 men, women, and children, led by Anderson, who blocked the road by lying down or standing in front of government trucks. At the same time, Seneca and Mohawk Indian people set up camps on the disputed land, challenging the state to remove them. Anderson and other leaders were arrested, but the media attention forced the power company to back down. The Federal Power Commission ruled that the Indians did not have to sell the land and the tribe did not sell. The *Buffalo Courier Express* reported that Mad Bear Anderson, more than anyone else, was responsible for the tribe's decision.[23]

Following the Six Nations' success in New York State, the Miccosukee Indian Nation of Florida summoned Anderson to help fight the federal government's attempt to take land from them as part of the Everglades Reclamation Project. In 1959, several hundred Native Americans marched on BIA headquarters in Washington, D.C., to protest the government policy of termination of Indian tribes and attempt a citizen's arrest of the Indian commissioner. In California, Nevada, and Utah, the Pit River Indians, led by Chief Ray Johnson, refused $29.1 million of claims case money awarded by the government and demanded return of their traditional lands. The Pit River Indian people carried on their battle for return of their lands until 1972, at which time they reached a negotiated settlement for partial restoration of land and a monetary settlement.

In the sixties localized Indian protest actions, such as the brief Indian occupation of Alcatraz Island in 1964, continued. Attracting a larger audience were the fish-ins along the rivers of the state of Washington, particularly the Nisqually and Puyallup Rivers south of Seattle. The NIYC sponsored fish-ins in support of the fishing rights guaranteed the tribes of the Pacific Northwest by treaties with the federal government. The fish-ins were designed to protest the treatment of Indian fishermen by the Department of Fish and Game, as well as sports and commercial fishing organizations that wanted to restrict Indian fishing rights while promoting increased fishing opportunities for themselves. The fish-in demonstrations provided Washington Indian youths with an opportunity to express their disillusionment and dissatisfaction with American society and also to actively protest the social conditions endured by their people. Celebrities such as Marlon Brando lent their names to bring national media coverage to the protest actions. Indian people who participated in the fish-ins would later lend their assistance to the occupiers on Alcatraz Island.

New Indian organizations also began to form during this period to support the growing activism and give voice to the rising militancy. Out of the Pacific Northwest fish-ins grew a group called the Survival of American Indians Association (SAIA). In the summer of 1968, UNA was founded in the San Francisco Bay Area. UNA had a pan-Indian focus and sought to unify all persons of Indian blood throughout the Americas and to develop a democratic, grass-roots organization. Its goal was to promote self-determination through Indian control of Indian affairs at every level. Many of the Alcatraz occupiers were members of UNA; many more were strongly influenced by the organization.

That same summer Dennis Banks, George Mitchell, and Vernon and Clyde Bellecourt founded the American Indian Movement (AIM) in Minneapolis. AIM began as a largely urban organization concerned with overcoming discrimination and pervasive police brutality. In Minneapolis where only 10 percent of the population was Indian, 70 percent of the city jail inmates were Indian. To divert arrests, AIM formed a ghetto patrol equipped with two-way radios that monitored police radios. Whenever a call came in involving Native Americans, AIM arrived on the scene first and prevented undue arrests or brutalizing of Indian people. The Indian jail population decreased significantly during the twenty-nine weekends of the patrol's operation. Out of the patrol grew the federally funded Legal Rights Center, where established attorneys donated time to counsel poor people. In 1971 AIM founded the Native Peoples' Survival School. Welfare rights and reform committees were established, as were jobs and job-training task forces. AIM addressed directly, and confrontationally, slum tenement housing, job discrimination, and overt racism against Indian people in the new urban areas. AIM ultimately became the most sophisticated and nationally recognized Indian activist group, with branches throughout the United States.

A confrontation between Canada, the United States, and members of the Iroquois Nation closed 1968. Canada had been restricting the free movement of Mohawk people (members of the Iroquois Nation) between the United States and Canada, demanding that the Mohawk pay tolls to use the bridge and pay customs on goods brought back from the United States. Members of the Iroquois League felt that this was an infringement of their treaty rights granted by Great Britain, and members of the Mohawk tribe confronted Canadian officials as a means of forcing the issues of tolls and customs collections. The Mohawk specifically protested Canada's failure to honor the Jay Treaty of 1794 between Canada and the United States.

A number of Mohawk people were arrested for blockading the Cornwall International Bridge on December 18, but when they pressed for presentation of their case in the court system, the Canadian government dismissed the charges. This protest action was not without precedent, however. In 1928, the Indian Defense League, founded in 1926, had argued that Native Americans should have unrestricted rights to trade and travel across the U.S.-Canadian border based on the Jay Treaty of 1794 and the Treaty of Ghent in 1814. It was not, however, until 1969 that the Canadian government formally recognized these rights.

The 1968–69 Cornwall Bridge confrontation also brought about the creation of *Akwesasne Notes,* an Indian newspaper that sought to inform Native Americans about the international bridge crisis by reprinting articles from diverse newspapers. Edited by Jerry Gambill, a non-Indian employed by the Canadian Department of Indian Affairs, *Akwesasne Notes* developed into a national Indian newspaper with a circulation of nearly 50,000. As a result, Cornwall Bridge became a prominent discussion topic of Indians across the nation. The influence of the Iroquois actions proved considerable. Out of this confrontation grew not only *Akwesasne Notes,* which would provide the Alcatraz occupation an Indian media voice, but also the foundations for the North American Indian Traveling College and the White Roots of Peace.

The North American Indian Traveling College, housed on Cornwall Island, Canada, was originally conceived by Jerry Gambill and Ernest Benedict, a Mohawk, as a mobile railroad car that would carry teachers of Indian traditions from one reservation to another, thereby networking Canadian Indian communities and fostering unity among native peoples.[24] Richard Oakes and other leaders on Alcatraz Island would draw on this effort and call for the creation of an Indian traveling college, similar to the Canadian version, during the nineteen-month occupation of the island. Its intent, like that of the earlier Canadian effort, was to foster pan-Indian unity and educate Native Americans throughout the United States about Indian issues, focusing on the Alcatraz occupation as a beginning of a new era in Indian opportunity. Indian people who had participated in the Alcatraz occupation would participate as teachers in the traveling college.

The White Roots of Peace harked back to an earlier Mohawk group, Akwesasne Counselor Organization, founded by Ray Fadden in the midthirties. The counselor organization had "traveled far and wide inculcating Indian pride among Mohawk youth . . . hoping to influence a group of young Mohawk . . . to take up leadership roles in the Mohawk Longhouse."[25] This was largely an attempt by Ray Fadden and other Mohawk to preserve and revive Iroquois lifeways. Jerry Gambill revived this idea by founding White Roots of Peace.[26]

Seeing the spiritual crisis caused by the death of key elders and young Indian movement away from the faith, Gambill founded this organization to bring back the Great Binding Law through speaking engagements to Indian and non-Indian communities and school audiences. In the process of touring, Gambill was purposefully trying to develop oratorical skills among his Mohawk troupe; he was also attempting to inculcate Indian pride and self-worth among the members, as well as to convey a certain political-religious message to his audience.[27] There can be no doubt that Oakes was motivated and influenced by the White Roots of Peace organization. Gambill, writing for *Akwesasne Notes,* reported that "Richard Oakes was one of the first people to help us get started. When the group known as White Roots of Peace made its first trip, we streamed into San Francisco in our aged motor home to stay for two weeks with Richard's family and his friends crowded into student housing on the San Francisco State College campus."[28] Ross Harden, a member of the Alcatraz occupation force, recalled that the members of White Roots of Peace "set our mood before Alcatraz when they came to visit us in San Francisco. They came out very heavily on the cultural thing. We were inspired by them."[29]

In addition to the rise in activism among the Mohawk, the Miccosukee, the Pit River Indians, and the Bay Area Indians, the Taos Pueblo Indians of New Mexico also reasserted their claims to ancestral lands in the sixties. In 1906, the federal government appropriated the Taos Blue Lake area, a sacred site, and incorporated it into the Carson

National Forest. In 1926, the Taos Indians, in reply to a compensation offer made by the government, waived the award, seeking return of Blue Lake instead. As a result, the Taos people got neither the compensation nor Blue Lake. On May 31, 1933, the Senate Indian Affairs Committee recommended that the Taos Indians be issued a permit to use Blue Lake for religious purposes. The permit was finally issued in 1940. On August 13, 1951, Taos Indians filed a suit before the Indian Claims Commission, seeking judicial support for the validity of their title to the lake. On September 8, 1965, the Indian Claims Commission affirmed that the U.S. government took the area unjustly from its rightful owners. Although legislation was introduced to return Blue Lake to the Taos Indians on March 15, 1966, the bill died without action in the Senate Interior and Insular Affairs Subcommittee. On May 10, 1968, House Bill 3306 was introduced to restore the sacred area to the Taos Indians. While it passed the House of Representatives unanimously, it once again died in the Senate Interior and Insular Affairs Subcommittee.[30] The return of Taos Blue Lake would become the centerpiece of Indian policy for the incoming Nixon administration.

The rising tide of Indian unrest and dissatisfaction with federal government Indian policy was not lost on the campaigning Nixon. On September 27, 1968, he sent a message to the delegates of the National Congress of American Indians gathered in Omaha, Nebraska: "The sad plight of the American Indian is a stain on the honor of the American people." Nixon proposed a bold new plan for Indian self-determination that would officially bring the Termination Era to an end and transfer responsibility for tribal affairs from the federal government to Indian people. He promised that if he were elected, "the right of self-determination of the Indian people will be respected and their participation in planning their own destiny will be encouraged."[31]

Nixon's proposal had roots deep in the sixties and numerous studies of the inefficiency of the BIA and its responsibility to Indian people. Of particular significance was a 1966 Presidential Task Force on the American Indian commissioned by President Lyndon Johnson that called for sweeping changes in Indian education, a strong disavowal of termination of Indian tribes as a government policy or goal, and a comprehensive plan to improve employment of urban and reservation Indians. The report called the deficiencies in the BIA "shocking." The substance of Johnson's March 6, 1968, message on Indian affairs had come from the task force's report and focused on "a new goal . . . that ends the old debate about termination of Indian programs and stresses self-determination; a goal that erases old attitudes of paternalism and promotes partnership self-help."[32]

Johnson's message was really a statement of goals rather than a plan of action. Johnson relied on congressional passage of legislation to increase funding for Indian programs, which would make reservations more economically viable. Unfortunately, only slightly increased levels of funding were approved, providing only for support of existing Indian programs and falling far short of the funds needed to have a meaningful impact on improved Indian education and self-determination. Nixon recognized the importance of Johnson's goals, however, and incorporated them into his own evolving Indian policy.[33]

Two other significant events had a strong effect on Nixon's developing policy. The first was the receipt of Alvin M. Josephy Jr.'s "The American Indian and the Bureau of Indian Affairs—1969: A Study with Recommendations." On January 16, 1969, James Keogh, special project manager for President Nixon, requested that Josephy, a well-respected author and citizen deeply involved in Native American affairs, conduct a study of the BIA and submit his report directly to the White House. Josephy's report chastises the federal government for its ineptitude in the handling of Indian affairs, specifically, the failure of the various presidencies to effect any change in the multilayered, bureaucratically inept BIA; the failure of the government policy in Indian education; and the high rates of unemployment, disease, and death on reservations as the result of neglect by the federal government. The Josephy report also points out that although the termination policy had been abolished in 1958, Indian people still feared it. Every new or proposed government policy was still viewed as an attempt to terminate their status as Indian people and further destroy their land base. Josephy found that a "termination psychosis" existed that "continued as a hobbling theme in all Indian affairs throughout the Kennedy and Johnson administrations and which in 1969 demands initial priority attention by the new administration."[34] In order to overcome this deeply imbedded fear of termination, Josephy recommended a *strong* presidential statement repudiating termination as a goal or policy of the federal government and an official pronouncement of self-determination for Indian people as a priority of the Nixon administration.[35]

The second significant event was the 1969 publication of Edgar S. Cahn's similar indictment of the BIA. Cahn presented a copy of *Our Brother's Keeper: The Indian in White America* to Leonard Garment, policy assistant to President Nixon, with the request that the book be passed to Vice President Spiro Agnew, who was also chair of the NCIO.[36] Recognizing that Indian people have been overanalyzed, the contributors to the book highlight the numerous studies, all conducted by non-Indians with one exception, and conclude that "recommendations have come to have a special non-meaning for Indians. They are part of a tradition in which policy and programs are dictated by non-Indians, even when dialogue and consultation have been promised."[37] Bradley Patterson Jr., assistant to Garment, wrote that he, Garment, and Agnew "were impressed by the case the Indian people made, by their articulation and their credibility." Patterson goes on to affirm that it was "with this meeting with Indian activists very much in mind that Nixon's plan for a major policy initiative on Indian affairs, and a major presidential message to congress developed."[38]

Nixon's concern and sensitivity toward American Indian people and their issues can also be traced to his college years at Whittier College in California. Nixon's football coach was a mixed-blood Indian, Wallace Newman, called "Chief" by his players. Newman was raised on the La Jolla Reservation near San Diego, was proud of his heritage, and had an influence on Nixon that would follow him throughout his life.[39] Nixon considered Newman a molder of character who instilled in him the ethic that "by hard work, training, and preparation, even the greatest of victories could be achieved."[40] Nixon developed a life-long friendship with Newman, who actively campaigned during the presidential election, and maintained contact with his former coach throughout his White House years. Newman was among the few personal friends that Nixon called around him following his resignation from the presidency. On a draft copy of his resignation speech Nixon wrote, "I have never been a quitter," a quality Newman had greatly admired in Nixon throughout his life. Following his resignation Nixon sought out Newman's wisdom and advice on how to fight back from the depression that overwhelmed him.[41]

During the protracted lobbying for the return of Taos Blue Lake Nixon was greatly influenced by the tenacity instilled in him by Newman. Nixon recognized that he had to make a stand for Native Americans and give substance to his stated policy of Indian self-determination. Taos Blue Lake would be that stand. The Blue Lake bill was once again introduced in the Congress in January 1969.[42] Thanks to Nixon's determination, on December 15, 1970, Taos Blue Lake was returned to the Taos Pueblo Indians.[43] During the ceremony Nixon spoke of the contribution of American Indians, who had given such great character to the United States, and ended with a reference to the "strong, indomitable character" of his old football coach, Chief Newman.[44]

Nixon's announced policy of self-determination would also be tested in California, particularly the Bay Area, which had become the hotbed for the newly developing Indian activism. Jack Forbes, a Powhatan/Lenape Indian and professor of Native American studies and anthropology at the University of California at Davis, became advisor and mentor to many Indian students. In the spring of 1969, Forbes drafted a proposal for a college of Native American studies to be created on one of the University of California campuses. Individual programs, which grew out of Third World student strikes, were already being formed on the various college campuses in California, such as the University of California at Berkeley, the University of California at Los Angeles, and San Francisco State College.[45]

On June 30, 1969, the California legislature endorsed Forbes's proposal. Forbes wrote to John G. Veneman, assistant secretary of Health, Education, and Welfare, and requested that Veneman look into the availability of 650 acres between Winter and Davis, California, as a possible site for an Indian-controlled university.[46] Additionally, in 1969, the Native American Student Union was formed in California, bringing together a pan-Indian alliance of the newly emerging Native American studies programs on the various campuses. In San Francisco members prepared to test Nixon's commitment to his policy before a national audience. For Indian people of the Bay Area the social movements of the sixties had not only come to full maturity but they had also come to a maturity that would include Indian people.

LaNada Boyer, Richard Oakes, John Trudell, Adam Nordwall (who later became Adam Fortunate Eagle), Grace Thorpe, and Stella Leach understood very well the plight of urban Indians and the power of the social movements of the area. All were products of federal programs designed to remove Indian people from reservations and relocate them to major urban areas, thus they had experienced firsthand the poverty, isolation, and helplessness of their people. They were students, members of Red Power organizations, business leaders, who helped invent the radical Indian right. In November 1969, they and all Native Americans moved onto the national scene as active participants in a war of their own. Alcatraz Island was the battlefield.

Notes

1. Albert and Albert, *The Sixties Papers*, 18.
2. Ibid., 22–23.
3. Cohen, *Treaties on Trial*, 69.
4. Cornell, *The Return of the Native*, 192. Cornell views the mobilization of African Americans as critical to the development of Indian activism: "Not only did it offer tactical lessons, but the magnitude of Black mobilization and its popular support forced government authorities to respond—however inadequately—to the issues it raises. This in turn encouraged similar actions by other groups, including Native Americans. . . . These developments further broadened the opportunities for Indian political action and enhanced the sense of power among Indian groups. Joined to the growing political capacities of tribes and other constituencies, to a heightened supratribalism and to the conviction among Indians that they had to seize the initiative in Indian affairs, they produced an explosion in Indian political activity of all kinds, which continued through the 1960s and into the following decade" (192).
5. Veterans Administration, Statistical Brief.
6. Wallace "Mad Bear" Anderson quoted in Steiner, *The New Indians*, 282.
7. Ibid.
8. Deloria, *Behind the Trail*, 34.
9. Clyde Warrior quoted in Josephy, *Fight for Freedom*, 84. Warrior, a Ponca Indian, was a leader of the NIYC upon its initial formation following the American Indian Chicago Conference in 1961 and is often referred to as the founder of the Red Power movement.
10. Brightman, "The New Indians," quoted in Forbes, *Native Americans and Nixon*, 28. Brightman founded and began publication of *Warpath* in 1968 and provided a voice for the rising urban Indian youth groups.
11. Melvin Thom quoted in Josephy, *Fight for Freedom*, 55.
12. Thom quoted in Steiner, *The New Indians*, 43.
13. Lyndon Johnson quoted in Senese, *Self-Determination*, 144.
14. National Council on Indian Opportunity, minutes, 3.
15. Ibid., 39.
16. Ibid., 16.
17. Ibid., 41.
18. Richard McKenzie quoted in Steiner, *The New Indians*, 45.

19. Walter Wetzel quoted in ibid.

20. Wallace "Mad Bear" Anderson quoted in ibid.

21. The Six Nations consist of the Mohawk, Oneida, Onondaga, Cayuga, Seneca, and Tuscarora of the northeastern United States.

22. Senese, *Self-Determination*, 146.

23. *Buffalo Courier Express* quoted in Senese, *Self-Determination*, 147.

24. According to Hauptman, the original idea was modified from a railroad car to a traveling college employing vans. The effort was successful and became a reality in 1968, and it is still a major Indian educational force in Canada. Hauptman, *Iroquois Struggle*, 222.

25. Ibid., 224.

26. Ibid.

27. Ibid. Hauptman points out here that White Roots of Peace had been strongly influenced by the North American Indian Traveling College.

28. Jerry Gambill, "He Liked His Mohawk Name, Ranoies—A Big Man," *Akwesasne Notes*, Oct. 1972, 13.

29. Harden interview, 13.

30. Gordon-McCutchan, *Taos Indians*, xvi-xvii. This book recounts the taking of Blue Lake and the Taos Indians' successful campaign to recover it.

31. White House, press release to the National Congress of American Indians.

32. Lyndon Johnson quoted in Senese, *Self-Determination*, 144.

33. Senese, *Self-Determination*, 144.

34. Josephy, *Bureau of Indian Affairs*, 3.

35. Ibid.

36. Cahn, *Our Brother's Keeper*, 187–90.

37. Ibid., 152.

38. Patterson, letter to Waggoner. In this letter Patterson describes the Indian people who later occupied Alcatraz Island as "fuzzy-minded radicals" and Edgar Cahn and his associates as "dissidents of a sort."

39. Gordon-McCutchan, *Taos Indians*, 218.

40. Aitken, *Nixon*, 34–35.

41. Ibid., 34.

42. Gordon-McCutchan, *Taos Indians*, xvi–xvii.

43. Ibid., 148–49.

44. Ibid., 218–19.

45. Champagne, *Chronology*, 356–57.

46. During this period, the University of California at Davis was also attempting to acquire the same site for its own use. It was the occupation of the intended site by Indian youth, some of which had been involved in the Alcatraz occupation, that ultimately led to success for the Indian-controlled university. In April 1971, the federal government formally turned this land

over to the trustees of Deganawide-Quetzalcoatl University (DQU), a joint American Indian and Chicano/Chicana University. One of the demands of the Alcatraz occupiers, both in 1964 and 1969, was the establishment of an Indian university on Alcatraz Island. While this never occurred, the establishment of DQU was seen by many as the fulfillment of that demand.

4

"We Hold the Rock!"
The Indian Occupation

.∧.∨.∧.

Throughout the cold and winter nights
We tended to our fires,
We drew our blankets close around
And watched the waves crash higher.

Though the cold waves beat on Alcatraz
Indian hearts are stout,
For white men think we'll go away—
But we'll live this winter out!

For the North Wind is our Brother;
We share his bitter shock;
Aii—we are the warriors of Alcatraz,
And we hold the Rock![1]

The manifesto of the Alcatraz occupiers was captured by Dorothy Lonewolf Miller in this poem and "We Hold the Rock" became their catch phrase during the nineteen-month-long occupation. The occupation was the dream of Indian college students such as Richard Oakes, LaNada Boyer, Joe Bill, and Ross Harden. They wanted to make a statement that would awaken the American people and especially the federal government. Although the older urban Indian community, including Adam Nordwall and the United Bay Area Council of American Indian Affairs, had their eyes on Alcatraz Island, it could never have carried out an occupation that would include living under conditions of severe hardship on a cold and isolated island for nineteen months. Additionally, the occupiers had to withstand a confrontation with the federal government. The young Indian college students who began the occupation and others who joined later had little to lose. The federal government could not take anything away from them because they did not own anything. They could sit on

Alcatraz Island and live off of donated food, clothing, and money and wait for the federal government to either agree to their demands or remove them from the island. The government, on the other hand, had its hands tied. The ongoing unpopular Vietnam war and the recent My Lai Massacre and shooting of college students at Kent State University resulted in an increase in popular support for the occupation force. The Alcatraz movement soon took on more than just a symbolic meaning as plans developed for the construction of an Indian university and a cultural center. But this occupation could not have been successful without the preliminary invasion earlier that month.

On November 9, 1969, a group of fourteen urban Indian youths, primarily college students from the Bay Area, occupied Alcatraz Island for nineteen hours. This preliminary invasion resulted not from one single spark, as some have intimated, but rather from several simultaneous events coming from several venues. The few researchers who have addressed this brief occupation generally focus on the fire that destroyed the American Indian Center in San Francisco on October 28, 1969, as the catalyst for the occupation. While the importance of the destruction of the Indian center cannot be overlooked and should not be downplayed, focusing only on this event obscures other important events and personages connected with the occupation.

Alcatraz Island was on the minds of Bay Area Indian people daily and served as a constant reminder of the broken treaties between the United States government and Indian people: "There it was, a dramatic outcropping right out in the middle of the bay. Every time you crossed the Golden Gate Bridge or the Bay Bridge, you saw that little spot in the water and remembered. Even at night the revolving searchlight on the Coast Guard light house beckoned to you. And you thought: 'Those twenty acres and all those buildings, all empty, falling apart from neglect. And we have nothing.'"[2]

In 1968, when Alcatraz was declared surplus property, many of the Indian people remembered the 1964 Sioux occupation, which laid claim to the island under the Sioux treaty of 1868. The government had dismissed the subsequent suit by Richard McKenzie for lack of prosecution and ruled that the provision of the Sioux treaty did not give Native Americans an extralegal right to claim unused surplus government land. Even so, the subject of Alcatraz continued to come up in meetings of the Bay Area Council. Still, talk was only tentative.

The council viewed Alcatraz as a "powerful symbol" and hoped to use its potential to bring together the urban Indian community and reach out to Indian people on reservations as well. After soliciting input from community members, the council began to draw up a formal plan for the use of the island, which included the development of an Indian spiritual center, ecology center, museum, and training school. The plan was refined to include the practical, historical, and political reasons why Alcatraz Island should be turned over to the Indian people. The submission of the formal application to the federal government was superseded, however, by the October 28, 1969, fire that destroyed the San Francisco Indian Center and by the city's announcement of Lamar Hunt's preliminary plans for development of the island.

On September 29 the San Francisco Board of Supervisors endorsed Hunt's bid for commercial redevelopment of Alcatraz Island despite Indian testimony and proposals. As a result of this decision, college students at the University of California at Berkeley and San Francisco State College resolved to conduct a demonstration on Alcatraz to emphasize the neglected educational needs of American Indians.

In 1969, Steve Talbot was a volunteer instructor in the developing Native American studies program at the Berkeley campus of the University of California. LaNada Boyer was among Talbot's students who had participated in the Third World strike on the Berkeley campus. Jack Forbes taught a class on Indian liberation at Berkeley during the spring term of 1969, and his class was visited by the White Roots of Peace. As a result, Forbes's Indian students were emotionally charged for participation in an event that would bring a national focus on Native American problems.

On the San Francisco State College campus Luis Kemnitzer, a professor in the Department of Anthropology, was teaching American Indian heritage in the newly established American Indian Studies Department. Twenty-seven Indian students were enrolled, and among the guests to appear before the class was the White Roots of Peace.[3] In Kemnitzer's classroom and that of Talbot, the planning for the student occupation of Alcatraz Island took place. Belva Cottier, a planner of the 1964 occupation, met with Oakes and other Indian students in the off-campus home of one of the San Francisco State professors as well. Cottier briefed the Indian students on the earlier occupation and advised them in the development of their occupation plan. Among Kemnitzer's students was Richard Oakes.

Oakes, a Mohawk, was born on the St. Regis Reservation in New York and credited the Third World liberation strike taking place at San Francisco State University, the need for an ethnic studies program to meet the needs of Indian students, as well as the various proposals for the use of the island with the motivation for the occupation. Convinced that taking Alcatraz would be a positive action, Oakes and his fellow students formulated plans to occupy Alcatraz during the summer of 1970. Other events would hasten the occupation date to November 1969.[4]

Joe Bill, a Hooper Bay Eskimo and a key individual in the November 9, 1969, occupation, recalled that the action was planned in a college classroom at San Francisco State University. Luis Kemnitzer allowed his Indian students to organize the class as a forum to discuss the direction of the newly formed American Indian Studies Department and to set their own agenda for the class. Following Oakes's lead, Bill and other students began planning for the occupation, which included meeting with Indian people from the various communities in the Bay Area.[5] Ross Harden, a Winnebago and a classmate of Joe Bill and Richard Oakes, explained that the psychology class was broken down into small discussion groups and it was in these group discussions that the idea of an Alcatraz occupation first emerged. Students from Berkeley were called and invited to join the discussions. In September a group of about forty students met at Fisherman's Wharf with their sleeping bags and blankets. Arrangements had been made for a boat to pick them up at seven o'clock and take them to Alcatraz. The boat failed to arrive so the occupation was called off. Undeterred by this setback, the students contacted others at the Santa Cruz campus and elsewhere in California. The taking of the island had become vital to the movement.[6]

From the various recollections and accounts, it is clear that more than one group was concentrating on Alcatraz Island as the focal point for Indian people in the Bay Area. Adam Nordwall and the Bay Area Council had discussed developing the island over the previous year. Some members of the council, such as Nordwall, wanted to occupy the island while others saw the island as a logistical challenge that was beyond their resources. If the federal government had been unable to maintain the facilities on the island it was doubtful that the urban Indian community was equal to the task. Still, they were mindful of the brief 1964 occupation, and each day as they viewed the San

Francisco Bay they were aware of the island sitting in the midst of the bay, wasting away.[7]

The young Indian college students from various California campuses were also somewhat familiar with the 1964 occupation and were motivated by Hunt's commercial proposal to develop Alcatraz Island, the seeming powerlessness of Native Americans in the area, the failure of the educational system to meet their needs, as well as the rising call for self-determination among both urban and reservation Indian people. Both Bill and Harden indicate that an attempt to occupy the island was planned as early as September or October 1969 by student groups but failed to materialize due to lack of logistical support. Events began to escalate, however, in October 1969.

In the early morning of October 28 a four-alarm fire destroyed the San Francisco American Indian Center, which served approximately 30,000 Indian people in the Bay Area; this coalesced the divergent groups with interest in Alcatraz Island. The Indian center, which was established in 1958, provided employment, health care, legal assistance, social programs, and an important meeting place for the growing number of relocated Indians living in the Bay Area. Earl Livermore, the Blackfoot director of the center, remarked in 1970 that before the fire, "we had a number of gatherings in which the students came upon the idea of occupying Alcatraz. Following the fire, we decided to draw up a proclamation of what use should be made of Alcatraz."[8]

The occupation planning moved forward at a rapid pace. Now meeting in the interim quarters of the Indian Center, the planners reached a consensus on who would represent them. The movement was to promote no one individual or one tribe, as the 1964 occupation had done, but rather Native Americans from all tribes across the United States; thus the name *Indians of All Tribes* was chosen to represent the occupation force. The proclamation drawn up to announce the group's plans reflected serious intentions, sarcastic humor, and hope for the future of Indian people:

To the Great White Father and All His People:
    We, the native Americans, re-claim the land known as Alcatraz Island in the name of all American Indians *by right of discovery.* We wish to be fair and honorable in our dealings with the Caucasian inhabitants of this land, and hereby offer the following treaty: We will purchase said Alcatraz Island for 24 dollars ($24)

in glass beads and red cloth, a precedent set by the white man's purchase of a similar island about 300 years ago. We know that $24 in trade goods for these sixteen acres is more than was paid when Manhattan Island was sold, but we offer that land values have risen over the years. Our offer of $1.24 per acre is greater than the 47¢ per acre the white men are now paying the California Indians for their land. We will give to the inhabitants of this land a portion of that land for their own, to be held in trust by the American Indian Government—for as long as the sun shall rise and the rivers go down to the sea—to be administered by the Bureau of Caucasian Affairs (BCA). We will further guide the inhabitants in the proper way of living. We will offer them our religion, our education, our life-ways, in order to help them achieve our level of civilization and thus raise them and all their white brothers up from their savage and unhappy state. We offer this treaty in good faith and wish to be fair and honorable in our dealings with the white men.

The second section of the proclamation emphasized the points they wanted the government and the American public to take special note of:

We feel that this so-called Alcatraz Island is more than suitable as an Indian reservation, as determined by the white man's own standards. By this we mean that this place resembles most Indian reservations, in that:

1. It is isolated from modern facilities, and without adequate means of transportation.
2. It has no fresh running water.
3. The sanitation facilities are inadequate.
4. There are no oil or mineral rights.
5. There is no industry and so unemployment is very great.
6. There are no health care facilities.
7. The soil is rocky and non-productive and the land does not support game.
8. There are no educational facilities.
9. The population has always been held as prisoners and kept dependent upon others.

Further, it would be fitting and symbolic that ships from all over the world, entering the Golden Gate, would first see Indian land,

and thus be reminded of the true history of this nation. This tiny island would be a symbol of the great lands once ruled by free and noble Indians.

The proclamation set forth the intended uses of the island as well:

1. A Center for Native American Studies which will train Indian young.
2. An American Indian Spiritual Center which will teach ancient tribal religious ceremonies and medicine.
3. An Indian Center of Ecology which will train and support Indian young people in scientific research and practice in order to restore Indian lands and waters to their pure and natural state.
4. A great Indian training school to teach Indian people how to make a living in the world, improve standards of living, and end hunger and unemployment among Indian people.
5. Some of the present buildings on the Island will be taken over to develop an American Indian museum, which will depict native foods and other cultural contributions. Another section of the museum will present some of the things the white man has given to the Indian in return for the land and life he took: disease, alcohol, poverty and cultural decimation (as symbolized by old tin cans, barbed wire, rubber tires, plastic containers, etc.). Part of the museum will remain a dungeon, to symbolize both those Indian captives who were incarcerated for challenging white authority, and those who were imprisoned on reservations.[9]

Once the occupation date and the proclamation were decided upon, the San Francisco media was brought in. A Halloween party at Tim Findley's home provided the forum. Findley, representing the *San Francisco Chronicle*, several reporters from other Bay Area papers, as well as radio and television reporters gathered around Nordwall and Oakes to hear the outline of the planned occupation. Since the occupation would not take place until November 9, the media representatives were requested not to break the story prematurely so that surprise would be on the side of the occupiers. The media members cooperated and the advance notice actually proved beneficial. Nordwall remarked, "We really did get more complete coverage than many of us expected from the establishment media."[10]

Although Oakes and Nordwall announced the occupation, no one person, organization, or group of people can properly lay claim to being "the original planner" or "leader" of the occupation. This issue became clouded when the news media, government officials, and various spokespersons sought out one person on whom to focus for answers and negotiations. The need by non-Indian society for a single leader or spokesperson was familiar and ironic to Indians. Upon early European contact in what is today the United States, many Indian groups had no one person, or "chief," with whom Europeans could negotiate for trade and land purchases. The position of "tribal chief" was often an artificial construction to provide an individual in a leadership position with whom the Europeans could conduct business. The Indian occupiers of Alcatraz Island attempted to maintain an egalitarian, democratic society without a single leader so that decisions would be made by consensus. The non-Indian press and the government system, however, were either unable or unwilling to accept this structure and continuously referred to specific individuals as "the leader" or "an Island spokesman," which later resulted in jealousy and dissension among the occupiers.

Initially, Richard Oakes was identified as the leader. It is inappropriate to identify him as a leader, however, without first acknowledging the importance of the leaders of the 1964 occupation—Belva Cottier, Allen Cottier, and Richard McKenzie. Adam Nordwall was a contemporary of Oakes and played a key role in the Bay Area Council planning effort and would continue to play an important role in logistical support. Others of importance in the planning of the November 20 occupation were Earl Livermore, the Bay Area Indian college students, and a Native American who has asked to remain anonymous.

Just as no one person can be called the leader, no one cause can be considered the catalyst of the occupation. Previous scholars and researchers have generally focused either on student unrest, Bay Area Indian problems, or the fire that destroyed the San Francisco Indian Center as single causes of the occupation. The occupation represented each of these concerns and was also a reflection of the time of rising social awareness in which it occurred. Bay Area groups and concerns coalesced in a single action.

Once the occupation date of November 9 had been established, planning began in earnest.[11] The occupation of the island would necessarily be done by boat, and Nordwall asserts that after he contact-

ed several charter boat companies, five boats were promised to transport some seventy-five people to the island.[12] Pier 39 on the San Francisco embarcadero was the planned debarkation point, and the various media were once again notified of the pending departure.
Difficulties arose almost immediately. Upon arriving at Pier 39 at approximately 10:00 A.M. on November 9, the occupation force realized
that the five boats were nowhere to be found. The press, however, was
present, and doubts arose regarding the occupiers' creditability. To
complicate matters further, a reporter from the Reuthers news agency and a television crew had preceded the occupation force to the island and were standing by to film the landing.

Nordwall states that he asked the Indian student groups, now growing in numbers, to keep the media occupied while he attempted to
secure alternate transportation. Oakes asked Nordwall for a copy of
the proclamation and permission to read it to the media. What resulted was an impromptu press conference formally announcing the occupation. At the moment the proclamation was read, Oakes became,
in the eyes of the media, the "leader" or, at the very least, "the spokesperson" for the occupying force. The reading of the proclamation was
followed by a brief period of singing and dancing, both to attract media
coverage and to stall for time.

Ronald Craig, the owner and skipper of a three-masted ship, the
Monte Cristo, was approached by Nordwall and asked for assistance.
Nordwall explained the predicament and Craig agreed to provide
transportation for the group provided that Coast Guard permission
was obtained and that rather than actually landing on the island the
boat would simply circle the island a couple of times. Craig feared the
danger of an attempted landing on the Alcatraz dock and that his boat
would be overcrowded. He limited the number of passengers to fifty.
Nordwall agreed to Craig's conditions and the *Monte Cristo* cast off
and headed for the island.[13]

According to Ross Harden, once the occupiers realized that the *Monte
Cristo* was not going to dock a small group of Indian men jumped from
the boat and began swimming. Oakes went off the boat first as it came
around the west side of the island, quite a way out. After Oakes jumped
some of the others started taking off their shirts and shoes. The next
one to jump overboard was a Cherokee Indian named Jim Vaughn, a
student from Berkeley. Joe Bill and Jerry Hatch from northern California soon followed. Harden was the last to jump as the boat circled the

island. When the swimmers reached the island the GSA island care-taker, Glen Dodson, confronted them and directed them to leave the island. Although Dodson had a dog with him, the dog came running over to the occupiers, wagging its tail and licking them on the face. According to Harden the group stayed on the island approximately ten or fifteen minutes, the length of time it took for a boat to come from the mainland to pick them up for the return trip. Once on the main-land, the group decided, "What the hell, these damn white people are laughing at us, let's go get the island again tonight."[14]

Richard Oakes provided his own insight into the November 9 landing:

> We were supposed to get dressed up in all of their "television costumes" and just make a pass around the island, to *symboli-cally claim Alcatraz.* But a lot of us were sick of doing things for the public; so when they sailed around the island, we decided to jump off the ship when it got close to Alcatraz, swim out to the island and claim it. When we got within two hundred fifty yards, I said, "Come on. Let's go. Let's get it on!" So I left all my stuff in the boat and dove into the water. Four others followed, but they went all the way around the island and jumped when the boat was closer to the dock, on the east side. I jumped when it was way out. The tide was on the ebb, going towards the Golden Gate Bridge. The boats, the main boat and the press boats, well, they just kept going. They went right on by. People on the boats saw me and yelled, "Man overboard, man overboard," but they just kept on going.
>
> Before jumping I felt a great sense of urgency. I felt I had to do it, so I just jumped off. I didn't have time to be scared. . . . I was too busy trying to get to the Rock, because that water was cold, and it was swift. I landed just to the left of the dock, on the rocks, I was being dragged in by the waves or the current, or something, underneath the barge. I was exhausted when I hit land. I've done a lot of swimming, but this was the toughest swim I've ever made. I crawled up on the rocks to rest, and a dog came up and began to lick the salt off my body. . . . I found out later that this was their "ferocious" guard dog. I found the other four guys. We claimed the island *by right of discovery.* We represented five different tribes, so we claimed it in the name of the Indians of all the tribes,

not just one tribe. That was the first time we used the name which would become our name on the island: "Indians of All Tribes." . . . After we were there for a couple of hours, their warriors, the Coast Guard, came and took us off.

That same night, students from San Francisco State College and the Berkeley and Santa Cruz campuses of the University of California set out again.[15]

It is important to note that Oakes claimed the island by right of discovery. The 1964 occupiers had based their claim on the Sioux treaty of 1868, which had been disallowed by the federal court system. Participants who joined the 1969 occupation after the initial landing on November 20 often indicated that they occupied the island under the Sioux treaty and therefore had a right to the island. This reasoning serves to differentiate those who were involved in the planning and early occupation and those who came later and were not well aware of the previous occupations.

The records of the regional director of PMDS, Richard F. Laws, verifies that the landing occurred at approximately 4:35 P.M. on November 9 but in error states that it was carried out by four young men who identified themselves as American Indians. The men were met by Glen Dodson, who asked them to leave, which they did after about ten minutes.[16]

The *San Francisco Chronicle* reported:

Four young braves dived off the barque *Monte Cristo* and swam to shore during that assault, but were taken back off again by a friendly yachtsman after a caretaker threatened to summon United States marshals. . . . Seventy-five Indians originally had intended to land on the island yesterday morning in an armada of five borrowed pleasure boats but the little fleet failed to show up, so the Indians made a quick bargain with Ronald Craig, 37, of Vancouver, the owner-captain of the 138–foot barque *Monte Cristo*. . . . Craig kept his passengers about 100 yards offshore, however. Although four or five stalwarts who jumped from the ship made it to shore and briefly claimed the island it appeared that the Indians would have to settle for less than complete victory.[17]

Accounts of events later that day vary. According to Nordwall, following this first, brief assault the Native Americans met at the temporary headquarters of the San Francisco Indian Center. Everyone wanted to go back that very night and land in force on the island. A fishing boat, the *New Vera II,* agreed to take the second occupation group to the island for a fee of $3 per person. The Indians gathered up sleeping bags and blankets, headed for Fisherman's Wharf, and began loading the *New Vera II.* In the rush, however, they managed to take aboard only two or three loaves of bread to eat. Nordwall maintains that although some two hundred had been prepared to assault the island, there were no more than twenty-five on the *New Vera II.* The boat had been forced to leave Fisherman's Wharf prematurely because of fears that the Coast Guard had been alerted of the impending event and would possibly intercept the occupation force.[18]

Problems with boat transportation continued to plague the occupation force. As the *New Vera II* reached the island, the tide swirled around the dock, making the captain's attempt to tie up alongside it extremely hazardous. Despite the captain's considerable skill, the *New Vera II* had difficulty remaining alongside the barge docked at the island even for a short period, but he eventually was able to tie a line to the dock. The captain had not been informed that an actual occupation was going to occur, however, and once the Native Americans began throwing sleeping bags and equipment onto the pier, the captain became agitated. "Realizing that he could be charged with aiding and abetting our takeover and concerned with the rushing tides and the possibility of being shot any minute by a panicked caretaker, he suddenly threw the gears into reverse once again." Again only a small portion of the planned occupation force had gotten ashore. Nordwall contends, "We were disappointed at being left behind on the boat, but we could count fourteen Indians, a sizable contingent, on the shore of Alcatraz. One was Richard Oakes; three were women. They all flew up the stairway of the old fort and quickly disappeared into the darkness."[19]

According to Harden, however, after the brief landing the group went back to the Indian center to meet, deciding that about twenty Indian students would go to Alcatraz again that night. They went through the details again, this time figuring that the government would not expect them to go back, especially the same night. The group set out on the *Vera II* at about six o'clock. The boat owner got scared when they started climbing off the boat so he began to back the boat away. Only fourteen of them made it to the island that night:

Jim Vaughn, Cherokee; John Martel, Cherokee; John Whitefox; John
Vigil; Joe Bill, Eskimo; LaNada Boyer, Shoshone-Bannock; David
Leach, Colville-Sioux; Richard Oakes, Mohawk; Bernel Blindman,
Sioux; Rick Evening, Shoshone; Fred Shelton; Linda Aranaydo; Kay
Many Horse; and Ross Harden, Winnebago.[20]

Joe Bill maintains that in the evening they hired a small fishing boat
and fourteen of the occupiers landed with only two loaves of bread
among them. That afternoon the GSA came and took them off the
island. The GSA spokesperson said they would not be arrested if they
left peacefully, and so they left and began planning an assault for the
week of Christmas, when all of the students would be out of school.
It was at this time that they planned to go on the island and stay
there.[21]

Richard Oakes recalls that they got a ride to the island with some
Sausalito sailors and landed at about six o'clock. The caretaker, his
dog, and three patrollers tried to find the group of fourteen who were
hiding in the grass and among the many buildings on the island. Oakes
states that at times they passed within inches of him and his fellow
occupiers.[22]

John Hart, the contract custodian on Alcatraz, was immediately
aware of the second November 9 landing. A GSA memorandum written by Richard Laws on November 19, describing the events of the
night of November 9, reported that at approximately 6:30 P.M., Hart
called Thomas Scott, the realty officer of the PMDS, and stated that
he was fairly certain that the Indians had once again landed on the
island. Hart called Scott again at 10:30 P.M. to confirm their presence
but did not know how many people were on the island. Scott told him
that U.S. marshals had been called and advised Hart to await further
instructions in the morning.[23]

According to his memoranda, on November 10 T. E. Hannon, regional director of GSA, went to Alcatraz to ascertain the intentions
of the occupiers and bring the incident to a close. He was accompanied by Thomas Scott, two uniformed GSA guards, the attorney for
the GSA, and some thirty-five to forty members of the press. After a
cursory inspection of the buildings, the fourteen occupiers came out
of hiding, made statements to the press, and presented Hannon with
a proclamation claiming the island by right of discovery. They then
agreed to return peacefully to the mainland. On a Coast Guard vessel during the voyage back Oakes accepted Hannon's invitation to

come to his office at a later time to discuss future plans. Hannon expressed his hope that Oakes and his group would not attempt to return to Alcatraz again. On landing, the occupiers disbursed. No arrests were made and no charges were filed.[24]

Oakes recalled that the occupiers had expected to be removed at sunrise. When Hannon arrived with the Coast Guard and a large number of reporters, the hidden occupiers could not be found. Finally at around noon the Native Americans went down to the prison exercise yard for a conference. Following the conference they went down to the dock and read their proclamation, claiming the island in the name of Indians of All Tribes and presenting their demands to the government. Oakes and the other member of the occupation force vowed that they would be back.[25]

Perhaps the best description of the first night on Alcatraz Island comes from Ross Harden. He recalled that immediately upon landing the Indian men and women ran around to the south and decided to make their way to the top of the island, where the main cellblock was located. Upon reaching the top, they noticed that the Coast Guard had started turning spotlights on different parts of the island. This indicated to Harden and the others that the Indians on the mainland had followed their prearranged strategy and notified the press of their landing. The occupiers then divided into three groups so that even if one group was found, the others would be safe. Harden's group decided that the old cellblock was an interesting place to see, and it was in the cellblock that they were discovered the following day by reporters. They advised Harden and his group that the GSA and the Coast Guard were down at the dock and were giving the occupiers a chance to get off the island peacefully before charging them with breaking and entering and trespassing on federal property. After a brief discussion Harden and his group decided it would be better to go. Prior to leaving, however, they read their proclamation to the GSA officials and announced that this was just the beginning of their protest. Harden explains, "We felt that fourteen of us would be easier to arrest than maybe about fifty or sixty people, and we wouldn't be doing the movement any good sitting in jail. Besides, this was just the beginning and there was a lot of planning to do. The most important thing in our minds was the fact that the Indians were getting stepped on and we wanted to make them aware of this."[26]

The following statement was then released to the press:

> Our people have suffered at the hands of the white man ever since we welcomed the Pilgrims to our shores. In return for our help and kindness, the white man has stolen our lands, killed our people and decimated our way of life. We have been under the Bureau of Indian Affairs for over one hundred years, and as a result we have the highest rate of unemployment, of illness, of poverty—of all the sickness of modern life.
>
> Now our young people cry out for social justice and for an opportunity to reclaim their proud heritage. The landing on Alcatraz Island is a symbol of our cultural right to land and to life. How are we to be charged with trespassing on the white man's land when the white man has taken all of this land from us?
>
> We propose to take control of our own lives and destiny, to assert our right to reclaim the tiny island of Alcatraz which once held our people imprisoned. We wish to develop on this island, Indian centers for the training and development of our Indian youth for a healthy and spiritual life.
>
> Our young people are only trying to reclaim Indian land for the betterment of all mankind. Their cause is noble and just. They should be treated as honorable warriors without weapons—not as criminals or as dogs.
>
> Hear our just claims; grant us social justice; restore our dignity and return us a symbol of our lost lands! We ask all white men of good will to join us in pressing our claim for Alcatraz Island and for a better life for all Indians.[27]

This was the first call by the occupying group for Indian self-determination.

Press coverage was objective and summarized the events of the two brief occupations in much the same manner as Harden, Ross, and Oakes have. On November 10 the *San Francisco Chronicle* carried the article "Indians Invade Rock; U.S. Counter-Attacks" and followed it up with "Indians 'Reserve' the Rock" and "Fourteen Indians Invade, Claim Alcatraz" on November 11. The *San Francisco Examiner* carried "Indians Invade Rock; U.S. Counter-Attacks" while the *San Diego Union* printed "Indians 'Reclaim' Alcatraz Island, Give It Back to the Indians" on November 10.[28]

The *San Francisco Examiner* additionally reported, "Authorities took a fairly light view of it [the occupation] until today, when the Coast Guard reported someone had broken into the lighthouse." This incident was mentioned also in the *San Francisco Chronicle.* Oakes contended that the occupiers had noted that a door had been jarred open, but the Indians had nothing to do with that. This charge may have been an attempt to focus negative publicity on the occupation force.[29]

The press identified Nordwall as instrumental in the preoccupation planning and support but focused on Oakes as the leader. The *San Francisco Chronicle* quoted Oakes as stating that the Indian occupiers had proven their point and that next time they would construct a new nation on Alcatraz. Oakes went on to say that if nothing else they had established Indian "squatter's rights" to the land. "If a one-day occupation by white men on Indian land years ago established squatter's rights, then the one day occupation of Alcatraz should establish Indian rights to the island."[30]

According to the *San Francisco Examiner,* Nordwall maintained "the landing party would remain until the claim is recognized," but added that the fourteen occupiers had arrived on the island without bedding or much food. Earl Livermore identified for the paper all fourteen of the occupiers as students of San Francisco State College or the University of California at Berkeley, sites for new programs of Native American studies.[31] Nordwall also verified for the *San Diego Union* that "at least 25 different tribes were represented in the group gathered at Fisherman's Wharf in view of Alcatraz Island."[32]

The planners did not take their actions lightly and fully realized that the occupation could be considered a criminal offense. Prior to landing, a representative for the Indian students engaged the services of the law firm Hodges, Houchins, and Zweig. A representative of the firm advised the occupation leaders that their planned peaceful demonstration would most likely result in citations for failure to comply with official signs of a prohibitory nature or loitering and disorderly conduct, none of which were felony offenses. However, the Native Americans were warned that there was always an inherent danger in any demonstration that a participant might commit a more serious crime without recognizing the consequences, such as forcible resistance to or assault upon any Coast Guard personnel, Indian field service officer, or marshal.[33]

Fears of government action against the occupiers proved unfounded, however. According to the *San Francisco Examiner*, the U.S. attorney's office had dismissed the invasion as a skirmish peaceably concluded and not worth pursuing in the courts. Oakes, on the other hand, pronounced that the Indian occupiers "had probably achieved their purpose with the publicity they received."[34]

However the U.S. Attorney's Office may have interpreted Oakes's statement, it soon became evident that Oakes did not mean that the Native Americans were abandoning Alcatraz Island without further confrontation. He considered the first two landings as reconnaissance missions, each group returning to confirm that they would be able to do the job. Oakes felt more people and more planning time was needed for the larger occupation he had in mind. He traveled to UCLA and made a speech about the occupations to Indian students, telling them that there was nothing to fear other than the hardships of the island itself. He said that he needed people who would be willing to live on the island. Oakes told the students that although it would take intense dedication to stay on the island, it would mean a great deal to all Native Americans. Eighty of the Indian students at UCLA decided to abandon their studies and travel to San Francisco to participate in the forthcoming occupation.[35]

Before dawn on November 20, eighty-nine Indian people occupied Alcatraz once again. In addition to college students, six children ranging from two to six years of age and several married couples came along. Traveling by boat from Sausalito, the landing force was met by a Coast Guard blockade. According to Oakes, the Coast Guard tried to take the boat carrying the Indian people that night, but some of the Indians jumped on the Coast Guard boat and said that if they tried to take the boat, they would take theirs. Oakes pronounced it a spectacle: helicopters circled overhead as the Coast Guard blocked access to Alcatraz. The island caretaker came out and started blowing his bugle, then called out, "The Indians are here, the Indians are here. I think they're here to stay." The caretaker told Oakes and the other occupiers that they were trespassing. Oakes recognized that he was trespassing, but told the caretaker that if he cooperated, the Indians would set up a Bureau of Caucasian Affairs and make him head of it.[36]

According to Nordwall, Oakes appealed to Tim Findley for help. Findley contacted Peter Bowen, who owned the boats that were utilized to carry the landing party. The occupiers were to meet at the

No Name Bar at approximately 2:00 A.M. and mingle with the closing crowd. Approximately ninety Indians including students from UCLA and the University of California at Santa Cruz arrived, gear-laden, and went to the Sausalito waterfront and loaded onto three waiting boats.

Nordwall's information was not firsthand because he had departed on another public relations effort to support the occupation. He had been invited to attend the first National Conference on Indian Education, which was being held in Minneapolis on November 20, the same date as the planned occupation. Nordwall saw this as an opportunity, however, to enlist national support:

> A meeting was held and I explained to the people that the Minneapolis conference would draw a large number of Indian scholars and tribal leaders and if we could give them first hand information about our cause they would take it back to their people. This would get us the national support and exposure just when we could use it to the best advantage and put pressure on the government. We would need a lot of copies of the proclamation for distributing at the conference. . . . The Scientific Analysis Corporation of San Francisco jumped into the breech by running off a couple thousand copies of the four page proclamation in time for me to take them to Minneapolis.
>
> While in Minneapolis I maintained constant contact with the activities going on in California. Bobbie [his wife] provided information for me to be able to pass on to the conference the moment this new invasion was effected. On November 20, I got the message, "The island is being taken again!" I went before this big assemblage of Indian scholars, educators, and community leaders and got the chairman to recognize me. I had the copies of the proclamation with me and I explained the purposes of the occupation and that we, in the Bay Area, would appreciate their taking copies of the proclamation and sharing them with their tribes. The response was incredible. All over that big auditorium was cheering as I ended my request of them. . . . The conference transformed our remote little Indian activity into a national movement with national support.[37]

Meanwhile, the large occupation force was met by a bleary-eyed caretaker, who stumbled out of his shack "with almost jubilant cries of 'Mayday, Mayday, the Indians have landed!' 'I don't really mind,' grinned deputy caretaker Glenn Dodson, adding with a sly wink to Oakes, 'besides, I'm one-eighth Indian myself.'"[38] Dodson directed the Indians to the island's most comfortable quarters, a three-story frame house that was formerly the warden's residence. There the Native Americans took advantage of the few remaining pieces of furniture to set up their headquarters.

The successful landing was celebrated with a victory powwow and ceremonial singing accompanied by a drum. Peter Blue Cloud described the following morning: as they walked uphill to the main cellblock the ocean breeze bathed them in a freshness which only the mountain, forests, and plains can know. The sun had risen, a huge red ball of fire. The waters of the bay were black, dark blue, green, and even white where the fog blanket was reflected. Choppy waves danced and the first sail boats caused the breezes to billow and pick up speed. A giant ship emerged from the fog and its horn blasted the seagulls screaming. They entered the main cellblock and walked through the cold, alien world of concrete and steel bars. On this first passage through the cellblocks they did not look too closely into the tiny cubicles which not so long ago housed human beings. Later, they would investigate this former maximum security prison and wonder at its many secrets.[39]

The occupiers explored the entire island, checking out the cell-blocks, walkways, and industry buildings. They wanted to generally familiarize themselves with the island, locate housing, and find possible hiding places in the event of attempted removal from the island, which they felt was imminent. As they explored, they also began to change the face of the island so that they could broadcast messages for those who would look upon the island during the occupation. By midday, flat cement spots on the buildings and road ramps displayed red-painted signs such as You Are Now on Indian Land. A sign on the water tower dominating the north end of the island read Peace and Freedom, Welcome, Home of the Free Indian Land. A warning sign for those approaching the island had been changed to read Warning Keep Off Indian Property.

The occupiers released a statement to the press that was an appeal for fair play, support, and understanding:

We, the members of the Indian Nations and tribes of North America, in an attempt to secure this island; in our attempt at asserting our cultural heritage; in establishing on this island an Institute responsive to the religious diversity of this Indian Nation; in the creation of a viable program of higher education serviceable to the needs of the Indian people; respectfully solicit your cooperation and expertise.

Indian people are desperately in need of self-assertion for their way of life and their desperate needs, both economic and political. The move to Alcatraz Island symbolizes what American Indians can get with mind power.

We are asking you to give back our honor and we won't need jails; give Indians a chance to come up and not have to stand behind any more.

We have been in this land for thousands of years. After a hundred years as prisoners of this country, we feel that it is time we were free. We have gone to Alcatraz Island to preserve our dignity and beauty and to assert our position with the new weapons we have come to learn how to use. These weapons are the same ones these invaders of our country used to take what they wanted.

These weapons are the laws and lawyers, and the power of the pen to tell our real story.

But in addition, we now have a more powerful weapon. The people of this country know a little of the real history and tragedy of the Indian people. What they do not know is the tragic story of the Indian people today. We intend to tell them that story. This is only the first stepping-stone of a great ladder of Indian progress.

We appeal to your sense of fair play and your desire to do what is right by all peoples. Indian people appeal to you to stand by us and help us in our hour of need.[40]

The government response to this new occupation was cautious. The Coast Guard established a blockade around the island to prevent augmentation of the occupation force. On the island Alcatraz chief security officer John Hart, who had been away on a fishing trip, returned to find the occupiers ensconced in the former warden's residence.

Hart, a gruff veteran of the busiest and bleakest periods on the Rock during his twenty-one-year tenure there, found the Native Americans awake and still singing in their paint-peeling sanctuary. A fire of branches and stray paper cups crackled in the fireplace and a large poster of the Apache chief Geronimo glowered from above the mantel. The Indians' food supply was laid out on one table—sandwiches, potato salad, and soft drinks. "Well, as long as you're here, you might as well be comfortable," Hart stated. He pointed out the accessible buildings with working plumbing and warned of some hazards on the crumbling catwalks and overgrown stairways of the hilly, deteriorating island.[41]

At 4:00 P.M., GSA regional administrator Thomas Hannon, who had visited the island that morning, returned with two attorneys representing the Indian occupiers—Aubrey Grossman and R. Corbin Houchins—and a representative of the Department of the Interior. Press members arrived on the island by helicopter and chartered fishing boat to record the events.[42] After meeting with the occupation force, Hannon delivered an ultimatum: the occupiers had until noon on November 21 to leave. One food supply boat would be allowed through the blockade but any other boats attempting to break through the blockade would be impounded. With one night's safety guaranteed, the weary invaders settled in scattered groups about their island. "'We won't resist,' said Dennis Turner, 22, a Mission Shoshone, 'but how will they find us? It's why we are here in the first place—we are the invisible Americans.'"[43]

On the afternoon of November 21 it became clear that despite Turner's statement the Indian occupiers would, in fact, resist removal from the island. Oakes and Houchins telephoned the following message to William T. Devoranon, regional coordinator of the Department of the Interior in San Francisco:

> To the Government of the United States from Alcatraz Island, Indian Territory.
>
> We native peoples of North America have gathered here to claim our traditional and natural right to create a meaningful use for our Great Spirit's land. Therefore, let it be known that *our stand for self-determination is on Alcatraz.* We invite the United States to acknowledge the justice of our claim. The choice now lies with the leaders of the American Government—to use violence upon us as before to remove us from our Great Spirit's land, or to institute a real change in its dealing with the American Indian. We do not fear your threat to charge us with crimes on

our land. We and all other oppressed peoples would welcome spectacle of proof before the world of your title by genocide. Nevertheless, we seek peace. We will negotiate with you on the mainland if:

1. Mr. Walter Hickel meets personally with our representative immediately upon his arrival on Alcatraz, San Francisco, and confers in good faith.
2. It is agreed as a preliminary to the meeting that the United States
   a. Return Alcatraz to the Indians within two weeks of this date, by transferring all its interest in the Island to an entity controlled and administered by American Indians popularly elected by the Indian people, without any participation in its management by any agency of government; and
   b. Provide that entity with funding for an Indian cultural complex, in sufficient amount to construct, maintain and operate a major university and research and development center for all Indian people, without participation in its administration by any agency of government.
3. The meeting take place in the presence of all Indians who are now on Alcatraz.
4. The subject of the meeting be the implementation of the preliminary agreement.
5. There be no interference with supply of necessary provisions for persons on Alcatraz.[44]

A press release calling for support for a prolonged occupation was also sent out:

Indian people are on Alcatraz in support of their assertion that they have the right to use the land for their benefit.

They went onto the island this morning with little hard supplies. They are going to stay.

Because they are going to stay they will need money and food. Canned goods and staples are sorely needed.

Because of the difficulty of getting to the island, perishables are not easy to carry to it. Frozen foods, bread, and other similar items will be difficult to carry out.

Money for building is also needed. The island is very run-down, and it will take much work to put it back into shape. Indians are willing to do the work, but they will need money to buy supplies, building materials, etc.

Food should be brought to the temporary headquarters of the American Indian Center, 3189–16th St. (at Guerrero) in San Francisco. Checks and money should also be sent to the Center and specify that they are for the Alcatraz Building Fund.[45]

Secretary of the Interior Walter Hickel replied to the Indian proclamation in a press statement, indicating that he would negotiate at any time but that the conditions set forth were unacceptable. Hickel noted that it was not in his power to transfer ownership of the island or to alter it in any manner. Hickel also hoped that the Indians would leave Alcatraz for safety's sake.[46]

Following Hannon's second visit to the island additional boatloads of Indians and reporters attempted to break the blockade and land on Alcatraz. In anticipation of further attempts, U.S. marshals were placed on the Coast Guard patrol boats circling the island. Hickel requested the GSA to do nothing to remove the Indians from the island until after 3:00 P.M. on Sunday, November 23, to allow for a cooling off period. The GSA honored Hickel's request.[47]

The Coast Guard blockade made it difficult to transport badly needed supplies to the occupation force, so most had to be brought to the island around two or three in the morning, when the guards were most vulnerable.[48] On November 23, a hot air balloon loaded with supplies for the estimated 120 Indians on Alcatraz Island was launched from the San Francisco Bay Marina. Unfortunately, due to adverse wind conditions, this attempt to avoid the blockade failed. Other attempts were more successful. Joe Bill slipped his canoe into the waters alongside Alcatraz and paddled to San Francisco, where he requested donations from the people on the mainland. A mercy ship came to Alcatraz that night and beached on the Golden Gate side of the island. From that side the upper levels of the island are inaccessible except by navigating sheer cliffs. The occupiers made a makeshift ladder and brought supplies from the boat up the ladder and over the precarious cliffs. To create a diversion, others started a fire on the opposite side of the island, throwing firebombs at the rocks alongside the shoreline to keep the Coast Guard busy.

According to Harden on one occasion the *Bella Donna* was waiting with nineteen Native Americans and a load of food and supplies. In order for the boat to land, the Indians on the island had to divert the Coast Guard's attention. The Indians got a can of diesel fuel from one of the abandoned trucks and some jars and made Molotov cocktails. They lit the cocktails, waited until the Coast Guard cutter could see the fire and sped up to investigate, and then threw a couple of cocktails onto the rocks below. The occupiers ran along the rocks throwing cocktails every twenty yards or so until they got to the south side of the island. The Coast Guard caught up with them and saw the Native Americans standing by the boat. The Coast Guard ship turned around to go back to the dock, but arrived just in time to see the Indians climbing off the boat.[49]

Despite the Coast Guard blockade surreptitious infiltration continued. One technique used was to join the other sailboats out on the bay and then sail by the island and throw supplies onto the Alcatraz barge, which was docked on the island. When this occurred the Coast Guard would sound a warning siren and attempt to prevent supplies from being landed. While the Coast Guard was pursuing that boat a waiting boat would come alongside and unload provisions onto the barge. A number of the Indian occupiers were standing by on the barge at all times to take donations from passing boats. Harden maintained that not only was the blockade ineffective but it also created a great deal of attention, favorable publicity, and support for the occupation. Although marshals made four arrests during attempts to bring provisions to Alcatraz on November 22, the blockade proved largely ineffectual and was lifted on Monday, November 24, after four days in operation. When the blockade was lifted, volunteer boats were standing by to provide food and water and to transport Indians back and forth between the island and the mainland.[50]

While the Coast Guard was busy attempting to maintain outside control, the occupiers were busy organizing themselves. Meetings were called as often as three times a day so that all Indian people on the island could be involved in the governing process. The meetings often focused on what should be done in event of a "rip off," a term the Indians used to mean their forcible removal from the island that reflected their fears. A council was selected to talk to the press and to the government. Although the men were organized into security, garbage, and clean-up crews, the women chose and volunteered their own work, such as cooking, sorting out the cans of food, and setting up the dining room. In the early days of the occupation security was the main concern and was provided both day and night. The security force was headed by Jerry Hatch, one of the men who made the initial landing. Lookouts were stationed on all corners of the main cellblock roof, where they could see all over the island.[51]

Although the federal government had not yet officially recognized the Indian occupation, the presence of U.S. marshals on the Coast Guard boats and Thomas Hannon's negotiation attempts provided tacit acknowledgment. Because of this delayed reaction, federal records from the first days of the occupation are sparse. The files of President Richard Nixon and the White House staff contain no information regarding the initial notification of or reaction to the November 20 occupation. In an interview with Leonard Garment, presidential special counsel during the occupation, Garment stated that in spite of Nixon's interest in Indian affairs, the president provided no direct guidance for handling the Alcatraz situation. Nixon presided over a daily 7:00 A.M. meeting attended by Assistant for Domestic Policy John Ehrlichman, Chief of Staff H. R. Haldeman, and National Security Affairs Assistant Henry Kissinger, which was followed by an 8:00 A.M. meeting chaired by either Ehrlichman or Haldeman with staff officers including Garment, his assistant Bradley Patterson, Ehrlichman's assistant Bud Krogh, Deputy Domestic Policy Chief Kenneth Cole, and White House intern Bobbie Greene. Any directions would have come down from President Nixon either directly to Garment or through the morning meeting from Ehrlichman to Garment to Patterson.[52]

In interviews with the author, neither Garment nor Patterson could recall how the initial notification came into the White House, nor do they recall having ever received special instructions regarding what was to be done, if anything, about the Indians on Alcatraz Island. Garment and Patterson both followed a "negative leadership" style in which they reacted to domestic situations based on their personal knowledge of Nixon's presidential policies. If they misunderstood or reacted incorrectly, they would hear "in one hell of a hurry" from the president. Patterson indicated that Ehrlichman "probably" briefed Nixon from time to time orally but that he and Garment ran the operation, being very sensitive to any instructions from Ehrlichman.[53]

In his book *The Ring of Power*, Patterson provides a firsthand illustration of the White House staff's role in this domestic crisis:

November 19, 1969: during the night a group of eighty Indian men, women, and children occupy long-vacant Alcatraz Island in San Francisco Bay. They issue a statement challenging the federal government: you can prove your title to Alcatraz by committing "genocide" against us, or you can send the secretary of the interior to meet with us in person after he agrees to give us the island and enough money to "construct, maintain, and operate a major university and research and development center there for all Indian people." Apocalyptic threat; theatrical demand.

Considering this to be simply a trespass, the real title holder to Alcatraz, Administrator Robert Kunzig of the U.S. General Services Administration, issues orders to his West Coast staff: get U.S. marshals to take the Indians off at gunpoint "by noon tomorrow."

Then the White House intervenes. Presidential special counsel Leonard Garment recognizes that this escapade is much more than an ordinary trespass, sees the GSA plan as pugnacious overreaction likely to spill blood and stir up an enormous public revulsion, and is sure that he has the support of the president. Garment telephones Kunzig and flatly instructs him to call off the marshals. Furthermore, the White House will need up-to-date information and will therefore want to be talking with GSA West Coast regional administrator Tom Hannon directly, for situation reports, but will keep GSA's Washington office informed.

Kunzig is furious; this is an unconscionable intrusion into his turf and his responsibilities; he finally tells Garment to deal with anyone he wants but never to speak to him again.

Garment's office promptly establishes communications with Hannon in San Francisco, keeping a Kunzig aide au curant as well. Why Hannon? Because he is the person on the front line of the crisis. . . . When Hannon comes back to his office phone, only he has the kind of immediate intelligence for which the crisis managers thirst.[54]

Neither the White House staff nor the Indians could have visualized that a symbolic statement for Indian self-determination would become a prolonged occupation of an internationally recognized federal facility. Oakes and others of the occupation party felt that removal from the island would come quickly, in the form of federal troops or, short of that, some type of negotiation. The federal government, however, could not afford a forced removal in which Indian men, women, and children might suffer injury or death. The war in Vietnam hung like a millstone around the Nixon presidency. The recent massacre of civilians by U.S. Army troops in the Vietnamese hamlet of My Lai and the shooting of college students at Kent State University by the National Guard dictated that an armed removal from Alcatraz was impossible. Instead, the government attempted to prevent supplies from reaching the island and thereby force an end to the occupation. Negotiations between the island occupiers and the federal government quickly became a problem. The occupiers recognized that they could bargain from a position of strength only as long as they physically occupied Alcatraz Island; they refused to leave peacefully. The government initially refused to negotiate unless the Native Americans left the island but subsequently agreed to meet with representatives on Alcatraz. Public pressure, newspaper articles, telephone calls, and telegrams to political leaders at all levels of state and federal government, including President Nixon, forced the concession. No points of compromise were reached. The occupiers remained fixed in their demands, so the government became equally fixed in its refusal. Since force could not be used, isolation, the passage of time, and the federal bureaucracy would be the weapons.

Notes

1. Dorothy Lonewolf Miller, "Alcatraz Rain."
2. Fortunate Eagle, *Alcatraz!* 38.
3. Kemnitzer, "Personal Memories," 107.
4. Oakes, "Alcatraz," 35–41.
5. Bill interview, 10.
6. Harden interview, 5.
7. Hauptman, *Iroquois Struggle,* 225. Hauptman affirms that Adam Nordwall realized that an occupation of the island would be a major media event: "Attempting to reverse the 'doctrine of discovery' in favor of the Indian, Nordwall . . . prepared for a landing in the summer of 1970" (225).
8. Livermore interview, 2.
9. Indians of All Tribes, "Proclamation."
10. Fortunate Eagle, *Alcatraz!* 50.
11. Very little written documentation of these efforts was made at that time, so most material is in the form of recollections of the participants. Four significant participants were interviewed: Joe Bill, a Hooper Bay Eskimo,

whose oral history was taken February 5, 1970; Ross Harden, a Winnebago, whose oral history was recorded on July 14, 1970; Richard Oakes, a Mohawk, whose recollections were recorded in late November 1969 and published in "Alcatraz Is Not an Island" in December 1972; and LaNada Boyer, whose oral history was recorded in December 1992.

12. Fortunate Eagle, *Alcatraz!* 52.

13. Ibid., 54–55.

14. Harden interview, 9–10.

15. Oakes, "Alcatraz," 38.

16. GSA memorandum, Nov. 19, 1969. This account coincides most closely with Ross Harden's.

17. "Fourteen Indians Invade, Claim Alcatraz," *San Francisco Chronicle,* Nov. 10, 1969. This article was under the byline of Tim Findley, the public relations representative for the occupiers. The events of the landing as reported in this article also coincide with those of Ross Harden's.

18. Fortunate Eagle, *Alcatraz!* 59.

19. Ibid., 63.

20. Harden interview, 10–11.

21. Bill interview, 10–11.

22. Oakes, "Alcatraz," 38.

23. GSA memorandum, Nov. 19, 1969.

24. Hannon memorandum, Nov. 11, 1969.

25. Oakes, "Alcatraz," 38.

26. Harden interview, 10–11.

27. Indians of All Tribes, press release, Nov. 10, 1969.

28. "Indians Invade Rock; U.S. Counter-Attacks," *San Francisco Chronicle,* Nov. 10, 1969; "Indians 'Reserve' the Rock," *San Francisco Chronicle,* Nov. 11, 1969; "Fourteen Indians Invade, Claim Alcatraz," *San Francisco Chronicle,* Nov. 11, 1969; "Indians Invade Rock; U.S. Counter-Attacks," *San Francisco Examiner,* Nov. 10, 1969; "Indians 'Reclaim' Alcatraz Island—Give It Back to the Indians," *San Diego Union,* Nov. 11, 1969.

29. "Indians Invade Rock; U.S. Counter-Attacks," *San Francisco Examiner,* Nov. 10, 1969.

30. "Indians Invade Rock; U.S. Counter-Attacks," *San Francisco Chronicle,* Nov. 10, 1969.

31. "Indians Invade Rock; U.S. Counter-Attacks," *San Francisco Examiner,* Nov. 10, 1969.

32. "Indians 'Reclaim' Alcatraz."

33. Houchins, letter to anonymous Indian leader. Courtesy copies were sent to Adam Nordwall and Earl Livermore, which indicate that they were working behind the scenes to promote the occupation and protect those involved.

34. "U.S. Waives Charges in Indian Caper," *San Francisco Examiner,* Nov. 11, 1969.

35. Oakes, "Alcatraz," 38. Records at the UCLA American Indian Studies Center indicate that Oakes did in fact recruit a large number of American Indian students from that university to participate in the occupation. The exact number is not recorded.

36. Ibid.

37. Fortunate Eagle, *Alcatraz!* 71–72.

38. "Raiders Capture Alcatraz—A 'Free Indian Land,'" *San Francisco Chronicle,* Nov. 21, 1969.

39. Blue Cloud, *Alcatraz,* 22.

40. Indians of All Tribes, letter to Whom It May Concern.

41. "Raiders Capture Alcatraz."

42. Hannon contacted the Federal Aviation Agency (FAA) to check laws governing helicopter landings on the Island. The FAA notified all local helicopter services and rental agencies that few if any had proper instruments required by law for flight over water, thus virtually eliminating further helicopter flights and landings on the island.

43. "Raiders Capture Alcatraz." The *Chronicle* reported that later in the day permission was received to land donated food from the Trident Restaurant and the Rock Island Health Food Store, both in Sausalito.

44. Indians of All Tribes, "Proclamation." It is interesting to note that in an interview with the author in December 1992 LaNada Boyer stated that self-determination *was not* an island concept. Boyer insisted that they did not know what they were doing, that they had "no grand plan." The dichotomy that seems to exist here may be because Oakes was a student at San Francisco State University while Boyer was a student at the University of California at Berkeley. Boyer did not travel with Oakes to UCLA when he recruited the largest portion of the occupation force and perhaps she was not present when the wording of the proclamation, which includes the specific word *self-determination,* was drawn up.

45. Indians of All Tribes, press release, Nov. 20, 1969.

46. U.S. Department of the Interior, press release.

47. Brant chronology.

48. Livermore interview, 2.

49. Harden defines "the movement" as follows: "When I speak of the movement, I mean Alcatraz, and the awakening of Indians." Harden interview, 13.

50. "Aerial Relief Fails," *Stockton Sunday Record,* Nov. 23, 1969.

51. Harden interview, 27. As will be discussed, women also served on the island security force.

52. Garment telephone interview and Patterson telephone interview. Ehr-lichman's presidential files contain no information regarding the Alcatraz occupation. Bud Krogh, Kenneth Cole, and Bobbie Greene would become involved in the Indian occupation as assistants to Garment, Ehrlichman, and Patterson as the occupation continued into 1970 and 1971.

53. Ibid.

54. Patterson, *Ring of Power,* 72–73. Patterson informed the author in a telephone interview on July 9, 1992, that the rift created in 1969 was never healed and that Kunzig never spoke to him or Garment because of this exer-cise of White House prerogative by the presidential staff.

5

The Occupation:
Logistics and Support

/.\.\.\

There can be no doubt that activities on Alcatraz received the majority of the attention from the government, the media, and the American public, and properly so. Credit must also be given, however, to the San Francisco mainland organization and support group that arose during the early stages of the occupation. The San Francisco Indian Center on Valencia Street had been a popular meeting place for various Bay Area Indian organizations, and the Intertribal Friendship House in Oakland had also been the site of meetings of various groups, including the Bay Area Council. The occupation of 1964 had been discussed and planned, largely, by Indian groups meeting at these facilities. The Indian studies centers in Bay Area colleges and universities also produced organizations that discussed and planned the series of occupations. Following the October 1969 fire that destroyed the San Francisco Indian Center, the temporary center located at 3189 16th Street became the local base of operations for the occupation. After the brief November 9 occupations, the Indian students returned to this temporary facility to plan the final, prolonged occupation, while Oakes traveled to UCLA to recruit Indian students. After the November 20 occupation, the temporary center became the initial point of contact between the occupiers, the media, the public, and other Indian and non-Indian people who wanted to become involved. As donations of food, clothing, camping supplies, and money began to stockpile additional space was needed. Joseph Morris, a Blackfoot Indian and member of the local longshoreman's union, acquired an empty space on Pier 40 on the San Francisco waterfront and with voluntary laborers including Earl Livermore, Charles Dana, Dean Chavers, and Shirley Keith turned the space into a logistical staging area from which supplies and people could be ferried to Alcatraz.

Everyone recognized the importance of establishing and maintaining a reliable supply network. The occupation would live or die based on voluntary donations. Everything required for life on the island, from the clothes the occupiers would wear, the food they would eat, to the water they would drink would have to come from donations and would have to be transported by boat. As the occupation continued logistical support became even more important as the federal government tightened the controls over Alcatraz Island and moved to restrict the flow of supplies.

As the volume of donations continued to increase, another facility was needed. Many of the occupiers slept and ate at the new facility provided free of charge by the Scientific Analysis Corporation (SAC) in San Francisco. Joaquin Ochoa and John Jimenez operated a two-way radio system between the SAC office and the island—a twenty-four-hour-a-day vigil. Among the handful of volunteers who lived and worked in the SAC offices were Peter Blue Cloud, Grace Thorpe, and Dorothy Miller. In these offices, funding for the occupation was obtained from many sources and an accounting system was established to keep track of public donations.[1] An account in the name of Indians of All Tribes was opened with the Mission Branch of the Bank of America in San Francisco. Mail and telephone services were provided from the SAC offices, as was transportation on the mainland. Food, water, and clothing were deposited in the SAC offices, and a distribution system to the island was established through the temporary warehouse facility on Pier 40.[2]

Richard DeLuca has indicated that public sympathy lay with the Native Americans. In the first week of the occupation, more than $4,000 was received by the American Indian Center, and on Thanksgiving Day, 200 complimentary dinners were prepared and delivered to the island by a local restaurateur. Public support was also evident in the numerous letters and telegrams that streamed into the offices of government officials, including the president.[3]

According to Dan Bomberry, a Cayuga Indian, there was widespread support for the occupation, but it came particularly from the Bay Area and northern California. People came from service clubs and down from out of the woods in northern California with food and supplies. Additionally, a large amount of money was donated to the Indians of Alcatraz so that a sizable bank account developed.[4] One anonymous donor provided $15,000 and Creedence Clearwater Revival, a rock and roll band, donated a $15,000 voucher to be used for the purchase of a boat to transport people and supplies between the island and the mainland. The *Bass Tub I* was purchased for $9,000 and the remaining money was deposited with a Berkeley food co-op and was used to buy food for the occupiers.[5] Lehman Brightman, president of the United Native Americans, added that a lot of the colleges and other non-Indian organizations collected funds and donations. Brightman recalled that they had over $17,000 on hand in January 1970.[6]

Rosalie McKay-Want, a Wintu/Wailaki and Pomo Indian, provided insights regarding the difficulties encountered in establishing an administrative organization that could properly handle and document the massive public interest:

> People came from all over the country. We had offices off the is-
> land and on the island both and the professional people kind of
> took over and ran everything and that was okay because nobody
> else knew how to do anything. The majority of us did not know.
> I was around the office a lot where I saw what was happening.
> And even though these people were more sophisticated than I
> was, I could see that they were learning too. They might have
> been working in offices but the majority weren't directors. There
> might have been one or two directors in the group but they
> couldn't do everything. We had to have a PR place because we
> just had letters, letters, letters. And, of course, the TV was out
> there all the time.[7]

An "Indian Desk" was set up at the SAC offices to handle public relations. The office was initially staffed by Livermore and other Indian volunteers. One worker summed up the efforts of the many volunteers: "Every day was HECTIC, but wonderful."

Thanks in part to the donated supplies more Indians took up residence on the island, including entire families. By the first weekend, the population had reached in excess of one hundred, and two hundred visited. The first requirement to support the growing population was housing.

Peter Blue Cloud recalled that sleeping quarters were everywhere. Each person felt free to decide where to live. Some of the occupiers lived in solitary confinement cells, the chapel, the warden's house, and the guard's quarters. Large rooms were claimed by groups and the rooms were named in bold letters of paint: POMO ROOM! DO NOT DIS-

TURB, MONOS, PRIVATE—PAIUTE, LONGHOUSE, LODGE OF THE CHEYENNE, AND SIOUX ROOM.[8]

These signs, setting forth ownership and boundaries within the island population, presented an early contradiction to the ethos of pan-Indianism and can be seen as antithetical to the collective spirit of the occupation force. Although they presented a pan- or supratribal appearance to the public, the Indians' loyalties remained first and foremost with tribal groups. This divisiveness, beginning with the first days of the occupation, would plague the island leadership for the duration of the occupation and result in what many have called factionalism. The word *factionalism* must be used with caution, however. In Indian society, consensus served as the governing style. When one person does not agree with the decision of the majority this should be construed as the exercise of consensus government, not factionalism.[9]

Because the group had already decided that the occupation would be an egalitarian effort, a seven-person elected council was established to determine which of the numerous issues confronting the occupiers should be addressed. Meetings were held on Friday of each week or more often as necessary, and the council gave voice to the decisions reached by the majority. The council members were required to be over seventeen years of age and have lived on Alcatraz for a continuous period of one week with no absence from the island for more than seventy-two hours. If the person was absent for over seventy-two hours, residency could be reestablished by remaining on the island for another continuous seven-day period. Elections to the council were held every ninety days, and council members could be reelected. Voting was open only to island residents. Each time a major decision was required the entire adult population was called together by the elected council. Coucil meetings were also meant to keep occupiers, as well as guests, informed of political strategies, current events, and other issues of concern. The first council consisted of college students Richard Oakes (Mohawk), Al Miller (Seminole), Ross Harden (Winnebago), Bob Nelford (Eskimo), Dennis Turner (Luiseno), James Vaughn (Cherokee), and Professor Ed Castillo (Cahuilla). Later members included Stella Leach (Lakota Sioux/Colville), Ray Spang (Northern Cheyenne), Judy Scraper (Shawnee), LaNada Boyer (Bannock), John Trudell (Sioux), David Leach (Lakota Sioux/Colville), Charles Dana

(Choctaw), Albert Montoya (Ute), Herbert Simmons (tribe unknown), and Vern Conway (Mission).[10]

A statement issued by Indians of All Tribes on November 21 provides more information regarding the island council:

> The Alcatraz encampment is governed by all the residents. The residents select seven Indian brothers and sisters to serve on the Council, which oversees everything that the island is doing. It's a big job and it's hard when maybe you've never had that type of experience before; but it's also educational.
>
> It's learning the operation and the functions of a whole new government and city. Council members have 90 days as their term in office and if the general membership should reelect them they will be back for another 90 days, but it's not the type of situation where people will remain on the Council forever unless their people want them and figure that they can handle the situation.[11]

Steve Talbot, a non-Indian observer of the Alcatraz occupation, held that egalitarian relationships between the rank-and-file and their leaders received strong support. Everything was shared—both the wealth and the poverty. The town meeting character of the ruling All Tribes Council was a logical extension of this principle. Even during bitter disputes that arose from time to time the Indians on Alcatraz did not abandon this egalitarian principle. According to Talbot, "when behavior did not conform to the egalitarian standards, such persons were said to be acting like White persons. One frequently heard the admonishment to think and act Indian."[12]

McKay-Want described the council meetings as follows:

> We had general meetings every day and we would talk about negotiations and other things. . . . The meetings were really a good thing because you got to meet a lot of different people. You didn't always sit by the same people so you got to exchange information on your tribe. The kids really benefited by realizing that there's so many tribes. The whole community was made aware of who was on the island and when and where the meeting would take place. At first we were going to put out an information sheet because rumors were being started all over the place. But it was hard because we didn't have any money to

print. . . . At meetings we always decided what was going to happen, whether we were going to set up a deadline or whatever. And
then whoever went to represent us followed our directions.[13]

McKay-Want was asked specifically about her role because wom-
en's participation in the occupation had become an issue. In most
Indian societies, except for those of the Iroquois, Navajo, and Pueblo
peoples, women rarely serve in political leadership roles. McKay-Want
insisted that there was always a good and amiable mix of men and
women and that women had been involved in the planning from the
very beginning. Many of these women were leaders in their own communities and had already served on community boards, such as the
San Francisco Indian Center Board. According to McKay-Want, once
on Alcatraz LaNada Boyer and Richard Oakes, one woman and one
man, emerged as leaders. They each had leadership qualities and were
able to hold a crowd's attention. Oakes, who traveled to Alcatraz,
would always open the island council meetings. Boyer, who stayed
on the mainland, handled public relations and dealt with government
officials.[14]

Earl Livermore affirmed that the occupiers held meetings practically every morning and it was there that they came up with a governing structure. First, all people would have a voice. The people in-
vested the council with the power to govern. The council, with
Livermore as coordinator, set up committees: public relations, health,
security, education, research and development, ways and means, food
supply, transportation, administration. Work assignments included
everyone. It was remarkable how most islanders took up their duties
in the kitchen, the clinic, the school, or the public relations office
without complaint.[15] One of the very first things the council did was
set up an ad hoc emergency committee of non-Indians and Indians to
elicit non-Indian support throughout the country.[16]

Another early action was the establishment of a security force. This
force of both men and women would serve several functions. In an
abandoned office adjacent to the boat landing, all visitors to the island, Indian and non-Indian, were required to sign a log. The log was
part of a series of rigid regulations adopted by the council to ensure
the protection and privacy of the occupiers and to ensure that no one
ventured into unsafe areas. The security regulations were drafted to
address problems that were either anticipated or had been experienced

by the occupation force, such as the introduction of alcohol on the island, the need for housing assignment and control, the need for specific control of children, and the assignment of jobs for both men and women. The regulations were also a precursor to the rise of the control of the island population by the security force, which would create resentment as the occupation continued.

The council also had to find a way to control the increasing horde of media representatives from all over the world. It soon became clear that it would be in the Native Americans' best interest to establish a public relations office on the island, operated by Indian people. Rosalie McKay-Want spent the majority of her time typing and answering letters. It was in working in the office that the impact of the occupation, the enormity of what they were doing, got to her.[17] The occupiers were receiving letters and donations from all over the world. Yet some donations offered levity to the otherwise momentous situation. Ethel Kennedy and National Football League commissioner Pete Rozelle presented the Indians on Alcatraz Island with a $600 color television from the Washington Redskins professional football team. Other donors decided to clear their attics of high-heeled shoes and formal gowns. McKay-Want admits that on occasion they would go to the gym and play around in the high heels and big, fancy hats.[18]

In addition to the public relations office on the island, two other national public relations efforts were undertaken. On December 22 "Radio Free Alcatraz" began broadcasting from the island over KPFA-FM in Berkeley. The Pacifica Foundation provided the occupiers with fifteen minutes of airtime daily at 7:15 P.M. KPFK in Los Angeles and WBAI in New York, both affiliated with KPFA, also carried the broadcasts to an estimated 100,000 listeners. John Trudell became the recognized voice of Alcatraz. Trudell interviewed residents, arranged dialogues about Indian culture, reported on national Indian affairs, and provided an ongoing docudrama of the occupation. His broadcasts often focused on problems Native Americans were having with the federal government, such as fishing rights or the taking of Indian land. He sometimes featured Indian elders telling stories that had been passed down from generation to generation.[19]

Another attempt to provide the public with information was the Alcatraz newsletter. In January 1970, copies of the *Indians of All Tribes Newsletter* were sent across the country, providing occupation history, news of events, poetry, and other items of interest to Native

Americans. Four editions were published before high costs forced its discontinuation.[20]

Talbot captures the importance of "Radio Free Alcatraz" and the *Indians of All Tribes Newsletter:*

> Educating the general public to the Indian condition meant breaking out of official channels and into the public news media. It meant speaking truth to power. The significance of Radio Free Alcatraz is revealed in this fact. For the first time Indian broadcasters reached people nationally on the critical issues in Indian affairs as the Indians saw them. The broadcasts also promoted cultural and political awareness among Indian people. The "Alcatraz Newsletter," beautifully illustrated, continued the communication theme.[21]

Information sheets highlighted the physical condition of the island and served as requests for specific items:

> Running an island operation for 100 people is like trying to run an entire village. We need a boat to commute to the mainland and enable the students who are still in school to keep on with their classes and enable us to keep in touch with the outside world. We don't want to isolate ourselves entirely. We'll need a water barge, too, eventually. . . . We'll need generators to hook up our electricity on the Island. We need stoves. We need furniture. We need supplies to fix up the Island with as best we can. The Island was in bad shape when we got here. The government really did a lousy job of getting rid of their garbage—they just dumped it over the cliff and all over the Island, so we have to clean that up as well as trying to make our living quarters as best we can. . . . We need a good pickup or jeep on the Island to carry garbage and we'd like to have a garbage scow come to the Island because we're not going to dump it in the Bay the way everyone else has. And we need food supplies . . . fresh fruits and vegetables, meat and fresh milk. And we need medical supplies for our clinic. For our nursery we would like to have things for our children, like a playground set. . . . For the children and for the school we'll need books, paints and blackboards.[22]

Many adult students, McKay-Want included, encountered many difficulties in attempting to continue with college:

At first at our meetings on Alcatraz we decided that the college students would have first dibs on the first boat out in the morning, and that worked out all right for awhile. I would go to classes and I was still keeping my apartment because I was in low income housing and I didn't want to lose my place, so I just kept on paying rent. And I was getting food stamps so we would donate our food stamps to Alcatraz whenever we needed food. But for awhile we really didn't need to because people were donating food and we had food galore.

Then some people started getting into trouble on the mainland . . . where they had to show up in court early in the mornings. So these people started taking the first boat and a lot of us who were taking classes started missing them.

I started doing really bad in my foreign language class because you have to be there everyday. . . . I went from being on the Dean's List to being on probation.[23]

Continuing education for adults was not the only concern. As an increasing number of Indian families moved onto the island, children needed to go to school as well. On December 11, 1969, the Big Rock School was opened in what had been the movie theater/meeting hall in the prison's main cellblock. The school concentrated on grades one through six but also had a preprimary education program in the same building. The first class of twelve was taught by Douglas Remington and Linda Arayando. Remington was a twenty-four-year-old Southern Ute from Denver, Colorado, and had a bachelor of arts degree in English education and a master's degree in theater arts. Arayando was a twenty-one-year-old Creek from Oakland, California, and a senior at the University of California at Berkeley in social sciences.

According to Remington, their immediate priority was to have the school accredited as a private school in the San Francisco School District. Without this accreditation, the children might be forced to return to the public school system, where they could be put back a grade or required to repeat a grade. City school officials, however, reacted favorably by officially recognizing Big Rock School and assuring Remington and Arayando that the students would not be assigned truant officers.[24]

Other teachers in the Big Rock School included Vicky Santana and Woesha Cloud North. Teacher's aides were Justine Moppin, Rosalie

Willie, and a number of teenage volunteers. Students concentrated on reading, writing, arithmetic, geography, health, and science studies. Native American studies courses, including history and culture, were also offered. Specific tribal information for each student was provided by the parents and others familiar with the material.[25]

In addition to standard texts utilized in the California public school system, a substantial amount of sophisticated tutorial material was provided by the Project Head Start program at St. John the Evangelist Episcopal Church in San Francisco. Educators at St. John wished to study the differences in intellectual and academic achievement between the Indian children on Alcatraz Island and Chicano, Black, and Indian children at St. John. Officials at St. John stated that it was in the interests of their study that they sent equipment of considerable value and expense to the school.[26] The study was never completed, however, because at the end of the occupation the school records disappeared.

An art school and crafts training center were set up by Earl Livermore for children as well as adults. The adults realized that neither they nor their children possessed skills or knowledge in the preservation of traditional arts and crafts. These skills, which were normally passed down from generation to generation, had largely been lost to urban Indians with little or no reservation or tribal contact. Francis Allen taught native arts such as beadwork, leatherwork, woodcarving, costume decoration, and sculpture. Dance and music instruction was provided by Meade and Noreen Chibatti, while two Tlingit Indians carved miniature totem poles.[27] Blue Cloud provides insight into the teaching atmosphere: "There was a gentle feeling of calm in the room where the young girls sat beading and making things from hides. Older girls and women taught, by showing, these ancient crafts. Voices here were very quiet. Young boys came to this room to watch, and soon they too were making headbands, or pouches. There is a very good feeling in working with the hands, your mind free to wonder and to dream."[28]

In addition to the the arts school, the crafts training center, Big Rock School, the security force, and the public relations office, many other services were needed for the island community to function smoothly. A kitchen crew was established to ensure that hot meals were prepared for the permanent residents three times per day. Although it was staffed primarily by Indian women volunteers, men also took part in the cooking, storeroom operation, and garbage removal. Women working in the kitchen complained that they could sense the spirits of the former Alcatraz prisoners and requested that the kitchen be moved from the original prison dining area to the lower apartment complex. Additionally, most of the island occupants had moved out of the cellblocks and into the old employee buildings, so the apartment complex proved more convenient for cooking and dining. Peter Blue Cloud recalled that the mess hall was a happy scene where men and women joked and laughed as they prepared the meals.[29]

After the basic requirements of shelter and food preparation were taken care of, more practical, day-to-day concerns quickly surfaced. The island had a growing population of Indian adults and children who brought with them various health care needs. In addition, the island presented numerous safety hazards: the former prison buildings had been constantly exposed to salt air and water and had badly deteriorated since the island's last use in 1963. To address these issues a health clinic was established in one of the buildings the day following the occupation and was operated primarily by Stella Leach, a licensed practical nurse who had been with the Well Baby Clinic in Oakland. Other clinic workers included Jenny Joe, a registered nurse, Dorothy Lonewolf Miller, and volunteer doctors Robert Brennan and Richard Fine. Stella Leach provides the following insight into health care on the island:

> I felt that perhaps some of our people might need medical attention, so with the assistance of Doctor Tepper, who is director of our well baby clinic in Oakland, we fixed up first aid kits and I attempted to come aboard the island. . . . After I arrived, the clinic was put into commission, and we found that there was a need for it here, because more and more families were getting through the blockade. So I stayed, and finally I got a three-month leave of absence and remained on the island permanently. My employer, Doctor Tepper, has since given one day a week to our clinic here on the island, and it might be interesting to the people to know that we have a doctor that comes every day. Six of these doctors are Jewish, and the seventh is Greek, Dr. Challes. These are people who have come from an oppressed background and I feel that they are sympathetic to us. . . . Of course, there are other doctors and nurses in the community who have donated large quantities of medical supplies.[30]

A nursery was set up in the office quarters of the main cellblock and later moved into the caretaker's building to care for the children whose parents had other duties. Nursery workers included Dagmar Thorpe, granddaughter of the Olympic athlete Jim Thorpe, Maria Lavender, and Lu Trudell. The nursery evolved into a preprimary institution, which enabled the children to learn through a wide variety of stimuli such as painting, modeling clay, collages, paper cutouts, block building, storytelling, and, most interestingly, song sessions in which Francis Allen sang Indian songs to the children.[31] Blue Cloud thought "it was reassuring to look into this room and see the many children playing, drawing, or being read to. These children were what the occupation was all about. It was for their futures that we had dared defy the government. To look at these children was to envision an Indian tomorrow of great hope."[32]

Hope was what buoyed the Indian people who planned, organized, and executed the November 20 occupation. They were very idealistic, yet sincere people interested in the problems faced by Native Americans throughout the United States generally and in the Bay Area specifically. They not only viewed Alcatraz Island as a symbol of Indian mistreatment but they also regarded the Alcatraz occupation as a symbol of Indian self-determination. Oakes focused on what he considered the main goal of the occupation: "We might—might—just wake up the conscience of America."[33]

The first island council members—Oakes, Miller, Harden, Castillo, Nelford, Turner, and Vaughn—represented the heart and soul of the island population in its earliest stages. The first council's tenure in November and December 1969 were the real glory days of the occupation—"days which raised us all above reality," wrote my confidential source. "If you came after New Year [1970], you were too late!"[34] The novelty of the event, coupled with the generous support of the Bay Area population, created unity among the occupation force.

The uniqueness of an Indian occupation of a federal facility appealed to the sensitivities of the new left generation that called San Francisco home. Support came from these people and life on Alcatraz, while uncomfortable at best, took on an excitement and exhilaration of its own. Thanksgiving Day, November 27, 1969, reflected both the support of the Bay Area community and the high spirits of the Native Americans. Six days into the occupation, Indian people gathered to celebrate a non-Indian traditional holiday feast:

It was cold on Alcatraz today, but there was warmth: the island was as bleak as ever, but there was pleasantness. The Indians who have inhabited the former prison island for more than a week settled down to a Thanksgiving feast principally provided by non-Indian sympathizers ashore.

Indians from more than 100 tribes were expected at the feast, many of them coming from distant reservations as representatives in support of the aims of the youngsters occupying the island. Richard Oakes, a Mohawk who often serves as spokesman for the group on the island, said that hundreds of letters had been sent to tribes on reservations throughout the country and that guests were due from Oklahoma, Washington State and other distant points.

"It will be our first Thanksgiving of a multitribal type. . . . We have something to be really thankful for that we are here together in our common struggle. This is a place where we can polarize our grievances and see if we can find a solution for them."

A Fisherman's Wharf restaurant had prepared enough food for about 200 people. This morning several power cruisers delivered large quantities of food, plus bedding and clothing. . . .

A rock group called the Cleveland Wrecking Crew also visited the island . . . and played a dockside concert for the Indians. . . . Though the Indians invited newsmen to be "pilgrims" at today's meal, they said they wanted no part of militants or hippies, nor of sightseers who might be tempted on the island.[35]

According to the Associated Press, the old prison exercise yard, site of the feast, had been cleaned and supplies were stocked in the old prison cafeteria as they were tossed onto the island by sympathetic boaters. Even though a Coast Guard cutter circled Alcatraz, it made no move to interfere.[36]

Following the Thanksgiving celebration, the occupiers began to settle into life on the island while awaiting the inevitable government reaction. A quick and forcible removal was considered a distinct possibility. Plans about hiding places and nonviolent responses had already been mapped out. Further actions to acquire title to the island would come through the courts. Although the occupiers hoped for acquiescence to their demands rather than to a forced removal, in that case they could capitalize on the attention and empathy amassed during the occupation and bring their legal grievances formally before the American public.

In the Bay Area and throughout the United States, initial support lay not with the federal government but with the occupiers. Supporters sent literally thousands of cards, letters, telegrams, and petitions to governors, BIA officials, members of Congress, senators, Pat Nixon, the White House staff, and President Richard Nixon:

> Mr. President and Mr. Secretary [of the Interior],
> Let us do something decent for a change! Return Alcatraz Island in the bay of San Francisco to the Indians of All Tribes for the development of a native American cultural center.[37]

> The President, The White House,
> For once in this country's history let the Indians have something, let them have Alcatraz.[38]

> Hon. Richard M. Nixon,
> I think the Indians taking over Alcatraz is the most *refreshing* thing that has happened to this country in years, and certainly hope you will find a way to let them have it.
> Our treatment of the Indians has been one of the most shamefull things in our history, and this is a glorious beginning to what could become something we could be proud of.[39]

It is unclear, however, if any of this correspondence actually reached the president. During the week of February 5, the president received 35,810 letters, 2,115 cards, and 5,156 telegrams. Although the mail was cataloged into subject categories including Vietnam, U.S. policy, State of the Union message, cut in cancer research, piano imports, and White House police ceremonial uniforms, no specific category was made for the Alcatraz occupation.[40]

It appears that all letters regarding the Alcatraz occupation were answered by Robert Robertson, acting executive director of the National Council on Indian Opportunity. A form letter was sent to each correspondent:

> Dear:
> The President has asked us to reply to your recent communication concerning Alcatraz Island.
> The Indian people who are demonstrating on the island have been warned that they are there as trespassers and that the Fed-

eral Government can have no liability attendant to their being there in this status.

Since the demonstration has been peaceful the Government has made no move to have them forcibly removed.

We are exerting every effort to resolve this situation satisfactorily and hope that the matter can be concluded soon.

Thank you for you interest in this matter.

Sincerely,
Robert Robertson
Acting Executive Director[41]

In the Bay Area the ground swell of support was not limited to local citizens. The Bay Area press adopted a supportive attitude as well. Articles appeared daily in the *San Francisco Chronicle* and the *San Francisco Examiner* that not only carried the Indian message to the public but also highlighted the needs of the Indians on the island. Between November 20, 1969, and January 10, 1970, over 125 articles appeared that fell into four basic categories: why the Indians wanted Alcatraz Island; what the Indians needed in order to remain on Alcatraz; what injustices had led to the occupation; how the government reacted, or did not react, to the occupation.[42] This support by the press and private citizens allowed the Native Americans to establish a form of normality in their lives as the reality of a prolonged occupation began to materialize. Life on the rock was still difficult because there were no natural resources, no fertile soil, no fresh water, no sanitation facilities, and no electrical power other than what was donated. On the island life was at times individual, pan-Indian, and tribal in nature. To understand what life was really like on Alcatraz Island we must hear the voices of the people.

Notes

1. An educational grant funded the school system on the island for the children. Fortunate Eagle, *Alcatraz*, 79.

2. Much of the information regarding the onshore organization was provided by an Indian informant who has requested to remain anonymous. The funds deposited in the bank account established through the SAC office were those received either in person or through the mail at the Indian Center or the SAC office. Mail addressed to the island or funds donated in person did not necessarily find their way into this bank account. Donations were dropped off at the Indian center or the SAC offices and then taken by boat to the island.

3. DeLuca, "We Hold the Rock," 14. It should be pointed out that this $4,000 represents only the money received at the Indian center and does not include any money delivered directly to the island.

4. Bomberry interview, 8.

5. Morris interview.

6. Brightman interview.

7. Rosalie McKay-Want, "The Meaning of Alcatraz," quoted in Antell, "American Indian Women Activists," 102–3.

8. Blue Cloud, *Alcatraz*, 25.

9. I do not use the word *factionalism* in this work unless the occupiers themselves used it to describe a particular event or group. It should, however, be noted that most of the occupiers were themselves urban Indians and could well have confused factionalism with consensus leadership.

10. Indians of All Tribes, "Why We Are on Alcatraz."

11. Ibid.

12. Talbot, "Free Alcatraz," 89.

13. McKay-Want, "The Meaning of Alcatraz," quoted in Antell, "American Indian Women Activists," 109.

14. Ibid., 110.

15. Talbot, "Free Alcatraz," 88.

16. Livermore interview, 10.

17. Antell, "American Indian Women Activists," 108–9.

18. Ibid., 111.

19. Trudell, "Radio Free Alcatraz," Dec. 22, 1969.

20. Through my contact with Indian people who participated in the occupation I was able to obtain copies of three of the editions of the *Newsletter* and draft copies of the fourth edition. I do not know of anyone who has a complete file.

21. Talbot, "Free Alcatraz," 90.

22. Indians of All Tribes, "Why We Are on Alcatraz," 3–4.

23. McKay-Want, "The Meaning of Alcatraz," quoted in Judith Antell, "American Indian Women Activists," 100.

24. Remington interview; Arayando interview. Regarding Arayando's concerns over accreditation and grade level, McKay-Want states that the children went back into the public school system following the occupation and advanced without problem into the next grades. She credits Indian sympathizers working within the school system for completing the necessary paperwork attesting that the children had indeed been in school while on the island. McKay-Want, "The Meaning of Alcatraz," quoted in Antell, "American Indian Women Activists," 101–2.

25. Fortunate Eagle, *Alcatraz!* 88.

26. Dzeda, letter to Warren.

27. Fortunate Eagle, *Alcatraz!* 88–89.

28. Blue Cloud, *Alcatraz*, 29.

29. Ibid.

30. Stella Leach interview by Trudell.

31. *Indians of All Tribes Newsletter*, Jan. 1970.

32. Blue Cloud, *Alcatraz*, 30.

33. "Oakes Has One Goal for Alcatraz: Unity," *San Francisco Examiner*, Dec. 7, 1969.

34. Confidential informant, letter to author, Apr. 25, 1992, and July 23, 1992.

35. "100 Tribes: Thanksgiving on Alcatraz," *San Francisco Examiner*, Nov. 27, 1969.

36. "Indian Squatters Feast and Dance at Alcatraz," *San Francisco Chronicle*, Nov. 28, 1969. In addition to the Bratskeller restaurant, the Trident restaurant in Sausalito also prepared and donated turkeys, as did numerous private citizens. See GSA Chronology.

37. Petition to the president and secretary of the interior.

38. Mander, telegram to Nixon.

39. Dawson, letter to Nixon.

40. President Nixon's handwriting file.

41. Robertson, form letter.

42. Copies of these newspaper articles are found in various locations. Perhaps the most complete are the files of the Bay Area History Project at the Intertribal Friendship House in Oakland. See also the Alcatraz Occupation File in the Alcatraz Library on Alcatraz Island and the Alcatraz File at the National Archives for the Pacific Sierra Region in San Bruno, California.

6

Voices from Alcatraz

.M.V.A

The problems, the joys, the heartaches of the occupation can be described only by those who lived through the euphoric days of November 20, 1969, to mid-January 1970 and by those who endured the tumultuous times of mid-January 1970 through June 1971. The living conditions on Alcatraz Island were never ideal and became more unpleasant as the occupation progressed. On November 20, 1969, phone, electrical, and fresh water services were provided by the federal government. By the summer of 1970, however, all of these services had been discontinued and the island occupiers found themselves on a barren prison island with no natural resources. Without running water, adequate sanitation facilities, and electricity and with a rocky and nonproductive land base, Alcatraz reminded the occupiers of most reservations. Winters were cold, summers were hot. Fresh water had to be transported to the island in barrels, drums, or plastic and glass containers. Meats and vegetables spoiled from lack of refrigeration. Sanitary facilities were nonexistent and water for bathing came from the ocean or an occasional trip to the San Francisco mainland. What began as a symbolic occupation soon became a test of fortitude, tenacity, and determination.

What follows are excerpts from interviews with Indian people who lived on the island, who believed in the occupation, and who devoted themselves to the ideal of achieving self-determination for themselves and other Native Americans by remaining on Alcatraz Island. The interviews were conducted between 1969 and 1994 by newspaper reporters, radio announcers, historians and researchers working for the Doris Duke Oral History Project, and scholars writing master's theses, dissertations, and books. Accordingly, some recollections are clearer and crisper than others; some facts may seem to contradict others; and the focus of all interviews is not consistent. These voices come from Indian people at all levels of society. Some are college students, involved in the campus and civil rights unrest of the 1960s and motivated by that experience; some are urban Indian people who would today be called the homeless. Without oral and written skills and the sophistication provided by education, their oral histories represent the truth of the failed federal relocation program of the 1950s, the program that brought them to the Bay Area. Other voices come from Native Americans who successfully assimilated into the dominant society only to have that assimilation shaken and challenged by a new Indian Red Power movement, led not by the elders, but by the young. Additionally, the voice of urban Indian youth, who were not raised in a traditional manner, in an Indian home, or on an Indian reservation is finally heard. Their confusion and struggle to find an identity and to fit within the Alcatraz movement is presented in their oral histories. Regardless of the participant, however, one theme emerges, never changes, and never loses focus. This constant is that those who occupied Alcatraz Island on November 20, 1969, and those who subsequently came to the island to support them and chose to remain did so in order to bring the voice of the American Indian before the larger U.S. audience, to dramatize the treatment of Indian people by the U.S. government, and to exercise the Indian right of self-determination by reclaiming Alcatraz Island by right of discovery.

Indians of All Tribes, Inc.

The first statement by the occupiers was a clear signal to the federal government, as well as to the American public, that the policy of handling Indian people was a dismal failure. Native Americans would no longer stand idly by and see tribal languages, customs, cultures, and religions destroyed. Indian people recognized that their future lay in their children. The statement was a clarion call for recognition of the failures of the past and a guarantee of the future for American Indian people everywhere.

> We came to Alcatraz because we were sick and tired of being pushed around, exploited, and degraded everywhere we turned in our country. We selected Alcatraz for many reasons, but, most importantly, we came to Alcatraz because it is a place of our own, somewhere that is geographically unfeasible for everybody to

come to and interfere with what we would like to do with our lives.... We can worship, we can sing, and we can make plans for our lives and the future of our Indian people and Alcatraz. ... The decision we want to make is in governing ourselves and our own people, without interference from non-Indians....

Our main concern is with Indian people everywhere. One reason we took Alcatraz was because the students were having problems in the universities and colleges they were attending.... We all realized that we didn't want to go through the university machinery and come out white-oriented like the few Indian people before us, or like the non-Indian people who are running our government—our Indian government—or our Indian affairs....

We were also concerned about our own lives and our children and what was happening on the reservations as well, because while we were physically away we still had our own families and people in our hearts and on our minds, the problems that they were facing and the frustration of not being able to help them. We needed attention brought to our people, and we needed a place to get together in the city so that we didn't become victims of assimilation. It finally all came to a point and we decided we would just go liberate our own land since all of our other lands had been taken away....

We feel that the island is the only bargaining power that we have with the federal government. It is the only way we have to get them to notice us or even to want to deal with us. We are going to maintain our occupation until the island, which is rightfully ours, is formally granted to us. Otherwise, they will forget us the way they always have; but we will not be forgotten....

We want to have our own Indian university because we need to develop things from our culture that are being lost, like our language. It is hard for us to go to the universities and have them tell us that we must learn a foreign language, when we know that English is a foreign language, and we have some native speakers of our own tribal languages. The tribal languages will eventually die out and we don't want to see it happen. We need an area of tribal languages so we can pass these things on to our children. We need legal studies too. We live under federal law and the state has partial jurisdiction as well, and city laws apply to us when we are off the reservation in the nearby towns. We never know what laws they're going to apply to us next because they manipulate the laws and do whatever they feel they need to do with us. We've got to understand those laws and the mentality behind them to help us deal with them. We've got to go back to the reservation and start fighting for our people back there. . . . The Constitution has not included us, as history will bear out.

We want to establish a center of ecology as part of our cultural complex. The cultural complex also involves the tradition of our religion. The basis of everything we do is our religion. We must have a place for our spiritual leaders and our medicine men to come. We also plan to have our own library and archives to help us document the wrongs that have been done in this country and the wisdom that has been lost. Also, we plan to have a place where we can practice our own dances and songs and music and drums, where we can teach our children and not let this die as it's dying on the reservations today. . . .

Our people want to start a university for Indians, a cultural center, an Indian bill of rights and a vocational rehabilitation program, which will involve major reforms in the way this country deals with the Indians. These are very big tasks. They require lots of planning.

We think the planning phase will take a year. It can be broken down into three phases. During the first phase of four months, we will recruit outside volunteers and consultants. We want the best people in the country to help us and other Indians throughout the country plan for the Indian's future. . . .

At the end of four months, we want a gathering of all tribes on Alcatraz and have representation from different tribes throughout the U. S. to talk, to review the preliminary plan which has developed, to ask questions, to outline the plans for the future. . . .

The final eight months, after working with our consultants, we will prepare detailed plans for our university, our cultural center, our bill of rights, a beginning, one beginning, of the answer to the question: What are we to become? Make no mistake about this. The day is over when non-Indians can answer this question. . . . Now, after Alcatraz, we, and the countless other Indians in this country will decide our future.[1]

Richard Oakes, Mohawk, early student leader on Alcatraz Island

Oakes's recollections of the occupation were published in December 1972 and in various newspaper interviews conducted between November 1969 and January 1970.

We couldn't have survived without all the people who ran that blockade, especially those first few days, that first week. I guess the people around San Francisco and the Bay Area saw the symbolic gesture of what we were doing, saw just how important this action was. . . . They made it possible.

Those were hilarious times. Someone donated a live turkey. That poor turkey. He didn't know what he was getting into. He had a beautiful coloring at first, white and other colors, but he soon turned gray, the color of concrete.

At first we did all of our cooking outside on an open fire. There was a big fire on the dock. The kids would fish for crab, and we would put a big pot on and cook the crab in there. Any fish that we caught were put right in tinfoil and directly into the fire. It was good. Everyone just came and ate the food that was there. There wasn't any sense of mine and yours. Everything belonged to everybody.

We did a lot of singing in those days. I remember the fires at nighttime, the cold of the night, the singing around the campfire of the songs that aren't shared by the white people, the songs of friendship, the songs of understanding. We did a lot of singing. We sang into the early hours of the morning. It was beautiful to behold and beautiful to listen to.

A few of us would go off alone and start talking about our experiences on the different reservations, about the more advanced problems and finding solutions to them. . . . We knew we had to bring the experience back home, to the reservations. We owed it to ourselves to keep it going. . . .

After Alcatraz was taken, Indians started coming in from all over. . . . They came from Canada, from Mexico, from South America, from all over. For some, it was the first time that they had met with the people of other tribes, the first time they felt a unity with all Indians. The getting together of all Indians was something undreamed of since the Ghost Dance of 1889.

Alcatraz was symbolic to a lot of people, and it meant something real to a lot of people. There are many old prophecies that speak of the younger people rising up and finding a way for the People to live. The Hopi, the spiritual leaders of the Indian people, have a prophecy that is at least 1200 years old. It says that the People would be pushed off their land from the East to the West, and when they reached the Westernmost tip of America, they would begin to take back the land that was stolen from them. . . .

When we first got there, Alcatraz was twelve acres of concrete, full of barbed wire. It just looked like an army concentration camp. Coming up from the dock, there was a stair that seemed to go right up into the wall. . . . I think they were made for giants. Walking into Cellblock One reminded me of walking into one of those huge airplane hangars . . . but there were no airplanes. We're the only kind of birds that do not fly, jailbirds. Jailbirds, wards of the government, prisoners of war. What's the difference? Before it was known as the Bureau of Indian Affairs, our "governing agency," it was under the War Department. We were called "prisoners of war" then. The two agencies are synonymous. During the Second World War, the Japanese prisoner of war camps were run by the same people that run the BIA. Somebody in Washington said, "Hey, this is a natural!" We still consider ourselves prisoners of war. We'll always be at war with the values of this society.

On January 3, 1970, our daughter, Yvonne, fell three stories down a stairwell in the officers' quarters. Five days later she died in a San Francisco hospital. She was just thirteen. About a week before the accident, my wife Anne told me of dreams and feelings of premonition she was having. She was afraid that someone in our family would be hurt if we stayed on the island. She felt that it was time to leave. I had been thinking about leaving to develop the idea of Alcatraz in other places. However, I put her off. I wish I had listened. Yvonne's death cast an air of gloom over the whole island. It was like a symbol of all the doubts we had hidden from ourselves during the whole Alcatraz experience. There had always been the possibility of failure as there is in every movement, but we had to suppress this idea in order to survive. This time was the test. It was a time to look inward. . . .

A few days after Yvonne died, we returned to the island to get our clothes and few possessions and left. We had to go. We needed to be away from there. We needed time to gather ourselves together. Leaving the place itself wasn't hard, and we have never left the people.[2]

In a December 1969 interview on "Radio Free Alcatraz," Trudell asked Oakes what had motivated him to join the movement.

I was involved in the 1959 struggle to blockade the building of the Lawson Dam, the seaway project which was taking parts of our reservation without compensation. Also the building of a bridge from the U.S. to Canada on the reservation and the building of facilities to house the maintenance men and the various aspects of the bridge, all on Indian land without just compensation, so it has really been a big part for me to try to rectify some of this. Now we feel we are in a position to do something about it. . . . As many people understand now, Alcatraz is not only here on the island, but it's a part of every reservation, it's a part of every person.[3]

Oakes continues in this interview to address the failure of the BIA boarding schools:

You see, the situation is that the whole school system, the BIA school system should be chopped, should be shelved, and restructured, but restructured in such a way that the Indian culture is revealed, so that the Indian person going to these schools, if these schools are still in operation, will get the knowledge and the understanding of who he is, what he is, and why he is in that situation, as well as an understanding of the different Indians surrounding him; the different Indians in the whole United States and Canada and Alaska. We have a great history and I think it should be brought forth.[4]

Newspaper reporters sought out Oakes for comment and quoted him frequently in articles. A *San Francisco Examiner* article on November 24, 1969, reported the following:

Richard Oakes, 27, Mohawk father of five and San Francisco State College student, a leading spokesman for several dozen tribes represented on the island, said the Indians plan to stay despite the hardships. . . . "We want this island," Oakes said again and again. "This is the beginning of our fight for justice and self-determination—and for Alcatraz. There is a dual sense of justice in this country, one for Indians, one for whites. If they're going to continue to treat us in this manner, why not set up dual government?"[5]

The November 28 *San Francisco Examiner* and *San Francisco Chronicle* quoted Oakes regarding the determination of the occupiers to remain on Alcatraz: "If they try to remove us we are going to barricade ourselves or go into hiding. The Indian people are definitely going to stay here."[6] "We're standing by our demands. . . . We have the support of all the Indian nations. We are willing to meet with Interior Secretary Hickel, but it will have to be on Alcatraz."[7]

According to the *San Francisco Chronicle* on November 29, the occupiers "want Secretary of the Interior Walter Hickel to personally come to the island to surrender it to the Indian people of America. Hickel is hospitalized in Washington, D.C. with a pinched nerve in his neck. 'I just wonder,' Oakes beamed yesterday, 'if that nerve happens to be his Indian nerve.'"[8]

In a *San Francisco Examiner* article on November 30 Oakes challenged the federal government: "'This time we have come to stay. The federal government is going to have to realize we mean business. We are not just children or wards of the State. What we are seeking as Indians is a real meaning in life, a challenge.'"[9]

Thomas Hannon, GSA administrator, invited Oakes to a December 1 meeting, at which Hannon said, "'The Indians were told they will have to leave, but we just haven't set the time.'" When Oakes was asked about efforts of the General Services Administration to induce the Indians to move off Alcatraz, he pointed to a button on his coat reading "We won't move." "'That answers the question,'" he said.[10]

On December 3 Oakes met with GSA representatives at the Federal Building in San Francisco. Following a 90–minute meeting, Oakes once again addressed the issue of remaining on Alcatraz Island.

"We're still going to stay on Alcatraz. Alcatraz offers us the insulation necessary for us to develop intellectually." Oakes stated that the Indians on Alcatraz invited all the Federal people they met with to come to the rock and talk to the Indians there. Oakes told newsmen the meeting "helped to open the lines of communication. The Federal Government has to respond to the needs of the people." Oakes told the Federal officials that white men receive one way of treatment at the hands of the law, while red men are not as solicitously handled.[11]

Oakes served on the island council, and he and his family remained on Alcatraz Island until January 8, 1969, following Yvonne's death. Oakes continued to be quoted almost daily in the San Francisco papers, always stating that the Indians would not leave the island and demanding that government negotiations take place on the island.

LaNada Boyer, Shoshone/Bannock, member of Alcatraz Island Council

The interviews with LaNada Boyer provide not only a history of her life on the island but also the events that led up to her involvement in the occupation. John Trudell interviewed Boyer on "Radio Free Alcatraz" on December 24, 1969.

Trudell: LaNada, being that you were one of the original fourteen to come out here, one of the invaders, why did you join this movement?

Boyer: Well, I guess it is a lifelong thing. It is hard to say that you just jumped into it or joined it. It comes from way back, from the reservation. The types of things you see your people going through. The type of things your family goes through. It has all affected me personally and I guess that is the reason I went into the area that I did, where I am going to major in law. . . . It's like I said, it's not just something you jump into. It's something that you have grown up with.

In response to a question by Trudell, Boyer provided insight into her experience in school and her relocation to the Bay Area:

I went to this high school and it is typical of BIA schools on the reservations, meaning that you don't have much of a choice as far as your education, the people who are in charge of you, the teachers, and all. They teach things in their classes, like no dogs and Indians are allowed, and you are the only Indian setting in the classroom. It really makes you feel badly. The only good Indian is a dead one. I was in a classroom when a teacher said that, and I nearly died of embarrassment. I did say something about it, and I got kicked out of the classroom and I had to go to the principal and they gave me a bad time there and I eventually got kicked out of school. From there on, I was too young to quit school, so my other alternative was to go to reform school, so with that choice then they offered me BIA school, so I said I would go to the BIA school. So, I went to South Dakota, the first time which would be up to a private Indian school, and I had problems there with people trying to regiment the girls. You had classes that were actually just taking care of the headmaster and head-mistress's home. It was actually only being their personal maids and servants. So I got expelled from there and I went to Oklahoma to Sherlock [Chilicco] Indian school, where I had problems there after about six weeks. They expelled me for inciting a riot which wasn't my fault either. I was just speaking up for what I thought was right. I got kicked out again, and they sent me to a school in Nevada, to Stewart Indian School, and I couldn't get in there because I didn't have any records or something like that, so I went to Carson City High. I went half a day, but by then my records were so bad they expelled me in half a day. . . . After I got back to my reservation, lucky enough my parents were under-standing and they didn't denounce me in the way the bureau did, and the rest of the people at the agency did. They said they were glad to know that "you are still you." I didn't know exactly what they meant at the time, but later on I knew that they meant that they were glad that I didn't get brainwashed. So it was all a part of the great de-Indianizing process, the brainwashing process that I went through. While in the boarding school, they sent me out in the summer time to live in a white home, where I earned $5 per week as a personal maid, and the money was sent back to the school, and the school didn't accept me back. They took all of that and it was really a hard blow on me psychologically. I never did finish school. I went to the 9th grade. I still didn't exactly want to quit there either. That's when I came out on relocation to the Bay Area and then I tried to get into the University of Califor-nia, where I was turned down. After a year or so, with the back-ing of some people in the Mission district of San Francisco, where most of the Indians are located, where they are centralized now, I got in as the "token Indian" in the Equal Opportunity Program, because they didn't have any Indians. That's where I first heard

about the plan to take Alcatraz Island. I knew then that I wanted to get involved, and I was, from the very beginning.[12]

Dan Bomberry, Cayuga Indian, occupation participant

Bomberry was interviewed on January 12, 1971.

Interviewer: You say you arrived there about a week after the takeover.

Bomberry: Yes, I got there the last week in November.

Interviewer: Could you tell us then how you got out to the island
and what the conditions are like there?

Bomberry: Well, we went out there in a sailboat. A fellow from
Sausalito, an old man . . . had donated his time and his sailboat
to take Indians back and forth from the island. . . . He wouldn't
take anyone unless they were Indian, and they had a security
guard set up at the dock to determine whether you were Indian
or not. We spent part of the night in the Indian Center in San
Francisco, or we spent a good portion, and then in the morning
we got up and helped them load food from the San Francisco Indian Center and rode down to the dock with an Indian who's a
veterinarian from the Bay Area. He had donated a bunch of stuff,
and he and his wife were heading out there. So we rode down
there, got on a sailboat and went out there. It was really a strange
feeling to be going out to the Alcatraz. When you got there they
had slogans painted on the walls, "Red Power," "Welcome to All
Indians," and lots of different signs painted all over the island in
huge letters. It was weird. It was like going to a reservation in the
middle of San Francisco Bay, because there were only Indians.
When we got there, there was lots of work to be done. You went
in and you checked in, and they usually gave you some kind of
job to do. Myself and Larry Benagas, we were assigned to a security job which basically was just checking out around the island
to make sure nobody was trying to sneak on the island like the
army or the navy, and we were assigned to one of the guard tow-
ers with a pair of binoculars to watch for any approaching vessels, military vessels. Things were pretty good then, because there
was lots of water; the Army Corps of Engineers had the regular
barge that they used when there was a prison to bring water out

there, and the people in the Bay Area had donated just tons of food. There was plenty of food and medical supplies coming in. Doctors had volunteered their time and that, to come out there and take care of the medical needs. The worst part was that there was no place to take a shower because there was no hot water at all, so what most people would do is go as long as they could without taking a shower until you just couldn't stand it anymore, then go into the city and go to the Indian Center or someplace and clean up and that and go back out there. That was the worst part; other than that it was pretty good. At that time it was probably upwards of 200 people out there. On weekends it would go up to maybe 500, 600 people. People were off work, and they'd come out there, and there was a powwow every weekend. Other than the fact that it was cold, things weren't too bad at that time, but they sure have deteriorated since then. There's a lack of water and electricity has all been cut off, and things have gotten a lot worse.

Interviewer: How many remained up till now?

Bomberry: I haven't been there in a long time, but I understand that there's around thirty permanent people living there and again that goes up on holidays and when people are out of school. People go back to Alcatraz during Christmas vacation, and on November 20, for the celebration of one-year occupation, there's a lot of people there. It goes up and down, but there's about thirty people who live there permanently.

Interviewer: What are the plans? Do they just intend to remain there as it is?

Bomberry: Well, the way I understand it, they're going ahead with plans to develop it; that's what they want it for—a culture center, a university, a training school, a vocational training school, a spiritual center, and museum. They've had an architect make up a model, and . . . I think they're now attempting to solicit private money to build this because it's pretty apparent the government doesn't want to do anything with it.

Interviewer: The government will let them go ahead and develop it then?

Bomberry: I don't know. I think they're going to try and force the government's hand. The government doesn't want to set a precedent, because we could claim a lot of land back. We could claim back the good portion of the United States and then use federal land. The government knows this, and if this ever gets into the courts I think we'll win. . . .

Interviewer: Well, the government's policy then is just kind of ignoring the whole thing?

Bomberry: Yeah, it's just like what they did to the Indians a long time ago, you know, put them on a reservation and keep them there and hope that they'll die out. That's what they're doing with Alcatraz, just ignoring it and hopefully people will give up, get discouraged and just go away or die out. . . . .

Interviewer: What do you think was the main purpose of the Alcatraz occupation?

Bomberry: The purpose was to get publicity, initially. It developed in a real short time into the cause of getting an independent educational system. That's the reason they want it now, to set up their own university plus various other things, a trade school, even. It's just under Indian control. It did get a lot of publicity; it did unify a lot of people.[13]

Grace Thorpe, Sax/Fox, occupation participant

Thorpe characterized Alcatraz as "the catalyst and the most important event in the Indian movement to date. It made me put my furniture into storage and spend my life savings."[14] Thorpe was interviewed by John Trudell on December 22, 1969.

Trudell: I would like to have Grace Thorpe give us her observations and views as to what is happening here.

Thorpe: Well, I read about it like most people, and I certainly heard it on the radio, too, and to me I think, it is about the most wonderful thing that has ever happened to the Indian people, and I just wanted to feel that perhaps I might be a little part of this great movement, that the young people, incidentally, this is a very young movement, with our young Indian students and they are the ones that are putting this together, and I think it is delightful.

Trudell: What do you think of the situation here?

Thorpe: I think it is basically a marvelous idea. I think it would unite the Indians. Perhaps we could have, like a Washington, D.C. bureau of Indian affairs right here, where all of the tribes would be united. And this, just the uniting itself is unusual within our Indian people. And this seems to be one thing that has brought a tremendous group of us together. And certainly we need to have an organization that would foster our Indian heritage, as far as our history, our religion, our cultures. I can visualize here, an Indian village perhaps, I can visualize in my mind the entire area run by Indian people, and it could be an education thing for the entire world. . . . The whole thing, it would be unique, and just Indian.[15]

Ross Harden, Winnebago Indian, member of the Alcatraz Island Council

Harden was interviewed on July 14, 1970.

Interviewer: How many Indians are now on Alcatraz?

Harden: It's hard to keep track because the Indians live all over the island. With people going to and from the mainland, some to work at the Alcatraz main headquarters, and some to take care of personal appointments. I would say between 50 and 76.

Interviewer: How would you appraise the movement, as you call it now. What is likely to be the future of the Alcatraz idea?

Harden: It's hard to say since the government is really supposed to make the next move. The island is incorporated so if and when the island is given to us, we will seek funds from different places to help us to start tearing down and building. We are utilizing the good buildings there. We have a nursery, a school for children, and a kitchen. The buildings on the top court have three condemned buildings and so everyone lives down on the second court. We have a cooking crew, and we also have a couple of vehicles that were built from a few old surplus trucks that were abandoned on the island. This was done by Indians who knew enough about mechanics to build these from parts taken from the rest of the trucks. The Coast Guard took our water and electricity, but generators were donated and we turned the lighthouse back on with our generators. Water is being donated to Alcatraz.

Interviewer: You have to haul in your water now and your food of course?

Harden: Food comes in every day. Not as plentiful as at first though; but it is still coming.

Interviewer: Where are the donations coming from?

Harden: From all over the nation, also the Alcatraz Relief Fund is being built up.

Interviewer: Are these coming from Indians or non-Indians?

Harden: Mostly non-Indians, but we don't like to ask the Indians to send money or food because we realize that they are poor and are in worse shape than we are. The movement was for them in the first place.

Interviewer: You mentioned that the Alcatraz movement resulted in bringing the Indians together in ways which haven't happened before.

Harden: Well, it's really not that obvious, except for the movements that went on out west, California, Washington, and all along there. The important thing is that these moves did happen because of Alcatraz.

Interviewer: Have there been any national movements or organizations grow out of the Alcatraz occupation?

Harden: Yes. One that I know of—Alameda, California; Dallas, Texas; Cleveland, Denver, and Chicago all had their BIA offices invaded by Indians on the same day. . . . I think all this protesting against the BIA is getting a few results. The BIA is now talking about contracting a few programs to various Indian organizations, to be staffed by Indians. . . .

Interviewer: Who are the principal people in the Alcatraz movement now?

Harden: John Trudell, an Indian from Nebraska was the main spokesman there when I left. He gets out what has to be said at press conferences and whatever the general membership tells him to put out. Not just anyone can hold a press conference. I don't know who the members of the council are now, but I do know that a new council is elected every three months. . . .

Interviewer: Ross, tell me, with the leadership, we've heard a good deal about Mrs. Thorpe on this one; what role has she played while you were there?

Harden: She had something to do with the public relations bit. This, I think, had to do with drumming up support for Alcatraz, with the TV appearances and that kind of thing. She later became interested in the Fort Lawton movement and went up there to help. She was arrested there.

Interviewer: If you were to name one man in the October, November movement, in terms of leadership, who spearheaded this whole movement in terms of leadership of this thing, who would you name?

Harden: There are a lot of people who played an important part, but I would name three people. I followed them all the way. Gerald Sam and Al Miller were the inspiration for quite a bit of the whole movement. Richard Oakes spoke for us. Gerald Sam and Al Miller had a lot to do with putting the words together. I must mention again that nothing was put out at that time without the consent of the general membership. . . .

Interviewer: You were talking about the people themselves, Ross, of the people in the San Francisco Bay Area who are Indian; generally how did they react to the Alcatraz movement? When you went back to the Indian community itself, what were the comments that you got?

Harden: A lot of them thought it was a good movement, an important movement, and many kept silent and waited to see what was going to happen and didn't want to get involved until they saw what was going to happen. Then there were the ones who said, "What the hell are you guys trying to do?"

Interviewer: How many supporters, active supporters did you think you had for this in the local Indians?

Harden: That question is hard to answer because who can say how many supporters we had unless we took all the names down and try to pick any percent out of the over 20,000 Indians in the Bay Area? I could say about one-third.

Interviewer: Then after the movement got started, then you said a lot of Indians came in.

Harden: There are only about two or three of the original invaders on the island now, but I told other people, too, that there are certain jobs different people can do and are best suited for. We were the people who provoked it and recruited the rest of our Indians for the invasion. All the invaders did a good job on that part of the movement. . . . The Indians on the island are doing their job now, as negotiators. . . .

Interviewer: With the matter of leadership, did you have the problem of fractionalizing once the movement had begun? Was it pretty consistent that everybody stuck together, or did it break up into factions once you got to Alcatraz? Did you have problems with that?

Harden: Well, we had potential problems. People we were warned about were spotted on the island, but we had a way of getting rid of them by isolating them from any communication we had with each other. We were accused once of being members of the mafia. We did lose a few supporters. I think I mentioned before that all these things that confronted the Indians was all new to us. We took things in stride and had quite a time handling it and of course through all this, mistakes were made, but we learned by mistakes. We took all kinds of precautions and was on guard at all times. . . .

Interviewer: What about the hippies movement? Is it very big in the Bay Area, Ross? Did the hippies' community offer you any support, or were they helpful to you?

Harden: The hippies are nothing but a bunch of spoiled white kids who are lazy and claim they want to go back to the ways of the Indians. They're all over San Francisco, wearing their headbands, vests with the fringe hanging all over them; they're buying bead-work, or trying to do beadwork. If they ever had a chance to change the color of their skin, they would never do it. Some of them were sympathetic, but then we never got much support from them. I figure they're a bunch of lost people, who don't know what they want. . . .

Interviewer: Question regarding leadership (unclear)

Harden: I'll mention here again, that I consider myself a follower and would follow people that I considered leaders and good spokesmen. Here again, I have two people in mind who are Gerald Sam and Al Miller. Gerald Sam turned down a position on the council because he thought there were too many people representing San Francisco State and Berkeley and thought UCLA and the other schools should be represented on the council too. This is how Gerald thought all the time. Richard Oakes, as it turned out, did most of the talking for the Indians of All Tribes, but the words were put together by the council, and of course, ideas from the general membership. When we had our press releases, all of the council members would be there, and people wouldn't think that only one person was leading the Indians. Richard Oakes never considered himself a leader, and we never considered ourselves leaders. The idea of leadership among the Indians came from the white people and newspapers, etc. They labeled Richard "Mayor of Alcatraz," "Chief Oakes," "President of Alcatraz," and different titles like that, and now when people ask me questions about Oakes, they refer to him as our leader. This is another major cause of a lot of our troubles, because Indians do not like to have leaders. Richard Oakes was not well known and he was being called an Indian leader. Indian people all over were wondering whether he was supposed to be leading them or who was he leading? Certainly not them. So the word *leader* came from people who are used to following a leader. I follow people, but once they start forgetting about the people who are behind them, then they're nothing. . . .

Interviewer: What processes did you go through and what units of organization did you create just to stay on the Rock?

Harden: When we first invaded the island, we immediately called a meeting every time we thought there should be one, which sometimes would be three times a day. In the meetings we would talk on plans of what we should do in case of a "rip off," which meant that the government would come after us. We selected a council of the members for spokesmen to talk to the press or to the government. We all had our plans laid out, and once in awhile we would receive word, which would turn out to be a rumor, that the "rip off" was coming. Everyone would grab their sleeping bags and be ready to hide. Everyone had their places picked beforehand, and would be ready to go there at a moment's notice. Some elected to do this and some elected to blockade themselves inside the main cell block and when the government did break through, we were to sit down and lock arms and let them carry us off. Our meetings produced crews such as security groups, garbage crews, clean-up crews, etc. Security was headed by Jerry Hatch, one of the men who swam with us. We had security both day and night. They were stationed on all corners of the main cell block roof, where they could see all over the island. . . . Security at that point was our main concern. . . .

Interviewer: Besides Gerald Sam, among the Indian community there, Ross, you say that he gave you inspiration; were there other Indian leaders that provided inspiration to the young men, the militants?

Harden: I said before that I was inspired by Al Miller, Gerald Sam, and Oakes. But I could see where all the invaders of Alcatraz had inspired the Indians that later came to Alcatraz. People would even come to me asking questions and wanting some kind of advice. I tried to give them the best advice I could but I'm not very good at anything like that. I was inspired by so many Indians who later came and started helping us and were very serious and proud of what they were doing. So inspiration came to us from each other, if you know what I mean.[16]

Judy Scraper, Shawnee Indian, occupation participant

Scraper was interviewed on February 5, 1970.

Interviewer: Can you tell me about the school?

Scraper: These teachers, not only do they teach regular academic subjects, but they also teach different Indian religions, different cultures, all types of Indian history. Everything that he can get from the kids and from the adults contribute to class, so then again you know, not only are they getting the education they need as far as education in the terms of learning, but they are learning what other tribes say, and what they are, so they can maintain our identity or the identity that they have. And the white man, by placing us in prisoner of war camps, which all the reservations were to begin with, they were successful to a certain extent of destroying what identity the Indians have, but even though they have destroyed a great deal of it, we have got enough identity if we salvage it.[17]

Peter Blue Cloud, Mohawk Indian, occupation participant

Blue Cloud wrote a memoir, *Alcatraz Is Not an Island*, that was published in 1972.

We liberated Alcatraz for everyone. . . . We came to Alcatraz with an idea. We would unite our people and show the world that the Indian spirit would live forever. There was little hate or anger in our hearts, for the very thought of a lasting unity kept us whole and in harmony with life. From this island would grow a movement which must surely encompass the world. All men of this earth must hunger for peace and fellowship.[18]

Blue Cloud kept a diary during the occupation that was published in his book.

The fishing boat drives steadily through the darkness. Aboard are Indians of many tribes on their way to visit Alcatraz Island. A Navajo mother with her baby, young warriors and women of the Sioux, Winnebago, Blackfeet, Apache, Cheyenne and Iroquois are aboard. An old man who is all of our grandfathers sits smoking his pipe, his eyes staring in contemplation through the dark. We are quiet as we head across the bay. Behind us the revolving beacon of the Alcatraz lighthouse and the mournful voices of the fog horns. The island is a black outline and we shiver in the cold breezes coming through the Golden Gate.

When we near Alcatraz, the boat circles the island and we begin to approach the water barge which is tied to the dock. A huge bonfire is burning and we can see many figures moving about. An amplified voice booms at us, "Indians only. If you aren't Indians, please keep going and don't try to land. If you are Indian, welcome to Indian land! Come ashore and join your brothers and sisters."

Many hands reach out to help us ashore. Everyone is milling and laughing. "Hey, Welcome! What tribe you from? Hey, come on and dance." It is like coming home after a long journey. Soon, all the new arrivals are laughing and joking with friends.

The security guards are everywhere in evidence, bright red head and arm bands, their badges. Like the warrior societies of old, their job is to see that all goes well. A round dance is in progress and the circle is the biggest we've ever seen. Old people, as well as children, hold hands with the young men and women and circle the fire. The deep throbbing of the drum demands that everyone dance and the fire casts long shadows upon the concrete buildings and the whole scene is of red and golds.

We join the dance and feel the magic which is passing from hand to hand. All tribes and unity are the words of the drum and all tribes in unity are the dancers. The vast distances separating our many tribes is forgotten, as are the man-made boundaries. Indians from Alaska to South America are here to dance as brothers and sisters. The ancient dream of Indian unity is begun. . . .

Isolated, we will learn unity and learn to speak out our demands to a deaf government. This temporary isolation is very necessary. We must build our strength. Self-determination is our goal. . . .

We walk uphill, to the main cellblock, a steep and winding road to the foot of the lighthouse. The view from this place takes in the surrounding bay and mountains, and we stop to look around. ... The waters of the bay are black, dark blue, green, and even white where the fog blanket is reflected. ...

We enter the main cellblock and walk through the cold, alien world of concrete and steel bars. ...

The odor of fresh coffee comes to us as we enter the large rectangular yard surrounded by high concrete walls. Three or four fires are going and the women are frying potatoes, bacon and eggs for breakfast. People stand all about sipping coffee and quietly talking. Members of the security guard are chopping up boards and wooden boxes for the camp fires, while others haul cans of garbage up the narrow stairway. There are children and babies, all over, some children playing with the ducks and turkeys which have been donated, and others eating bowls of cereal. We join the long line of those waiting for breakfast. Afterwards, the new arrivals find chores to help with camp life. Cooking, dish washing, serving food, hauling garbage, security, and the hauling of groceries are shared by men and women. In the main cellblock, men and boys take on the task of sweeping.

A first aid station, manned by volunteer doctors and nurses, has been set up in solitary confinement. Bright blankets bring life to this very depressing cellblock. Children wander in and out of the cells, little wondering that the doors are solid sheets of steel with tiny openings. ...

Sleeping quarters are everywhere, each person free to decide for themselves where they will live. Solitary confinement cells, the chapel, the warden's house and guard's quarters are all taken and made use of. ...

Security has an office to keep track of all necessary chores. Public relations has an office next to security to handle the hordes of newsmen and photographers demanding immediate admittance and permission to roam the island at will.

Darkness is a welcome end to the busy activities of the day. In those first few weeks dances were held nightly and the drumming and singing were the pulsing of our very sleep.

In front of the main cellblock is a concrete area overlooking the bay and the Golden Gate. Railroad ties were placed in a wide circle and a fire built in the center. In the first cool evening breezes we sat, huddled in blankets to rest from the day's activities. Children grew quiet and sat close to their parents as a drummer began, soon to be joined by others in song. Above our heads the lighthouse beacon circled. Between songs the voices of the security guards could be heard. We stared into the embers of the fire and listened to the drum and the song. . . .

Indians of all tribes, who were we? From reservations and urban settlements, government boarding schools, street gangs or giant cities, plains, and desert, horse people, sheep herders, fishermen of the coastal rivers, hunters of the frozen north, we had come. Never before had the dream of Indian unity been put into reality in such a sudden way as at Alcatraz. . . .

We had come home. This cold and windswept island was ours. Unwanted and unknown by the strangers who now lived upon all parts of our continent, we had come home. Our earth mother wanted us here, for we are of the land. . . .

Negotiations between Indians of All Tribes and the government were taking place on Alcatraz. Self-determination, an Indian university, library, housing, spiritual center and all to be run by Indians, we said. . . .

The government representatives did not even offer us beads or blankets, as their fathers had. They sat like dummies being manipulated by others. . . .

These representatives of the government returned to the mainland and wearily told the press of the Indian's lack of understanding and of their unreasonableness. Didn't they, the government, know what was best for the Indian, they asked?[19]

Blue Cloud sent a letter to the Urban Indians of New York clarifying the situation on Alcatraz:

You say that information you receive is that factionalism and petty feuds are destroying the Alcatraz movement. But let me reassure you that though there are always those present who would ruin things—the majority, those dedicated to the true aims of our occupation, are seeing to it that these spoilers are made true believers, or asked to leave.[20]

Rosalie McKay-Want, Wintu/Wailaki/Pomo Indian

Text of an interview with McKay-Want appeared in a 1992 dissertation.

When we first got to the pier, it was real dark by then, and there was a bonfire going and Indians were standing around. Then we started walking up these stone steps and it was a real long walk up. And the steps were high. And we were going along like that and I heard some Indians talking in the background and the sound of Indians is so different than when white people talk. And it felt so good, it just felt like I was home. And we ended up stayin' there just a long, long time.

The best things that we ever got there were from the Asians, the Japanese-Americans. They sent us some really good, warm cardigans. It was really thought out, what they were going to send us. They brought produce over that was firm, juicy tomatoes. Everything was the best. I don't know the name of the group, but when we went to the dock to pick things up they had a banner out there that said "The Japanese-Americans support the Native Americans." . . .

Interviewer: I asked Rosalie to tell me what she remembered feeling on this November night, in the middle of the night, when it was dark and cold and she was surrounded by strangers, going to a place and to an event where she had little notion of what to expect.

McKay-Want: I knew I was lonesome, but I didn't know what it was. I didn't know that just being around Indians again. . . . I felt good because there was nothing but Indians around at the Indian Center and when we were down there at the pier, all the Indians standing around. When we got to Alcatraz it was real dark and there was a bonfire going and Indians were standing around. Then we started walking up these stone steps and it was a real long walk and the steps were high. When we got to the top and started signing in, there was a Blackfeet girl there named Vickie Santana. She said, "I have some room in my area. Come on and I'll show you where you can sleep tonight. You can stay there if you want." So we went to the main cellblock, the front part of it. I don't know what those rooms might have been. It was on the second floor towards the front. They had blankets. It was a room, probably 16' x 16' and they had it all sectioned off with blankets, a little cubbyhole. Vickie had one corner of the large room and we ended up staying there the first time around. We stayed there a few months, in fact. And then one of the houses got clear so we ended up going down to the house. But it was such a good experience for me and my kids. Later we talked about it and I'm so glad that I did it. It was just the right move. I was surprised that all these Indians, so many of them, had been living in the Bay Area and I hadn't known how to contact them. . . . Well, it got harder and harder to leave the island when we would come on the boats to the mainland to do laundry or to pick up my food stamps and pay my rent. And as we would come into dock all these white people would be out there staring or taking pictures. That constant clicking of the cameras just drove me into a frenzy after awhile. . . . In the final analysis, however, the occupation of this small territory could be considered a victory for the cause of Indian activism and one of the most noteworthy expressions of patriotism and self-determination by Indian people in the twentieth century.[21]

Al Miller, Seminole Indian, occupation participant

Miller was interviewed by John Trudell on "Radio Free Alcatraz" on December 22, 1970.

Interviewer: Al, I believe you were in on this from the very beginning, weren't you?

Miller: Right. . . . We started out originally with thirteen or fourteen people that were obsessed with the idea of taking Alcatraz, and those thirteen or fourteen people were motivated by the incident in 1964, when the Indians laid claim to the island. They did it under the provision of a treaty made in 1868, which stated that all unused federal land would be reverted back to the Indian. . . . Well, in 1964 when the Sioux tried to assert their rights under these treaties . . . the Indian claim was sort of treated as a big joke. . . . In 1969 they started accepting proposals again for Alcatraz, and Hunt and all these millionaires just wanted to turn it into another site of American garbage. That's when these two people, they contacted about all of the universities and got all of the young people . . . and we came out and laid claim to the island.

Trudell: What possibilities do you foresee we can do with this island as far as for the people on the island and Indians throughout America?

Miller: I have one of the original plans. It is still probably the best one for use of the island. The five uses we have down on that plan, among all those, the spiritual center and the university of higher learning would probably be the two most prominent features we would have here on the island. Indian people, they have always wanted something since the days of her [Grace Thorpe's] father. Something with an Indian curriculum, developed by Indian people.[22]

Earl Livermore, Goshute/Blackfoot Indian, member Alcatraz Island Council

Livermore was interviewed on April 8, 1970.

Some of the problems that came about, it was a tremendous challenge from the very beginning. In the main, we had set up an office in which we had to take care of the many calls that came from throughout the country, the donations, and so we met this challenge. . . . Some of the things that were needed was water, we had to bring our own water supply. We had to bring out some gas heaters, or whatever, and we had to bring out our own butane tanks for cooking, and we also brought our own water tanks and hooked all of these up for hot water for the kitchen, and we had to take care of the plumbing facilities, and we had to work on generators to get our electrical supply, because it was not fixed for over about five years. Some of the things, naturally, we had to try to get organized, some of the things we did in the very beginning was set up details, and this was the cooking and garbage and security and whatever, and then we finally set up committees. Then we needed a governing body. We had meetings practically every morning in which in setting up our governing body we came upon this type of structure. . . .

We also had an all Indian conference held on December 23 [1969]. One of the prime reasons was to get ideas from Indian people themselves, just what to do with the island. We set up committees and got about our business and had very good constructive ideas which we can use in our proposals. We set up the legal committees, admissions and qualifications, staff and physical operations, finance, and overall aims and goals. Some of the things that came out of this was, for example, in the design and layout, the plans that the building and grounds must express the unique purpose that Alcatraz Island is dedicated to the American Indian people locally, especially those who made the landing. The plan will solve the problems of lack of fresh water on the island, its natural limitations, its size, and rocky surface, and steep terrain, etc. . . . We had a number of ideas, but the whole idea was that it would be expressed Indianness. We also expressed the idea, the desire to set up a center of ecology. And, so we also found with it, in the line of our planning as far as transportation, we would have electric cars to avoid carbon monoxide, air pollution, and sanitation, chemical garbage disposals and so on and so forth. So, the whole thing was, the idea was similar to a small model city . . . and a number of things we had, cliff dwellings and round houses, so the whole island would be a culture center and everything would be in the design of Indianness. . . .

So, after less than two months we set up our articles and corporation by-laws, in which we are now incorporated, and it is called "Indians of All Tribes Incorporated." We also realized that we needed legal support, and we received legal support from Arnold Porter, one of the largest law firms in Washington, D.C. . . . We found that we needed to set up a task force of lawyers in the Bay Area because . . . a lot of people were going in freelancing and making a lot of money which we weren't seeing anything of, so now one of the committees for one of the lawyers was to work with contracts or any fund-raising or anything like this; and so the idea was for anyone who wishes to make any show, any film or documentary, or sign a letter of intent, or do any writings, they have to go through the council first and then it goes to the lawyers; from there it is brought to the general assembly for final approval.

On December 2, 1969, the San Francisco Regional Office of the General Services Administration, along with the members of the Department of Labor, Adult Education, Welfare, Housing, Urban Development, and EOC, met with the representatives from Alcatraz to determine what, in the way of assistance, can be properly provided by the federal government, to the Indians, in establishing a cultural center to meet their needs. So, we did generate some type of rapport with the federal government and also we were in constant contact with the federal government. . . .

One of the most beautiful things that came out of the occupation of Alcatraz was the fact that, because we have so many problems in the Bay Area and many of the Indian organizations were not really in communication; one thing came about was the fact that all Indian organizations banded together, primarily because the federal government wanted to speak with Indian leaders in the Bay Area. So they banded together under one organization called BANAC. . . . And from there the Indians began negotiations with the federal government. . . .

We had a lot of people come out to the island, so we have wonderful media coverage, and these people, one of the beautiful things, we brought a lot of attention to the world about the problems the Indian people are having in this country. We had a number of architectural firms and engineers that were offering their services . . . and we have had a number of resolutions, some were submitted by unions, Indian organizations, private organizations. But anyway, the support, we received a lot of support which was beautiful, from private citizens, private foundations, Indian organizations, and a lot of unions supported us: United Auto Workers, Cleaners, and whatever. And United Auto Workers gave us enough people to work and help us with some of the generators, and they also sent donations. We have had a number of celebrities on the island, we've had Anthony Quinn, Buffy St. Marie, Jonathan Winters, Candice Bergen, Merv Griffin, and Jane Fonda. We have had wonderful cooperation from the news media, radio and television, and from the international news media from Japan, Italy, France, Sweden, and England. . . .

We had petitions from all over the country, also, donations to our relief fund, and we are still receiving a lot of donations, which we are still badly in need of, because our budget is quite high, we have to rent our own boat service and everything.

In general, I would like to sum up the fact that we are not militant, we are only seeking a small part of that which we feel is rightfully ours. . . . Alcatraz has already served a number of purposes; it has served as an awakening to the general public and the world of the many injustices done to the American Indian in both the past and present. It has shown that we are proud of our culture and heritage and wish to retain it. It has shown that we can organize and develop unity. It has forced the federal government to recognize the problems facing the Indian community in the Bay Area. . . . This symbolic act by the original fourteen, who came to the island has been effective. There are few Americans who are not aware of the occupation or that there are many problems facing the American Indian people.[23]

Joe Bill, Eskimo, occupation participant

Bill was interviewed on February 5, 1970.

Interviewer: Well, what exactly do you think you are going to gain by getting the island?

Bill: A new school.

Interviewer: Well, morally as well as physically?

Bill: I suppose it will be the biggest unity fight the Indians ever had.

Interviewer: In other words, you are pushing this many tribes together as an aspect, instead of just one separate tribe against the government?

Bill: Yeah, because this is the reason why we signed the paper, the proclamation to the great white father, and signed it Indians of All Tribes. . . .

Interviewer: What is this meeting that is going to happen this weekend that you were talking about earlier?

Bill: Oh, I just heard that it was federal people meeting here in town and at the same time they had a meeting in Washington, D.C., and we might have our answer this week.

Interviewer: Do you have any hopes? I mean, any more than hopes, do you have any inkling of what is going to happen? I mean, do you think that you are going to win? Seriously?

Bill: Well, if we don't win, they are going to give us a good fight in getting us off.[24]

Stella Leach, Colville/Sioux, member Alcatraz Island Council

Leach was interviewed on February 4, 1970.

Interviewer: When did you come to Alcatraz?

Leach: Well, I was over there [San Francisco], and they called and said people had landed on Alcatraz and that they needed food and so we started getting that together and we were going to help. This was on the Saturday after they landed on the island on Thursday. So we went over to the Indian Center in San Francisco, and I helped out there before actually going on the island.

Interviewer: Do you think that Alcatraz is going to answer a lot of these problems that Indians are facing in the Bay Area?

Leach: In my mind it does, especially the isolation. That is what I like about it. I mean, it is obvious that white people can't come here, because an island, you can keep it more separate than you can a reservation. Myself, I was working in the All Indian Well Baby Clinic in Berkeley, and then in the clinic a couple of our Navajo girls and a couple of our Sioux girls helped me organize, and . . . I have been working there and I took three month's leave, came over to Alcatraz, and I just got involved in this thing and here I am, still here. . . . I think that as far as our main problem of securing the island is concerned, I think that the government is going to give us the island, and I think that they are going to be pressured into it by outside elements, because the middle class Americans are really becoming aware now. And it is surprising how much support that we are getting from more of the working class man. Of course, now all of the unions have come in to back us, and the map up there, a map of all the unions that are participating now, fund raising for us, and if they do that all over the United States and in Canada, and Alaska, and clear down to Mexico City; it's the longshoremen in Mexico City, the national local there. People are supporting us all over now. I think this is going to put pressure on the government, to give the island to the Indians. . . .

Interviewer: The young Indians on the island are, how would you say, educated, kind of sincere.

Leach: Well, I think most of the kids here are sincere. What is really remarkable as far as I am concerned is the change that you see in the kids that are here, and they don't come on really sarcastic and skeptical about the whole thing: What are you damn people trying to do here, play Indian, or what, really sarcastic. It is really surprising some of the changes that have come over the kids you know, like some here you know, they did come on here with some weird ideas, you know. I came to see what the action was all about, and who these nutty Indians were, you know, and soon they're involved in it, too, and here they are, here to stay. That is good, though, we are happy. I think that we are beginning to get together, you know.[25]

Marilyn Miracle, Mohawk Indian, occupation participant

Miracle was interviewed on February 5, 1970.

Interviewer: Why don't you give us a story about what is going on, on the island?

Miracle: Well, we're moving; trying to make it possible to live on the island. Of course we don't want to get wiped out because of lack of interest. . . .

Interviewer: What about tribal leaders all over the country? Have they supported you?

Miracle: We have had letters of support from tribal leaders across the country, involved in different organizations, from tribal councils; we have had visitors from the All Pueblo Council. . . . I don't remember what the names of the men were. Representation from the American Indian Movement in Minneapolis was out here; about fifteen of them came out and spent a week out here and they may be back. While they were here, they offered us assistance in writing proposals and working on security force, working in the kitchen, just organizational type things that we desperately needed. . . . We have had letters from the Sioux tribe, signed by, I think it was fifteen different people there.

Interviewer: Have you sent out literature to these various reservations?

Miracle: When we get letters coming in from reservations, we generally send out either a newsletter or an information packet. Now on the mailing list for the newsletter, I think our mailing list right now is over 3,000. That has to be sent out, and, unfortunately, in addition to sending these to individuals, we try and send them to universities and organizations where they can give support for the expensive postage and for printing and things like this. These are the types of organizations that we want to contact, you know. . . . But right now, this is one of the big problems that we have in operating. It was not set up beforehand to really, like we are attempting to organize and get things straightened around, while at the same time, continually just handle all the things that we get. And it really takes three times as long to get everything going. We are trying to develop, we have a couple of people working on the national committee, of Indians throughout this country, to give their support and also to use us kind of as a bargaining deal with the federal government.

Interviewer: In San Francisco itself, what is the feeling about it?

Miracle: Generally, I would say, people here in the Bay Area definitely support us. On our mailing list, as far as the list of donations, we have most of it from San Francisco and the California area. That way we get money. People are continually calling and donating food and supplies, blankets, clothes, and this is really business like. They want to know how they can contact us, how can we get this stuff to you, what is happening. There is a great deal of interest. . . .

Interviewer: Do you get a lot of curiosity seekers trying to get out here?

Miracle: Yeah, very simple, there is one rule, the only non-Indians allowed on the island are government people and the press, who come up to the pier with proper credentials, and they are issued a pass. . . . The only non-Indians allowed to spend the night on the island is like lawyers or doctors. We have some trouble sometimes with people that go out there, like these photographers with four or five cameras, and like one day we had to ask them to leave, because there are restricted areas on the island, that is, that they are not allowed into. And like, a lot of times, they will want to take pictures of people, and a lot of people don't want their pictures taken, and you have got to be there to tell them you can't take pictures unless you ask that person. . . . And then they say that we are censoring them, because we don't let them take any pictures. Like, for instance, you are not allowed in the private homes, unless the person living there invites them; they are not supposed to be in even certain parts of these cell blocks. . . .

Interviewer: Question unclear.

Miracle: If we get the island, I'm really certain we eventually will get it by some means or other, legally get that; then this will be the first step and it will establish a precedence in court, or in the law, for other people to work from in different areas. This is one thing that you have to be careful of, you know. As far as handling politicians and handling a lot of people, is that this is one thing that is saving them, the precedence. They can say, you know, let them have Alcatraz, but then when they start claiming other lands, all of a sudden they begin to worry about setting a precedence.[26]

La Rayne Parrish, Navajo Indian, occupation participant

Parrish was interviewed on February 5, 1970.

Interviewer: What relationship do you have with Alcatraz?

Parrish: Well, I guess my whole life revolves around what is happening on Alcatraz. I have been involved with the movement for about two and a half months now. And overall I feel it's a beautiful thing, and a movement like this is long overdue, but I guess it has always been the nature of Indians not to jump into things until the time is right. My total relationship has been more of doing a visual anthropology kind of thing. I have been filming and photographing what's been happening out on the island for some time, interviewing people, finding out how they feel about what is happening at all age levels. I have talked with a number of older people that have come from the rancharias in California, that have come from the reservations, from states all across the nation. . . .

Interviewer: How does the rural Indian fit into this picture of Alcatraz?

Parrish: I think it was an urban movement initially. I mean it was started by urban Indians, but it doesn't end there. What's happened to the urban Indians is a result of what has happened on the reservation, and that alone, that movement alone is symbolic of the need for attention on the rural areas and reservations in the United States. . . .

Interviewer: Some of us weren't particularly impressed with some of the Indians we met today. Can you give us some kind of comment on what you feel, the kind of students that are being attracted to this movement? Are they, by and large, pretty sincere, or are a number of them just coming because of the publicity and that sort of situation?

Parrish: No, I don't think so. I think the majority of the people that are now involved as residents and as leaders are very serious about what has happened. A lot of the people have experienced reservation life; they know what it is like to, they know what the feeling is when their parents have to live on welfare, when they have to depend on the BIA and their services, their families and relatives have to depend on the reservation, the BIA and Indian Health Service, and government employment services, just for a job, just for a livelihood to exist. I think a lot, the majority, I think maybe half of the students are family, are students that have been through the reservation schools. . . . We have all kinds of people involved in the movement. Initially it was like, educated Indians out there doing their thing, some with bourgeois backgrounds, some like LaNada Boyer, who have been through the Indian ghetto scene in the Bay Area, but because of her wanting to liberate her own people, she is out there fighting. Some of these people, before the movement, hung out in the parks, out on the streets, without a damn thing to do. That is why the movement is happening, because of people like that. Whether they are aware of their behavior now, or whether they are aware of the way they treat other people now, they are bound to learn from it, in a few months or in a few years. But what's happening out there has just been tremendous. Really, I think that everybody that has been involved in the movement one way or another, with all the hassle, and we will all have learned from it you know, it is just tremendous.[27]

Wilma Mankiller, Cherokee, occupation participant

Mankiller wrote me a letter about Alcatraz on November 27, 1991.

The occupation of Alcatraz was an important event in the overall development of Indian policy. I visited the island many times during the occupation and was a supporter. I'd never heard anyone actually tell the world that we needed somebody to pay attention to our treaty rights, that our people had given up an entire continent, and many lives, in return for basic services like health care and education, but nobody was honoring those agreements. For the first time, people were saying things I felt but hadn't known how to articulate. It was very liberating.[28]

When members of the American Indian Movement took over the former prison at Alcatraz, "she experienced an awakening that ultimately changed the course of her life."[29]

Mankiller further discusses the impact of the Alcatraz occupation in her book *Mankiller: A Chief and Her People:*

When Alcatraz occurred, I became aware of what needed to be done to let the rest of the world know that Indians had rights too. Alcatraz articulated my own feelings about being an Indian. It was a benchmark. After that, I became involved. . . .

They took over the twelve-acre island to attract attention to the government's gross mistreatment of generations of native people. They did it to remind the whites that the land was *ours* before it was *theirs* . . . . The name of the island is Alcatraz. It changed my life forever.[30]

George Horse Capture, Gros Ventres, occupation participant

Horse Capture wrote about his impressions in 1991.

The word quickly spread across the waves and on the moccasin telegraph—"The Indians Have Landed." There was universal rejoicing from the Indian reservations in the country to the Indian centers in the cities. For the first time since the Little Bighorn, the Indian people, instead of passively withdrawing and accepting their fate, had stepped forward in the bright sunshine and let it be known that they were Indian and proud, and their present situation must and would change. . . .

The first Thanksgiving on the island drew international attention as journalists and media crews from around the world attended the Indian event. Empathetic citizens and organizations sent water and food, including scores of baked turkeys, on boats and barges as the Indian people told their story to the world.

In the following months, the movement continued to capture public attention, and non-Indians learned more than ever before about the hundreds of years of injustice to the Indian people. More important, the occupation by the young warriors forced the Indian people themselves to reexamine their acquiescence to the non-Indian world and seek to determine their own social and cultural responsibilities.

Though not members of the original landing party, other Indians from all tribes came to take part in this epic historical declaration, as I did myself. One night, an Indian arrived on the last boat from the mainland. When I asked what he thought of the island, he exclaimed in wonderment, "I don't believe it. It's incredible, I just hitchhiked from my home in New Mexico to see if the news was true. I have to return tomorrow. It is true. We did it!"[31]

John Trudell, Sioux, member of Alcatraz Indian Council

Trudell was interviewed on "Radio Free Alcatraz" and as its primary announcer conducted numerous interviews.

December 1969

This is John Trudell speaking to you on behalf of Indians of All Tribes. . . . I am going to use the time this evening just to answer some questions I have received in the mail, and talking to various people. One of the first questions to pop up is, people want to know if we are serious about our university on Alcatraz Island. Well, the way it stands today, the longer an Indian student stays in a BIA school, the further behind he becomes in his education. . . . So yes, we are serious about an Indian university. . . .

There have been newspaper reports about our organization falling down on the island. . . . We are not disorganized on the island. On the island right now we are functioning better than we have ever functioned from November 20th up to this date. The only disagreement we have on the island would come under the everyday hassle of 150 people living together, and most of these people didn't live together before. We have many different backgrounds and many different ideas. But we don't have anything that is damaging us. We work out all of our problems, as I mentioned before. [T]he Council on the island holds general meetings, where all the people attend. Any issues or policies that are to be decided or made for the island, concerning the island, are decided on by the people at these meetings. Everyone has the chance to have his say-so. Everyone's opinion is respected. And then, we vote on it. The majority vote carries and the council acts on that, what I believe is called a democracy. And that is what we are trying to have here. . . . All we are asking for right now is time to get ourselves together.[32]

January 20, 1970

Interviewer: This is Johnny YesNo, the host of a radio program here in Canada. First let me begin by asking you a few questions. What is the population of Alcatraz?

Trudell: I would say roughly around seventy-five people at this time. We lost quite a few of the younger people who had to go back to school at the beginning of the quarter or the new semester, and especially some of the young men who are of draft age and their draft status is kind of uncertain, so they had to go back to school.

Interviewer: What are some of the tribes that are represented at Alcatraz?

Trudell: We have Eskimos from Alaska. We had an Aztec from Mexico, we've had Seminoles, we have people from Florida, New York, the midwestern states, and I believe we have two gentlemen here from Canada.

Interviewer: I would be interested in finding out just how you people are surviving out there. For instance, how are you getting your food supplies, heating, lighting, and this sort of thing?

Trudell: OK, with the heating, we don't have any central heating at all. Our best bet is to find a warm building, if possible, and some of the buildings have fireplaces in them. So this would take care of the heating needs, and we have a clinic that has a heater that we can use, an electric heater. It has to be used very sparingly because we do not have much electricity. We have, a few of the buildings have electricity and the rest of them don't have any. And as far as food, we received quite a bit of food stuffs as donations, like canned goods, so we use these, and we have to buy all of our fresh foods daily because we don't have any refrigeration. Also, we have to buy the fresh meat and bread and milk and things like that.

Interviewer: How about the general public, the white sympathizers. Have you had much support from them?

Trudell: Yes, the more they find out about what we are doing here, the more support we are getting from them. Right at this time we don't have any enemies or people who are against us. The reaction from the white people that I have had is that they are eager to find out, find the answers to a lot of questions. But on the whole they agree with us.

Interviewer: I understand why you took over Alcatraz, one of the things you wanted to do was turn it into a cultural center. How was that thought of?

Trudell: The cultural center would include a museum of Native American history, it would have an ecology center, a spiritual center, a free Indian university that would stress both academic training and vocational training. It would be up to the individual student. At this university we would allow Indian students to come and attend this school, regardless of age or prior education, because many of our people have not received proper education. We hope that once we get the question settled with the U.S. government about giving us the island, then we hope to go through private grants and even ask the government for money to develop the island, when they give us the island.[33]

March 1970

Good evening, this is John Trudell . . . . We have been lucky here, we haven't really had a lot of cold weather. And we've got, let me see, about a week ago, we received $15,000 worth of medical supplies and beds from Los Angeles. I think George Brown donated it to us—he brought it up here to us, that I know. We've got things pretty well in shape here. Our biggest hassles right now are with food supplies, fresh foods, and we have a boat problem yet. We are still chartering a boat, but we are looking into all possibilities now of buying a boat of our own, because that is our biggest single expense. . . .

We also are working, so that we can send runners out to the people who are associated with the Alcatraz movement, to go visit as many of these Indian people as possible, so that they can answer the questions that are asked, and so that they can get this information out and start building our ties a little stronger. We haven't been able to do this very effectively in the past because it runs into, it takes money to do these things. We see a real big need for this, so we are trying to tie everything in together here. We are sending our speakers out nationwide. So while the people are on the speaking engagements, we are trying also to send our runners to the reservations and urban Indian organizations, to where our speaking engagements may be. We are learning to use all the resources and take advantage of everything that is given to us.[34]

April 30, 1970

As far as the island, we're holding up pretty well. We have been working pretty closely with the [Bay Area Native American Council] organization here. . . . BANAC was formed by the Indian groups and the service organizations in the Bay Area to deal with the Alcatraz situation, and Alcatraz is a part of BANAC. . . . BANAC has helped us to establish a refrigerator over at the depot, on Pier 40, and things can be brought there, contributions, whatever you feel that we deserve, and we will try to liberate ourselves from the federal government and gain some kind of self-determination. Meat, things like that, and also we could use tools, things like working implements, if we are going to start remodeling the island. We are going to liberate the land now from some of these buildings here, very shortly, because there are many of these buildings that are unsafe. We need things like cutting torches, to start cutting down some of this old barbed wire, and these big fences. Not only will it make things a little safer here, but it will give us something to do here while we are waiting for our dear old uncle out there to start acting like he should, to start coming around and start dealing with us. . . . We are asking for self-determination, and we are asking for jobs for Indian people, and that is part of the symbolism of Alcatraz. . . . Alcatraz is all of these things you know, it is social, economic, and to an extent political self-determination. . . . We want to be free, we want the right to live like free men, as a free people. I've talked to different people, you know, and immediately they want to put it in the context of militancy. . . . Militancy is just another white word like democracy is, equality too, all of these beautiful words. We don't want words, we want self-determination. If you believe strongly in anything, you have the right to be militant. When your back is to the wall, how do you expect people to react? . . . So everything here is cool, we're still here and we're still holding out, and we haven't changed any of our ideas about what we want. Someone mentioned to me, not too long ago, about America having an Indian problem. America doesn't have an Indian problem, Indians have an American problem.[35]

May 27, 1970

T. E. Hannon made a statement yesterday that they had met with us over thirty times, you know. That's kind of weird, because I've never seen him around except for about three times that I can actually name things that were said. Yeah, well, anyway, we told the government, no, we don't plan on leaving. Well, the situation was, they said that it's [Alcatraz] going to be a national park with an Indian flavor and that they were removing their officials from the lighthouse. They encouraged us to leave too. So today they cut off the electricity, and yesterday they took our water barge . . . they were going to take our water barge away so that we would be sure to get it back by today, so we would have plenty of water for the weekend. This is the story we were told, then they ripped us off. . . . They took off with that water barge. Took the GSA personnel off the island. There are only Indians here now. . . . So we have a good food supply coming, and water is limited now because of what they left us with. We are starting to ration the water, but the morale is really high you know. Everyone is starting to pitch in when the boats come in down there. I don't think we will be losing any people out of it—the intimidation[s] they have put on us. I don't know, I think things are going to start getting tight now, but then actually to me they are just intimidating us, you know, waiting for us to make some kind of move, because we have been out here six months and they haven't done anything. So I feel they will continue the waiting game in hopes that we will all give up and go home. I feel they will probably come in here and rip us off, because ripping us off the island, really, because they've done everything else in the last couple of months and have gotten away with it. . . . But we need water. So anyone out there, jump in your boat and bring us some water. We will let you land. Yeah, I mean we will let you come in and give us some water anyway. Because water is going to become a problem. If we have any big problem, that is going to be it, water.[36]

June 2, 1970

Here is what happened last night, June 1, 1970. We had a fire that burnt down the warden's, the warden's home, the old clinic, and the old lighthouse building. All that is left of the lighthouse building or the lighthouse is a long skinny thing with a light on the end that sticks up in the air, and that is all that was burned. The next question was how did the fire start, or do you know that? No, we don't know that. All we know was that at about 10:30 last night that it started and that it finally died out this morning. We tried to keep the lighthouse from going, but it went, and there was nothing we could do about it. We didn't have any water to fight it with, and by the time the Coast Guard came, it was too late for them to do anything, so we didn't let them come on the island. They asked if they could land, and we told them no, and they stayed off, stayed away from the shore. . . . They couldn't save the buildings, they were already too far gone to be saved, and we didn't know what was coming off. We didn't know if they were going to try to take us off the island, or what, and we didn't want all of those government people running around at night, so we just kept them off. . . . We've got it all under control, everyone got a little more excited about it than we did. We moved all the women and kids into one building, away from the fire, and we decided to just let it burn out. We made an attempt to stop the lighthouse fire. We couldn't do that, so we just let it all go.

I heard this morning, one of the reporters from the Associated Press told me, that a man by the name of Laws, with the GSA, said that we started the fire and I don't know anything about that, and I would like to say right now, there have been no Coast Guard or GSA personnel on the island, so he cannot say that, because he doesn't know. But this is the kind of thing that he [Laws] is putting out right now. . . .

I think the fire just got started and the whole deal is like, the way I look at it is, the fire did us a favor. It just burned down two buildings that we were going to have to tear down, and that's exactly the way it is. . . .

We are going to be in dire need of water here now, because we had some water in the tank, but when the clinic burned down it ruptured a couple of pipes and we have been losing water most of the night and I don't know how much we have left. I don't think we will have any left, not at the rate we were losing it. . . . People can bring it down to our loading dock there next to Capinolas, down on Fisherman's Wharf, and if the people have boats and they want to come, they can bring water and we will let them land.[37]

June 1970

The fuel and food situation is still the same on the island. Bottled water is still being brought onto the island. The reaction from the people in the Bay Area has really been great as far as water, because every day we have people coming by and carrying anything from two gallon containers of water to fifty gallon drums of water. . . . As far as electricity goes, we have a generator to supply power for the lighthouse. That's the way it is running now, I believe. One of our Indian electricians on the island hooked that up and we have a small generator that supplies power for our mess area so that we have a TV in there and we have enough electricity in there for the people cooking. We are trying to get more generators so that we can hook up more power.[38]

June 1970

Right now everything on the island is fine. We are in, as far as the people are concerned, I mean, we are in good shape morally, morale is high, and we are still in the same position as far as electricity goes. Things like, we had our lighthouse burned out, we blew some bulbs a couple of nights ago when we went without a lighthouse for a night, but things are running all right again. . . . But our biggest problem we have now is running into this deal abut water. We are out of water. I think we have 500 gallons of water left and that is it. So now our biggest worry is getting water. We need water because we have children out here. We need the water for them, we need the water for ourselves. We need it for sanitation purposes. We can't flush toilets. Cooking, washing dishes, we need water for these things also. The government hasn't released their hold on giving us water. They gave us 500 gallons of water a long time ago, and we haven't heard from them since then. They gave that to us as a sign of good faith. But that's as far as it got, a sign of good faith, one trickle of water. But we'll find a way to get water. If nothing else, we have to haul it ourselves in one-gallon containers. We discussed it last night at our meeting, that we're not going to back down. Water or no water, we're still going to go all the way. . . . But other than that, everything on the island is going, it's going just fine, other than the small water problem. Morale is high, very high. Everyone is still determined that we are going to stay, that we are going to stick around for awhile. No park, that's the number one thing. We still want the deed to Alcatraz Island so that we have control over it, that Indian people have control over it.[39]

July 1970

Everything out here is in good shape except for our water supply. We are running into a hassle on that. The government still hasn't eased up on us and given us any water. But the morale is still high. Everyone is still behind what we are doing. We are making arrangements now to see what we can do to see if we can get someone to intervene and maybe supply us with some water. The weather has been cold, except for the past couple of days the sun has been shining. The cold weather has been to our advantage, because, without enough water, if the heat were to come out here we would be in real trouble. But with God on our side, the weather has been cold, although it is kind of a hardship at times. We could use wood, I guess, things to burn.

Another bit of good news is that we are expecting to have a birth out here on the island, sometime within the next, the doctor said today, within the next forty-eight hours. . . . It's my wife who's going to be giving a son maybe, or something.[40]

July 1970

Well, I guess the biggest, the one biggest piece of news or event that has happened out here this past week is the birth of a new boy, Wovoka. My wife had the baby, Monday evening . . . . There are some really good feelings out here. The feelings were already here and they seem to have been strengthened. . . . His name is Wovoka, no middle name, no last name, and he is about what I would call the first free Indian born in the past 500 years, because the government is not going to get him. . . .

We have somewhere around sixty or seventy people out here. We're all hanging tough. Water is still our big number one problem, and rapidly the number two problem is becoming electricity, because our generators are, we have two generators that are working right now, two large generators and one of them is supplying power to the lighthouse. The other one is being used down on the mess decks where we are eating and the generators are pulling a lot of duty, so I don't know how much longer they are going to last. . . . We had visitors last night, we have about forty visitors from the Hemisphere Indian Convention, in Tallalup, Washington. These were people with Mad Bear Anderson. Mad Bear is a medicine man from the Iroquois people. Charles Kills

Enemy, a Sioux medicine man from Pine Ridge was also here, and one of the chiefs of the Iroquois Six Nations, and the head chief was also here. They were out last night and we had a ceremony on the island, it was a religious ceremony. We had that last night. We have a teepee out here, it was set up in Tallalup, for the convention, and Mad Bear said that there were over sixty tribes who came and paid honor to the teepee and they brought the teepee home. So now it is set up on Alcatraz once again.[41]

July 1970

It's been kind of warm out here the last couple of days and the water has been bad in the late afternoon. Our boat is barely holding together at some times, but we make it. The situation is still the same as far as water and electricity with the government. We had a man come out and repair some of our generators, so our electrical situation isn't as bad as it was last week. Buffy St. Marie bought us 400 gallons of water and sent it up, and we are working right now in any way possible to pick up some more, some way. . . . Oh yes, another bit of news here. We are going to be applying for foreign aid shortly. And I guess we are going to have to turn and ask other governments to do what the U. S. government should be doing but neglects to do. This isn't entirely our decision. Somebody out there helped us make it. The decision was made because we came here in November, we came out here and voiced our opposition to what was going on and we had all of these people say, yeah, right on, we support you, you are doing right. Indians have been screwed, so what you people out there are doing is really wonderful, and we are behind you all the way. But we look back at what has happened since last November and somehow this support does not overly warm my heart, because we have all this support and yet the government has come in and taken away the water, the government has come in and taken away all of the electrical power. The government harasses us in the small ways. When we went to purchase our boat, they asked questions like, are Indians citizens, and they make us prove it. And I think the biggest burn is the fact that we do have women and children out here, and we've committed no crime, we haven't advocated the overthrow of the U.S. government by force, or by any other way. We have simply said that there are things that must be changed. And yet, we have whole families out here and the government comes in and just rips off the water, shuts it off, and America just sits back and says, How you doing without water? Do you have enough water? Well, whether we have enough water or not, that is not the issue. The issue is that there is such a thing as right and wrong, and it is wrong to deprive people of water. . . . We are protesting, which, according to the Constitution of the United States, the people have the right to do. We are protesting injustices that have been directed towards us and this is what we get. . . .

We are going through this period now, I read in one of the papers or magazines that right now the government is at a policy of not doing anything to upset the American people. They don't want to rock the boat, so they're not going to come in right now and rip us off the island, because they don't want to rock the boat. The American people would get upset if the government would come in and arrest us. But they don't get upset by the fact that we don't have water out here. They don't get upset over the fact that it is unsanitary out here without water, that we can't keep the places as clean and healthy as they should be, and we would like it to be. We're out here, and we've got things like fire hazards, there's no water out here to put out things like fires. The water that we do get is brought in small containers, and if anything bad happens, there's not much defense we have against it right now, but then, it's not my conscience.[42]

August 4, 1970

Number one, everything on the island is in pretty good shape. Everyone out here is in good spirits, good mood, high morale, the baby is fine. . . . Quite a few things are in the news today, I guess. The number one thing was in yesterday's newspaper, I believe, or on the news yesterday, about the government, Congress, has authorized the Coast Guard, or someone, to restore power to the lighthouse because of the pressure put on them by the unions, the waterfront unions in San Francisco, the maritime union. And that is really pretty strange, you know. All of these unions in San Francisco can put pressure on the government to restore power. But Indian people can't put enough pressure on the government to give Indian people title to the island. Pretty strange, kind of makes one wonder with all of the support we have. And also, one other thing on that, Congress decided that it was too dangerous for the boats out here, but maybe they didn't care what we were saying on May 31st, when we said that this is our island, and they forgot to ask us about restoring power to the island. And the whole thing on this is, that the Coast Guard has told us that they are going to rehook up the electricity out here, but that we can't have any of it. Then I'm afraid that they are not going to put any electricity back out here. We are not going to allow them to put electricity back to the lighthouse and the foghorn, if we the people can't have any of it. It is our island, so we will make them a trade. We'll let them rent, or lease, the lighthouse area and the foghorn, if they restore electrical power to us and bring the water barge back. Otherwise, we are just going to have to hassle this out and see what happens, but that is only what is right. We are out here, we're people, and we've got a say-so. That's the way we see it.[43]

August 11, 1970

Well, I guess there has been what you would call quite a bit of action going on concerning Alcatraz, a lot of activity somewhere. On the island itself, we are in good shape, we have quite a few people, morale is high, everyone is happy, so I guess we really couldn't ask for much more than that. Well, we could, but we've got a working system going here and we are content with that. As far as the other side, now, we have been getting a lot of attacks, verbal attacks by Thomas Hannon, the GSA regional director, here in San Francisco. . . . He is trying to paint a really ugly picture of us so that he can justify something that is going to happen to us, something that is not going to be too good for us I guess. I don't know. We will see what happens. We had an incident last week about an arrow being fired at one of the ferry boats that go by here, by the island, by one of the ferry boats. And we noticed that it got quite a bit of play in the paper. Mr. Hannon from GSA made a big to-do about it, and how dangerous it was. We would like to remark on that also. We admit firing the arrow and if we had to do it again, we would do it again. The arrow was fired because these people wouldn't listen to us, and we had to have it happen some way. Every time these harbor boats come by the island, they come in close to the island, they come in twenty to thirty yards off. And these are big boats, and these boats leave these tremendous wakes behind them, which send the waves rippling out from behind the boat, and when our boat is in, tying up, these captains, these harbor boat captains, have no consideration at all. They just come in as close as they can possibly get, because they are loaded to the gills with tourists who want to see the Indians on Alcatraz. So these boats come in as close as they can. And when our boat is tied in close to the dock, this is dangerous, because we are loading and unloading people from our boat. If someone falls because of this wake that is left behind, if someone falls between our boat and the dock, that is it, you see, because these waves cause our boat to smash up against the side of the dock. It is damaging to our boat, and it is very hazardous to our people. We asked the people from the boat companies to stop it. We asked the Coast Guard to have it stopped. And then we said that we wanted it stopped, and nothing was ever done about it. So, we bought one forty-two cent arrow, shot it in the middle of the night, and that stopped it, and that is all there is to that, to the whole thing. I mean we are not out to start any, I mean we didn't mean to start a general alarm or anything. But we are not fooling around.

There has been a lot of talk about how dangerous it was to fire that arrow at that boat. Well, we fired that arrow in the middle of the night, when the boat wasn't loaded. We could have done it in the middle of the day when the boat was crowded, which would have increased the chances of somebody getting hurt. We did it in the middle of the night. We accomplished what we set out to do, and that's all there is to that.

But anyway . . . we haven't changed our position on anything. We still want the deed to the island. And if the government wants to restore power to the lighthouse and the foghorns, then we want them to return our water. We will take care of the electrical part of it all, but that's the way it's got to be. We're not going to allow anything to go on until we get our water supply back. We're willing to work with the government because, last week, we told the government that we wanted the power returned to us and our water returned to us. Well today we've made our own arrangements for power and to help ease our power shortage, so now we've extended what we call a hand, and if they slap it, then we won't extend it again, that's all there is to it. . . .

We've got, this is a July issue of the *Los Angeles Herald Examiner* and we don't usually get into things like this, but this is something here, we know that we have listeners in Los Angeles, and we would kind of like to clarify this up a bit. It's the headlines. It made the headlines. The headline is "Alcatraz Indians, The Shattering of a Dream" by Robert Schwartz. . . . Schwartz said that "when I visited last Thanksgiving day, there were 700 happy men, women, and children on the island. There was feasting, merriment, and high hopes. This week I counted twenty persons, there is no electricity, no gas, little shelter. The proud Indian leader lies near death in a San Francisco hospital. His twelve year old daughter died in a fall several months ago. There are no more high hopes. Nine months ago there were high hopes and great plans. Incorporation papers were drawn up in January and filed in Sacramento. A newspaper was printed and distributed, a radio program carried the news of the Indians of Alcatraz daily to its listeners. A school was established on the island for the many children there, and a clinic was open seven days a week. Tragedy came in the form of a great fire that wiped out the warden's mansion, and with it the best shelter. It has come in different form. Tragedy came in the form of death, when the thirteen-year-old daughter of the leader, Richard Oakes, the occupying Indian, was killed in a fall. There are several versions, she was sliding down a banister when she fell, she fell down some steps in the old guard's quarters, she fell from the second story of a balcony in the main cell block, she fell sliding down a banister in the old guard's quarters. Tragedy came when some of the water sent from the mainland was contaminated. Practically everyone on the island fell ill. And lastly, tragedy fell when Richard Oakes was beaten nearly to death and hospitalized in San Francisco. He was their president and firm leader. Despite the persons remaining here now, the island seemed deserted and lifeless, despite the fact that John and Lu Trudell will have their baby here, sometime around July 20th, there seems to be a lack of objective. Perhaps LaNada Boyer expressed the thoughts of the group in a conversation held over breakfast while waiting for a boat to take us out. 'The original landing force, most of them have gone out to continue the work around the country. There are eleven areas now being occupied by Indians; Rattlesnake Island, Pit River area, Lassen Park, Fort Lawson, and the Washington state fish-ins. Indians there are being arrested for fishing, but under treaty there, Indians could fish there as long as grass grows and water flows. The fires on the island were started by self-appointed vigilante types and rich boats firing at us. We have nothing to negotiate, we plan on sending letters to countries all over the world to approach the United Nations for help.'"

I don't know what the man was looking for when he came out here really. He came out here with both eyes closed and ran into a wall. But we have a reply, and this is a letter that was written by my wife, and a copy has been mailed to Mr. Schwartz and any of the Mr. Schwartzes that might be out there and are looking at us through his type of eyes.

"Mr. Schwartz: It was only this evening that I read your article that was printed in the July 19th issue of the *Herald Examiner*. No, Mr. Schwartz, our dream is not shattered. Perhaps if you lived here you could see this. But then, the heart of a man is not visible. It might help to say that our newsletter, paper, is still printed and distributed, or that our school is resuming in three weeks, after a well-deserved summer vacation, or that Indian land radio is still broadcasting on Thursday evenings at 6:15 on KPFA and KPFK in Los Angeles, or that the clinic is still here, with visiting medical and dental personnel, or that Indians of All Tribes is still incorporated. You stated that tragedy has come to Alcatraz. Yes, the warden's mansion burned and so did two other structures with it. But that was on the upper level where no one resided, and Mr. Schwartz, that was not a tragedy. If tragedy came, when supposedly contaminated water was brought here from the mainland, neither my family or myself felt this tragedy. Neither myself or friends felt this tragedy. The death of the young girl in January was tragic, as is the hospitalization of Richard Oakes and the events leading to the hospitalization. The Indian has had a tragic past Mr. Schwartz, needless to say, a tragic present. But we are here on Alcatraz, and Rattlesnake Island, and Pit River, to prevent a tragic future. This is our objective and if you could search our minds and hearts, that objective is there, even if it is not visible to you. There is definitely no one leader or president here, Mr. Schwartz, nor has there ever been. We have a seven-man council, but none are so-called leaders or chiefs. The leaders are the whole body, the whole population on Alcatraz, for without them there would be no Alcatraz, and there would be no hope. It would be good if you could understand that a diminishing of the population does not mean desperation, nor a lessening of activity, the vanishing of hope. It could be good if you could realize that we have not lost our chance, but are starting to regain it. It would be good if you could see our dreams, but you see only what you wish to see. Incidentally, Mr. Schwartz, the young Indian rumored to have committed suicide did not and is alive and well, and the day after your article was printed, I gave birth to a beautiful baby boy here on Alcatraz. That, Mr. Schwartz, is hope. Sincerely, Mrs. Lu Trudell." . . .

As for us, I will call Mr. Schwartz a liar in the fact that there are more than twenty people here and more than twenty people in July. There were more than that at that time, and there have always been more than twenty people here. Maybe there aren't 700 people here anymore, but we're not trying to confine our people, we're not trying to lock them up and say, look, you've got to live on this island, you've got to be this way because everything depends on it. They're Indians, they're people, they are free, and there are other things in the country to do, and other places that they've got to go and work, and as long as they are involved, and they are becoming involved in these areas, it's—Alcatraz is here and it's open to Indian people who want to live here and we'll do what we can with it, and we are doing it. But it's not the hope, the hope being gone. That's not it, that's not where it's at. And we're going to hang in there.[44]

November 20, 1970

Interviewer: Well, you have been here for almost a year and you have seen a lot of changes on the island and a lot of people come and a lot of people go. . . . Can you think back to November 29, 1969, when you arrived and what it was like back then?

Trudell: Back in November, last year, when I first came out here, there was a lot of excitement, there were a lot of people out here. The occupation was very new. We had large numbers of people here, living out here, anywhere from 200 to 300 people living out here at a time. Then after that came school, quarter breaks and semester breaks, whatever, and we had more people coming out. . . . And that time of the year when the occupation first started, we were more concerned, we were very concerned with how the public would react to what we were doing. We kind of patterned our occupation so as not to offend the public too much, because that is where our support was, our sympathy you know. It allowed us to stay here. From that time, we have kind of evolved into the period we are in now, where we are not so much concerned with what middle class America thinks about it. We are concerned with our image with Indian people. We are here under the name of Indians of All Tribes, so what we are now working to do is to create that good image with our own people. We are not so much concerned with what John Q. Public thinks anymore, because John Q. Public is just that, while Indian people are our own people. What we are working for now is—we would like to see a strong sense of Indian nationalism built and I think Alcatraz is starting to do that. . . . I see the Indian unity coming and that's what our whole objective is now. Whatever we do, do it for Indian people. Because eventually, I imagine, I don't know, but I know what the government solution to this is, that is come and take us off, and if that happens, we win, and if they give us the deed to the Island, we win. So that is a pretty good feeling, we win, a damn good feeling. We don't want just the small little battle, we are shooting for the whole works, we are shooting for the overall victory and in the process of doing so, this hasn't changed from the beginning to now. . . . We won't deal with the government, it's just as simple as that. We are tired of being lied to and about. Now if the government ever wants to sit down and talk about serious issues, what we want to talk about, and they send someone with a little authority to deal, then maybe we'll sit down and talk. . . .

Interviewer: What is life like on Alcatraz now? Roughly how many people are there here and are living conditions acceptable and so on?

Trudell: Well, we still have about eighty people here. You know, the number changes throughout the year from a large population to a small population. We are back to almost the same number we started out with a year ago. And out here, now that the government took the water away and shut our power off, we haul our own water. Sometimes we have difficulty with heating, like getting firewood is a hassle. So we started tearing down wooden cottages on the island for firewood. For electrical needs we have a generator, a thirty kilowatt generator, that was bought for us. It supplies most of our electrical needs. That is all taken care of, so I don't know, it is very—I compare it to living on a reservation. You know, we are better off than some reservations even though we don't have a lot of things. We are used to it, we are used to living this kind of life. You know, it's not like we all left good homes and came out here and all of the sudden started enduring hardship. These aren't hardships to us. To a great deal of white society, it would be, but to us it is natural. It's just like our culture. It's our culture almost to the extent that this is what we have always lived in. The biggest thing that I am pleased with here is our children. The fact that our children are free. We have a lot of reporters and people come out here and say: what kind of education are you giving your children? When they think of education, they only relate to the class room, you know. They relate to propagandizing, and what we are trying to relate to out here is real education. We try to see to it that the children get reading, writing, and arithmetic, and whatever, spelling, some of the basics, so they can survive out there if they choose to do so. But the rest of the education is an education of freedom. These children living out here are never going to forget what the government has said or done. These kids will never forget it. They are growing up with it. We are not pumping political awareness into their heads, but it is there. It is available for them to pick up onto. . . . This is part of what makes our determination hang in there, you know, we look at the physical or the lack of materialism, physically and the lack of luxuries, such as running water and all this, but then we look back at what we got as people, you know, and it all balances out, you know. . . . Here we've got a sense of security. We expect one day, the man to come in and try to rip us off. But when he comes, he has got to come and get us all at once. It is directed so that we have a sense of security in a very insecure situation, because as long as we are here and as long as he doesn't come to bust us, nothing is going to happen to us out here. We are free, and that's what the whole thing is all about.[45]

Darryl Wilson, Pit River Indian, visitor to Alcatraz Island

The final voice from Alcatraz is that of Darryl Wilson, a California Pit River Indian. Wilson presents a different view of the occupation, a discordant voice that reveals leadership problems associated with the Alcatraz movement and that shows respect for and concern that the indigenous people of the Bay Area, the Ohlone, were not represented on Alcatraz Island, an island that was part of their traditional homeland.

It was ten days before Christmas 1969, and I was standing upon the little island of Alcatraz. I did not know the real name of it, because I did not know any Ohlones who remembered all of the details, but my people called it Diamond Island. . . .

From a distance I watched a news conference. The Indians of All Tribes were squatting here and there, the feather and bell-spangled leadership was arguing who was going to talk with the news media and who had the most important information for the entire world to know. Soon, the discussion over who was going to represent the people escalated into an argument. . . .

The scene eroded into chaos, and I am sure that the American viewing public, who never had to be presented with all of the knowledge the leaders were vehemently trying to offer, were spared and thankful. Moments after the leadership realized that the TV crew had packed up and left for San Francisco, they rushed here and there looking for a way to get back to San Francisco, too. It was apparent that the "leadership" lived in the San Francisco area and ventured to the island only when there was to be a press conference. . . .

A boat pulled into the dock area. It was laden with old clothes. This must have been about the 100th such expedition. The island was littered with piles of old clothes. . . . And, as evident by crazy piles of old and rusted, labelless cans, the people of American also thought the Indians could make use of their old cans of food that they no longer could identify—they had worn out their welcome in the good old American styled bomb shelter. . . .

Now that the "leadership" had gone back to San Francisco, the island again took on a pleasant atmosphere. . . . Watching the Tlingits, the Siouxs, the Hopis, the Navajos, the Cheyennes, and the

Arapahoes wander almost pointlessly around the island, shadow-ing into buildings, kicking the piles of clothes, digging through the labelless cans of goods, and seeking wood for a fire, I wondered about this little island. I wondered about the people who should be here to claim it. I thought this was Ohlone country. By the oc-cupation and the attitude of the leadership, a person could very easily be convinced that California was a land that was claimed by the relocated elements among the original natives, and it should not be recognized as an element of the Ohlone history and the Ohlone future, or related to the California natives. . . .

. . . But this is the land of the Ohlones. Today I am like a strang-er. There is no council fire where the governing body of the Oh-lone gathers. There is no way to ask permission to stay upon the little island. There is no one speaking the original language that is familiar with this area. Everyone is laughing and shouting in English. Yes, it seems like a group of strangers whose "leadership" appears once a week to talk about their adventures, a movement separate from the Ohlones and the other California natives.[46]

The voices of Indian people deeply involved in the Alcatraz occu-pation speak to the central importance of the Alcatraz occupation as a new symbol of long-standing Indian grievances and increasing im-patience with a political system slow to respond to Indian rights. The voices present a poignant sense of life on the island with campfires, singing, and dancing—a syncretism of Indian cultures, beliefs, and practices from across the Americas. Through these voices we can feel the chill as Richard Oakes, Joe Bill, Jerry Hatch, and Ross Harden jumped from the deck of the *Monte Cristo* and swam to Alcatraz Is-land. We can smell the fresh coffee brewing the following morning as the occupiers walked up the winding road to the main cellblock where they were assigned their duties on Alcatraz. We can gather around the open fires where Indian women fried potatoes, bacon, and eggs. We can watch the Indian children running around the prison courtyard, happily chasing ducks and turkeys. Tragically, the voices also bring to stark reality the death of Yvonne, the collapse of the ini-tial occupation leadership, the frustration of failed negotiations, the shortage of supplies, the difficulty of daily living, and above all else the shared joy over the birth of Wovoka. Together these voices give depth and breadth to a movement so strong that it would launch a new era in Indian activism. Because of the Alcatraz occupation Indian people throughout America experienced an awakening that ultimately changed the course of their lives.

Notes

1. Indians of All Tribes, "Why We Are on Alcatraz."
2. Oakes, "Alcatraz," 38–40.
3. Oakes interview.
4. Ibid.
5. "Alcatraz Indians Call for Help," *San Francisco Examiner*, Nov. 24, 1969.
6. "U.S. Hint to Indians—Get Off Alcatraz," *San Francisco Examiner*, Nov. 28, 1969.
7. "Alcatraz Gathering of Indian Tribes," *San Francisco Chronicle*, Nov. 28, 1969.
8. "Alcatraz Indians Invite Interior Secretary Hickel for Meeting," *San Francisco Chronicle*, Nov. 29, 1969.
9. "The Week's News in Review," *San Francisco Examiner*, Nov. 30, 1969.
10. "Indians Told: Go, Then Talk," *San Francisco Examiner*, Dec. 1, 1969.
11. "Powwow on Indian Justice," *San Francisco Chronicle*, Dec. 3, 1969.
12. LaNada Boyer interview by Trudell.
13. Bomberry interview, 1–6. In the early period of the occupation to which Bomberry refers, everyone arriving on the island was required to sign a log book on the Alcatraz landing dock. Attempts were made to keep the occupation an "all Indian occupation" during this early period. The island log book is in the possession of one of the island occupiers.
14. Chavers, *Indian Voice*, 31.
15. Thorpe interview. Thorpe also recognized that the occupiers had more to struggle with than just the government.
16. Harden interview, 16–25.
17. Scraper interview, 13–14.
18. Blue Cloud, *Alcatraz*, 9–30.
19. Ibid.
20. Blue Cloud, letter to Urban Indians of New York, quoted in Igler, "This Land Is My Land," 34.
21. Rosalie McKay-Want, "The Meaning of Alcatraz," quoted in Antell, "American Indian Women Activists," 58–60.
22. Al Miller interview.
23. Livermore interview, 4–8.
24. Bill interview, 12–13. Bill obviously recognized that the struggle would not only be one with the government for possession of the island but would

also be one of unity among the various tribes coalescing under the umbrella Indians of All Tribes.

25. Stella Leach interview by Boyd, 10–12.

26. Miracle interview, 16–18.

27. Parrish interview, 1–3.

28. Mankiller, letter to author, Nov. 27, 1991.

29. "She Leads a Nation," *Parade Magazine,* Aug. 18, 1991. Mankiller became the first woman chief of the Cherokee Nation and gives credit to the Alcatraz occupation for her rise to this position. In the *Parade* article, Mankiller gives the American Indian Movement credit for the occupation, which is incorrect. As stated previously, the occupiers formed an incorporated group called Indians of All Tribes, which had no connection with AIM.

30. Mankiller and Wallis, *Mankiller,* 189–96.

31. Horse Capture, "An American Indian Perspective," 188.

32. Trudell, "Radio Free Alcatraz," Dec. 1969.

33. Trudell interview by YesNo.

34. Trudell, "Radio Free Alcatraz," Mar. 1970.

35. Ibid., Apr. 30, 1970.

36. Ibid., May 27, 1970.

37. Ibid., June 9, 1970. It remains uncertain as to who started the fire that destroyed the buildings on the Island. There are no reports that tie the fire to the Indian people on Alcatraz. No reports of official investigations exist and no one was ever charged in connection with the fire. Several of the occupiers state that just prior to the fire starting they heard a popping sound followed by the sound of a departing motorboat.

38. Ibid., June 1970.

39. Ibid.

40. Ibid., July 1970.

41. Ibid. Originally only a midwife was to assist in the birth of the Trudell child. Linda Rae Brown came to the island and resided in the former warden's quarters for two weeks. Just prior to Wovoka's birth Dr. Larry Brillant came to Alcatraz and assisted in the delivery.

42. Ibid.

43. Ibid., Aug. 4, 1970.

44. Ibid., Aug. 11, 1970.

45. Trudell interview by unknown interviewer.

46. Wilson, "Alcatraz."

Belva Cottier and Chicano friend. Belva was instrumental in the planning
of the 1964 occupation of Alcatraz Island. (© Ilka Hartmann 1996)

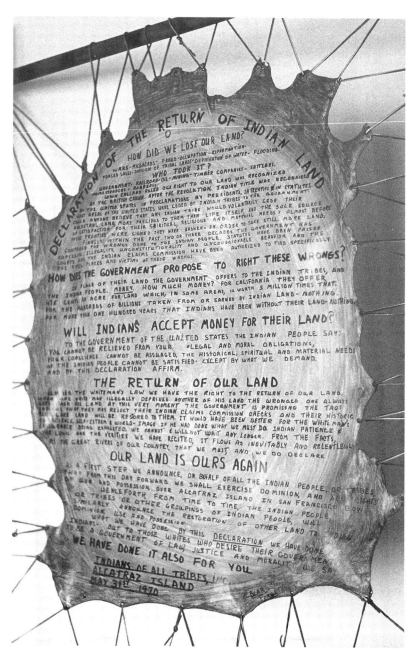

The Declaration of the Return of Indian Land spelled out the rationale for the Indian rights to Alcatraz. (© Ilka Hartmann 1996)

Once on Alcatraz Island the occupiers set out to establish ownership and painted signs welcoming other Indian people to the new Indian land. (Courtesy of Michelle Vignes)

Occupiers hang a sign over the entrance to the main cellblock claiming ownership of the island. (Courtesy of the *San Francisco Chronicle*)

A sign that formerly read *Warning* Keep Off U.S. Property
was changed to read *Warning* Keep Off Indian Property.
(Courtesy of the *San Francisco Chronicle*)

A Coast Guard blockade necessitated that supplies be carried up steep
ladders. Richard Oakes, often identified as the student
leader of the occupation, is third from the right.
(Courtesy of the *San Francisco Chronicle*)

Communal meals were prepared in the prison kitchen and courtyard.
(Courtesy of the *San Francisco Chronicle*)

An Indian flag flies from the guard tower on Alcatraz Island.
(Courtesy of the *San Francisco Chronicle*)

In June 1970 a fire on Alcatraz Island destroyed three historical buildings. (Courtesy of the *San Francisco Chronicle*)

A Coast Guard cutter, a clenched fist, and the burnt-out hulk of the former warden's quarters give an ominous cast to Alcatraz Island. (Courtesy of the *San Francisco Chronicle*)

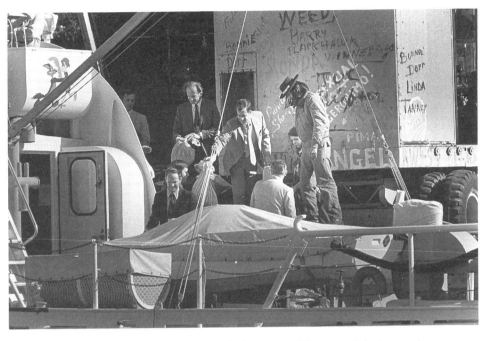

In June 1971 a force of U.S. Marshals, General Services Administration
Special Forces, and the U.S. Coast Guard removed the
final fifteen occupiers from Alcatraz Island.
(Courtesy of the *San Francisco Chronicle*)

One of the last occupiers leaves Alcatraz Island, June 11, 1971.
(© Ilka Hartmann 1996)

Overcoming exhaustion and disillusionment, young Atha Rider
Whitemankiller stands tall before the press at the Senator Hotel after the
Indians were removed from Alcatraz. His words about the purpose of the
occupation—to publicize his people's plight and establish a land base for
the Indians of the Bay Area—were the most quoted of the day.
(© Ilka Hartmann 1996)

Eighteen-year-old Oohosis and friend stand at Pier 40 after the removal. "The Indians were finally standing up and really doing something against what the government has done to us." (© Ilka Hartmann 1996)

The 1969 occupation of Alcatraz Island became a springboard for Indian activism that lasted into the mid-1970s and continues to inspire Native Americans today. Indian people in this photograph carry a drum to the upper level of Alcatraz where they began the 1979 Walk for Survival from Alcatraz to Sacramento and on to Washington D.C.
(© Ilka Hartmann 1996)

7

Trouble on Alcatraz

ᐱᐧᐱᐧᐱ

The optimism of the occupiers ended quickly as divergent voices began to make themselves heard on the island. The solidarity shown by the Indian students who successfully carried out the occupation was compromised by the arrival of Native Americans unaware of the Bay Area Indian problems and unwilling to learn about the original motives for the occupation. A struggle for leadership ensued and the Indian people were distracted from their original, more altruistic vision of the occupation and concentrated instead on access to power and money. The new leadership and population viewed Alcatraz as a haven free from state or federal government control, with a sympathetic national audience providing donations of cash and provisions. The security force originally formed to protect the island population became a feared enforcement group that resorted to brutality to gain island leadership. Gone was the opportunity for compromise between the occupiers and the federal government because the new leadership refused to negotiate and became firmly entrenched on the island. As a result of the breakdown in negotiations the federal government discontinued electrical power to the island and the water barge, which provided the only water to the island, was removed. Following these events, on the night of June 1, 1970, a fire destroyed three historical buildings on the island. The federal government blamed the Native Americans while the occupiers blamed government saboteurs who were attempting to shift public support away from the occupation. Government officials and the general public soon became aware of the divergent voices and the growing dissension on the island following the death of Yvonne Oakes, the thirteen-year-old step-daughter of Richard Oakes.

On Saturday, January 3, 1970, Yvonne Oakes fell down a stairway in an empty apartment building on the island. Yvonne never regained consciousness and died on January 8, 1970, from head injuries sustained during the fall. Reports state that "the girl was apparently sitting on the landing, her arms draped over the last rung of an iron pipe railing, when she somehow slipped and plummeted down the stairwell, landing on her head."[1] It appears that Yvonne had been playing with a group of children on the third floor of the vacant apartment building with little or no supervision. Stella Leach stated that "she had warned the Oakes child and several other children several times away from the stairwell and corridor before the accident occurred. About three minutes after the last warning, she heard a cry outside of her clinic door and went out and found the injured child."[2]

Richard Oakes and his wife, Anne, suspected that Yvonne's death was not accidental but was, in fact, the result of jealousy arising because of Oakes's recognition by the press and government negotiators as "leader" of the Alcatraz occupation group. Following Yvonne's death, Oakes requested that both the Federal Bureau of Investigation (FBI) and the San Francisco Coroner's Office investigate to ascertain if Yvonne had died as a result of foul play. There was insufficient evidence for either agency to determine that her death was other than accidental.

> On 1/3/70, YVONNE SHERD, age 13, the stepdaughter of RICH-ARD OAKS [sic], a Mohawk Indian and the first leader of the Indian occupation of Alcatraz, fell down a stairwell of an abandoned apartment building on Alcatraz, and she subsequently died at the Public Health Hospital, San Francisco, on 1/7/70, as a result of injuries from this fall. On 4/2/70, OAKS made a complaint to General Services Administration (GSA), San Francisco, saying he thought there might have been foul play, in his step daughter's fall. OAKS and a 14 year old cousin of the victim, who was with YVONNE when she fell, were interviewed by Bureau Agents and they had no evidence to indicate there was any foul play in connection with YVONNE's fall. OAKS' only reason for making any complaint was that he felt that he was hated by some of the other Indians on the island and he thought this might have something to do with his stepdaughter's fall. . . . Based on interviews by Bureau Agents, there was no basis for any further investigation.[3]

In a videotaped interview conducted by the U.S. Park Service on Alcatraz Island on July 25, 1988, Thomas Scott, who was the PMDS realty officer in charge of Alcatraz during the occupation, alleged that there were, in fact, eyewitnesses who saw Yvonne pushed to her death. Scott offered no explanation as to why a further investigation was not conducted. One occupier who requested to remain anonymous stated that he was in the group of children playing with Yvonne. There was one other playmate between he and Yvonne going up the stairs to the top of the third story of the abandoned building. Yvonne got to the top of the stairs and the next thing that he saw was Yvonne falling down the stairwell. He said that he did not see if she was pushed or fell, but when I asked him about this possibility, he stated that they frequently played in the abandoned buildings and that Yvonne was not the type of person who would have fallen.[4] It is my opinion after having discussed Yvonne's death with a number of people who were on the island at the time, and taking into consideration the hostile atmosphere toward the Oakes family, that Yvonne Oakes most likely was pushed to her death on Alcatraz Island.

Upon hearing of Yvonne's death, Leonard Garment sent Richard and Anne Oakes a letter of condolence. Garment was optimistic because the negotiating process was "useful and promising . . . but such a personal tragedy as this is crushing and sorrowful." Garment assured the Oakes family that "there *will* be a brighter day for the urban Indians of the Bay Area and of the nation." Garment's letter was followed by a personal visit by T. E. Hannon. Anne Oakes informed Hannon that she had wanted to leave the island "for some time and the accident settled it."[5] Their other children had been getting a lot of verbal abuse and their oldest son had been seriously beaten two weeks prior to Yvonne's fall.[6] According to Anne, some of the Indians on Alcatraz hated her husband and were jealous because "Richard was the leader." This jealousy was reflected in the attitude of the adults toward her and in their criticism of Richard. Anne declared that "there was a lot of dissension among the Indians on Alcatraz, fighting, drinking, etc., and that nothing was going right."[7] The criticism directed toward Richard came primarily from the new island residents. Most of the college students who had carried out the occupation returned to college in January 1970 and a new type of occupation emerged that, according to Anne, was filled with dissension. To the new occupiers, Richard represented a threat and an obstacle to their control of the island.

Tim Findley, in a *San Francisco Chronicle* article dated January 7, 1970, announced to the public, "Like an ancient tragic curse come back to haunt them again and again, Indians on Alcatraz are apparently approaching a crisis in leadership that may determine the future of their six-week-old occupation of the crumbling island." Findley reported that the cause of the dissension was "booze, boredom, and, most seriously, bickering." He had observed broken windows in his trips to the island and had heard about the use of drugs and intoxicants, fights, dissension, and a split-up of leaders.[8]

Findley mistakenly classified Oakes as the leader of the Native Americans and claimed that after Yvonne's death and the departure of her family, "if there is a single 'leader' on Alcatraz now—and the Indians insist that no one person can claim that role—it is Stella Leach, a 50–year-old Sioux woman with an arrow-sharp tongue and a strong aggressive personality." Findley continued to classify Oakes as the old leader of the occupation despite Leach's assurances that "Oakes never had any particular status, he was elected spokesman for a while, and that's it."[9]

According to Findley the real leadership had passed from Oakes to Leach and her son David. Al Miller, a former member of the council, was still on the island but was dominated by Leach, as was Earl Livermore, who came back and forth to the island as "coordinator." Dennis Turner, one of the original occupiers, returned to the island on January 5, "probably to find out where he stood in the new lineup."[10]

Findley claimed that there was "no communication between the mainland and Alcatraz Indians and dissension . . . about how money being received is to be spent."[11] Although Leach and other Native Americans said most of the original occupiers had simply had to return to the mainland to attend classes or their jobs, Findley characterized them as abandoning their trouble-ridden cause. Findley prophesied: "The Indians were losing friends, and the council was losing control."[12]

The following day Findley asserted that observers likened the situation on Alcatraz to the social drama portrayed in William Golding's nightmarish *Lord of the Flies,* about an island society destroyed from within. At the beginning of the occupation, liquor and drugs were banned; however, their prohibition was now often violated, and the militant young Indians on the island's security force were the worst offenders. Findley characterized the island security force as an exclusive group of militants whose power on the island rivaled that of the elected council.[13]

The change in the role of the island security force from one of pro-
tector to one of militant is not a new phenomena and certainly cannot be restricted to the Indians on Alcatraz. In 1972 Philip G. Zimbardo, a professor of social psychology at Stanford University,
published the results of a study observing the behavior of mature,
emotionally stable, white men who were placed in a prison guard role.
After only six days the experiment had to be discontinued because
the results was shocking. About one-third of the guards became cor-
rupted by the power of their roles and tyrannical in their arbitrary use
of power while those who maintained some sense of fairness failed
to prevent or report the actions of those displaying this pathological
behavior. Zimbardo states that this pathology is not predictable and
is extreme enough to modify fundamental attitudes and behaviors.[14]
Clearly, although Findley's portrayal of island behavior may be accu-
rate, it is in no way unique to Alcatraz.

Jeff Sklansky claimed that no institution on Alcatraz was so imi-
tative of modern non-Indian society as the security force, aptly named
the "Bureau of Caucasian Affairs." The roughly ten members of the
force bought themselves army fatigue jackets emblazoned with red
emblems and, according to Anthony Garcia, one of the first members
of the occupation, then decided to become the police. Overcome by
their own sense of importance and free from any constraining forces,
they started pushing others around and used what were described by
several members of the occupation group as "Gestapo tactics."[15]

On February 17 Thomas Scott issued a memorandum concerning
the power struggle among the island occupiers: "Many Indians are
disgusted with the breakdown in their organization and are leaving
the movement. There are apparently two factions now battling for
leadership—one group is Stella Leach and the other is made up of
leaders of the various California tribes. It appears that neither group
can get the support needed to gain leadership."[16] The GSA caretaker
on the island had reported to him incidents of inebriation and that
the occupiers had set up a house of prostitution.[17]

Richard DeLuca avers that problems of leadership and behavior
cropped up soon after the occupation began:

Factions had already begun to form among the seven-member
elected council, some of whom were resentful of councilman Richard Oakes, who had captured a disproportionate amount of

media attention. As the occupation wore on, boredom also increased, and as one result, the island's security force became more vocal and militant. Pointless vandalism began, reporters were occasionally harassed, and the proclaimed ban on liquor and drugs was openly violated. And under the surface was the unresolved tension between the . . . Bay Area Indian groups . . . and the younger, more aggressive factions on Alcatraz.[18]

The Native Americans on the island did not want to acknowledge to the general public that dissension existed. Trudell handled the issue on "Radio Free Alcatraz" by claiming, "Things couldn't be running more beautifully than they are right now. Everyone seems to be fairly well, happy, and contrary to all reports you may be receiving . . . everyone is getting along fine." Trudell's broadcast was largely a public relations facade intended to ensure continued support.[19]

Peter Blue Cloud similarly attempted to assuage the rumors of factionalism and feuds by writing to the Urban Indians of New York. Blue Cloud claimed that although the press had reported alleged instances of factionalism and petty feuds, the majority of the occupiers were dedicated to the original goals and those who were not had been asked to leave the island.[20]

In fact, those who did not agree with the council were dealt with much more strongly than that. Maria Lavender, who operated the island nursery, and her non-Indian husband, Carlos, were among the early occupiers of the island. Carlos fell into disfavor with the island council because he talked openly to newspaper reporters about the conditions on the island and the dissension on Alcatraz. Carlos reported to Don Carroll, the GSA caretaker, that his life had been threatened because of his disclosures. Maria was physically removed from her position in the nursery. At one point, Maria missed a doctor's appointment on the mainland so Carroll went to the Lavender apartment on the island and reported, "Checked it out—one Indian and one Indian security in her apartment holding each other to a stand still—she was OK."[21] Out of fear for their lives Carlos left Alcatraz on February 8, and Maria and their children followed on March 3. When she left, Maria said she was leaving because there was too much dope being dispensed, and she just could not take any more of the life on the island.[22]

Following Oakes's resignation from the council and departure from the island, there was a lack of strong, focused leadership. Not only

was Oakes instrumental in the development of the occupation concept but he was also the unifying force that galvanized the student
participation and population. Oakes was also the link between the
occupiers on the island and the urban Indian organizations as represented by Adam Nordwall. Once Oakes left Alcatraz, a state of dis-
array and confusion engulfed the occupiers. Although the council
continued to function, the direction of the occupation had been lost.
What had begun as a symbolic action to benefit Indian people of all
tribes quickly became a struggle for individual power, self-aggrandizement, and money. The occupiers found themselves in a position none
of them could have ever envisioned. They were free from city, state,
and federal control, could come and go as they pleased, answered to
no one, and had a large amount of cash that they did not have to account for to any agency. This license would eventually lead to the
downfall of the occupation.

The leadership vacuum created by Oakes's departure was filled by
Stella Leach. During the struggle for the change in leadership, Leach
was supported by a group called the Thunderbirds, who arrived on the
island in January 1970. This militant group was allegedly heavily
involved in heroin trafficking and was known to be extremely tough.
On the island they were reported as being armed with chains and pipes
and beat up Indians opposed to Leach. "This same group, led by the
island nurse, was dispensing pills (narcotics) and selling marijuana in
her apartment. Some of the leadership objected to this, and that, again,
created open conflict."[23] Don Carroll reported that the Thunderbirds
had begun to beat other Native Americans. One Indian man came into
Carroll's office with his nose pushed clear over against his cheek. The
man said that the Thunderbirds had beaten him over the previous
weekend. Additionally, Carroll reported that Bob Bradley, the Indian
public relations representative, had informed him on about April 2
that a shipment of heroin, valued at $150,000, was being handled by
the Thunderbirds. Carroll also had personally seen evidence of hard
drugs on the island.[24] Carroll stated that at times it was impossible
to find a lucid Indian on the island because they were on either drugs
or alcohol. Carroll said that "the two sons of Stella Leach appear to
be the main fermenters of trouble on the island."[25] My confidential
informant also felt that "Stella Leach was a really bad influence on
the Island. She and her gang (Indian bikers) set up a dope center there,
which really pissed me off. They led a welfare-bums occupation—

every Indian derelict in the country swarmed out there later on for the 'free lunch.'"[26]

LaNada Boyer, however, disputes this negative portrayal. She maintains that Leach and her sons tried to hold the organization together after Oakes departed. According to Boyer Leach had nothing to do with drugs or any movement against Oakes. The Thunderbirds was a group of Vietnam veterans and unemployed youths, some of whom were also bikers. According to Boyer it was not an enforcement gang against Oakes nor a support group for Leach, but rather a group formed by her brother Dwayne, who came to the island, under protest, to look after LaNada and her sister Claudene. Boyer further insisted that Leach did not remain on Alcatraz long, perhaps eight to ten months, at which time she left because nothing was being done by the government to meet the demands of the island occupants.[27]

Further difficulties arose in December 1969, when a brother and sister, Tom and Torrie Mudd, donated $16,000 in negotiable stocks to the occupation, "to be used in the best manner for the Indian people."[28] A committee was created and a meeting called to decide the best use of the money. Composed of Charles Dana, Earl Livermore, Dean Chavers, Richard Oakes, and Adam Nordwall, the committee represented the interests of both the island occupiers and the mainland Indian population. The island representatives had decided in advance that they were going to use the money to hire a director for the Alcatraz occupation group and to carry on island programs. The mainland group, however, wanted to use the donation to establish a Native American scholarship fund or a student aid fund and raised concerns over the accountability of the funds already donated to the occupation force by the public. Ultimately, the committee decided that the money would be used to establish an American Indian scholarship fund to be administered by the Bay Area Council, directed by Nordwall. The argument and the obvious differences in priorities deepened the growing rift between Indian people on the mainland and those on the island.

Because of the large number of people involved in the handling of Alcatraz mail, and because inadequate accounting records were kept, it is almost certain that no one will ever know exactly how much money was donated through cash, checks, and negotiable stocks. Complete records simply do not exist. Initially, cash or checks were mailed or simply dropped off at the San Francisco Indian Center or at Alcatraz Island. As the occupation progressed, donations were received by cash or check through the mail addressed to Alcatraz Island, to Indians of All Tribes, or directly to Richard Oakes, who was most readily identifiable with the occupation. A bank account was opened in the Mission Branch of the Bank of America. Prior to that time, however, no records exist regarding the amount of donations, nor their disbursements.

Donations from a variety of entertainers supported the occupation force. Dick Gregory donated a substantial amount of money to the Indians, and the San Francisco cast from the production of *Hair* took up a collection. On November 28 and 29, 1969, a benefit rock concert featuring a group of popular rock bands from the Bay Area was held at Bill Graham's Fillmore. The folksinger Malvina Reynolds gave $1,000 and donated one year's royalties from her song "Alcatraz," and Buffy St. Marie, a Native American recording artist, donated concert receipts of $2,500, which were deposited into the Alcatraz bank account.

In a 1992 interview, Horace Spencer, one of the original occupants and one of the island council members, stated that he had estimated the amount of money donated to the occupiers to be between $20 and $25 million. Leach had previously informed Spencer that the total was in excess of that amount. Spencer concluded that "several people got rich off of donations to the Alcatraz movement."[29]

Ed Castillo, one of the original occupants and also a member of the island council, expressed doubts about this estimate but did provide some insight into the problems of financial accountability. At the time of the occupation Castillo was married to Luwana Quitiquit, who worked in the mail sorting room. Quitiquit opened all of the incoming mail except that addressed to Richard Oakes. According to Quitiquit, Oakes apparently took all mail addressed to him and kept the contents. Castillo recalled that when he went into the mail sorting room, there would literally be "stacks of hundred dollar bills on the desks."[30]

Earl Livermore noted that "a lot of people were going in free-lancing and making a lot of money which we weren't seeing anything of."[31] McKay-Want stated simply, "We had a lot of money coming in, and we just didn't know how to handle everything and some of it got lost. I think that was our downfall."[32] Whatever the amount of money donated to the island may have been, it did not remain on the island long. A large portion was spent to charter boats to transport people and supplies. Additional funds were required to purchase fresh food and water. A GSA memorandum dated May 15, 1970, states, "Funds are very low. It has cost $44,000 so far to occupy the island, $12,000 for the Indian boat alone."[33] Because of an increasing need for money, some Native Americans stripped copper pipes from bathroom fixtures as well as copper electrical wiring to sell on the mainland as scrap metal. The government became aware of these activities and arrested and charged those involved. On June 12, 1971, Eugene Cox, John D. Holloran, and James Robbins were arrested by the FBI and charged with stealing and selling 1,665 pounds of copper from the prison's electrical system. The men were tried on February 25, 1972, by the U.S. District Court and found guilty of selling 1,664 pounds of copper for $600.

The stripping and selling of copper from Alcatraz Island was a coordinated effort and a memorandum "To the Silent Miners of Alcatraz" set forth the procedures. "Indian" Joe Morris, a Blackfoot, wrote the guidelines:

> Scrapping is a silent word. The "word" should only be whispered among Alcatraz people only. Don't breath the word scrap or mining on the Main-land. It is against the law. It is an act of *pillage.* Until the Indian people are given the title of ownership of this government owned Island.
>
> *SCRAPPERS MORATORIUM*
> Any boat hauling metal shall be paid for by the scrapper. Empty water containers will be loaded with the first load of scrap. The second trip which is a survival run, will carry food, water and Indian passengers.
>
> All tools and equipment shall be furnished by the miner. These will be bought from the profits from his scrap.
>
> No scrapping on Sunday—if anyone is seen, they will be asked to leave the Island on that date. No scrapping.
>
> Your Alcatraz Representative,
> Joseph L. Morris
>
> P.S. Joe Morris, who has been on the Alcatraz movement for sixteen months, who heads Pier 40 and a main land representative, I make a motion not to haul or put any scrap on the main deck

of the Alcatraz Boat (Clearwater). Keep the boat as designated—hauling water, food, and transporting the people. Keep the boat tied up at Fisherman's Wharf at the end of each day. It is not to be moved until the following morning. Then everybody will be happy. Thank you. Joe Morris.[34]

Given that the occupiers resorted to selling scrap metal, demanded $300,000 from the government to develop an Indian university and cultural complex that included a library, archives, and ecology center, asked for $130,000 to operate the proposed facilities for one year, and requested another $42,000 to cover consultant fees, it thus seems highly unlikely that donations could have reached the levels estimated by Spencer and Leach. Some rumors of extravagance did emerge, however. Leach allegedly purchased a new station wagon shortly after her rise to power on the island,[35] some suggest that Oakes misappropriated island funds, while others have stated that picking up incoming mail served as an opportunity to divert funds prior to their arrival on the island. There appears to be no way to determine how much money was actually received and how it was disbursed.

In addition to finances, further problems arose over the composition of the occupation force and the occupation itself. The Ohlone people considered Alcatraz to be a part of their traditional homelands, land they had never relinquished to anyone, Indian or non-Indian. The occupation organizers did not consult with this indigenous group or ask any members to join the occupation. On December 25 the American Indian Historical Society wrote a letter to President Nixon advising him that if possession of the island was to be given to any of the "original Americans," then certainly it should go to the descendants of the Ohlone people, some of whom still resided in the Bay Area and none of whom were on the island. According to the letter, the American Indian Historical Society, representing the Cahuilla Band of California Indians and the Ohlone Indians, was prepared to make a formal request that the federal government transfer a portion of Fort Mason to the California Indians for use as a national historical, educational, and research complex.[36]

On the same day Rupert Costo, a Cahuilla, and Philip Galvan, an Ohlone, requested that the president deed the land by executive order and declared: "We expect to fund our activities in connection with the establishment of an educational and research complex at Fort

Mason through our own efforts, through public and Foundation contributions, and through our activities."[37]

The Ohlone people continued to express their opposition to the
island occupants and to the president. In a letter dated January 22,
1970, they clearly expressed their views regarding ownership of the
island and their views toward the Indian people on the island:

> We are Ohlone Indians, also known as Costanoans. We Ohlone
> are opposed to the occupation of Alcatraz. It is wrong. . . .
>
> Those on Alcatraz say they speak for all Indian people every-
> where. They do not. They have no authority whatsoever to speak
> even for a single tribe. They are misinforming the public about
> Native American culture, history, and beliefs. They are destroy-
> ing what we Indian people have been fighting and dying for these
> hundred years. . . .
>
> The Ohlone people discovered, owned, and occupied the land
> from Pleasanton in the East Bay to the Coast, and southerly to
> Monterey, including the islands along the coast, Alcatraz and
> Yerba Buena among the others. If any Native Americans have a
> right to claim these lands, we Ohlone are the only ones.
>
> There is not one Ohlone Indian among those now on Alcatraz
> Island. Those who are squatting on this rock are mainly from
> other states, other tribes and reservations, other peoples and dif-
> ferent ancestry. One may not trespass upon or claim land owned
> by another tribe, according to the laws of the Native. . . .
>
> If the United States is ready to deed this land to anyone, we
> claim that right. We will immediately restore it as a natural wild-
> life sanctuary, and a way station for all people navigating the
> Bay.[38]

In addition to the petition to the president, the Ohlone people wrote
a letter to the island occupants on January 22 expressing the same
theme. They closed by stating that the current occupiers should end
their trespass and return to their jobs, their colleges, and their universities.[39]

The growing population on the island during the early period of the
occupation created a problem for the Indian council as well. While the
actual number of Native Americans living on the island was slightly
in excess of 100, the number of transients—those who stayed for only
a few hours or perhaps one or two nights—swelled the population to

over 200 on weekdays and as many as 750 on weekends. By December 4, the permanent population had leveled off to approximately 250; however, more were expected to arrive in the very near future. Security was tightened to ensure, so far as possible, that the alcohol, drug, and gun ban was enforced. Housing on the island had to be allocated, and work assignments had to be made so that an egalitarian and consensus community could be established and maintained. Additionally, the growing population, most of whom came with no provisions, soon taxed the food and water supply on the island.[40]

Excerpts from the notes taken during a GSA telephone conversation with the caretaker on Alcatraz provide keen insight into the comforts enjoyed by those 250 occupiers. On December 4 all power on the island was out, there was a water leak in the primary water main on the island, a leak in the diesel fuel line developed leaving only one day's supply, the auxiliary power generators were inoperative, steam return lines were leaking, incoming phone service had been discontinued at the direction of the GSA, and a spoilage of fresh food had been experienced as the result of lack of electricity and refrigeration.[41]

By December 11, the discomforts and growing dissension had caused many of the permanent residents to leave the island. In a handwritten letter to the White House, Hannon reported that the permanent residents, then between fifty and seventy-five, were "orderly, making efforts to curtail use of liquor and drugs by occasional unruly Indians and non-Indians who go to the island." Hannon indicated that some organized Native Americans on the mainland had disassociated themselves from the Alcatraz situation because of dissension; he also stated that there was some dissension among those on the island as well.[42]

On January 15, 1970, the San Francisco Regional Council of the National Council on Indian Opportunity convened a special session to select representatives to present the needs and priorities of the Bay Area Indians to federal agencies. William Oliver, acting area director of the BIA, provided Hannon with the names of Indian leaders and influential members of Bay Area organizations, including Alfred Elgin Jr., director of the Intertribal Friendship House in Oakland; Adam Nordwall, chair of the United Bay Area Indian Council in San Leandro; Ray Billy with the Intertribal Friendship House in Oakland; Rupert Costo of the American Indian Historical Society; Lehman Brightman, president of United Native Americans based in San Francisco; Earl Livermore, all-tribe coordinator on Alcatraz; Charles Dana, affiliated with the Indian Center in San Francisco; Don Patterson, president of the board of directors of the San Francisco Indian Center; Richard Oakes, representing the Native Americans on Alcatraz; John Jacobs, director of the Alcohol Center at the Intertribal Friendship House in Oakland; Norm Rambeau of the Oakland American Indian Association; and Alfred Bergen with the Association of American Indian Affairs. Of this group of fourteen, only five—Nordwall, Brightman, Livermore, Dana, and Oakes—represented the Indians on Alcatraz and only Oakes was an active participant in the occupation.[43]

On January 6 Adam Nordwall provided Hannon with the names of a group he claimed was "organized as a body to administer a trust fund and who could represent local Indians in an initial meeting with the Regional Council." Those names were Adam Nordwall, Richard Oakes, Dorothy Miller, Earl Livermore, Don Patterson, and Charles Dana.[44] Although four were active participants in the occupation, only Oakes was on the island.

The Indian leaders who were ultimately selected to attend the meeting were Elgin, Nordwall, Brightman, Patterson, Rambeau, Costo, Miller, Oakes, Livermore, Dana, Ray White from the San Jose Indian Center, and Horace Spencer from the Navajo Club in Oakland. Three additional Native Americans attended as observers: John Trudell, Stella Leach, and Grace Thorpe. The presence of these three observers (all of whom lived on Alcatraz island at that time) and the comments made the day prior to the meeting demonstrated the tension that existed between the more conservative Bay Area Indian groups, who had been supporting the occupation from the mainland, and the younger, more aggressive occupiers. In a telephone conversation with Robert Robertson of the National Council on Indian Opportunity Nordwall asserted that the occupiers felt that the government was undermining their goals by asking Indian representatives of other groups to attend the regional council meeting. Because the occupiers considered these groups more concerned with urban problems than with the Alcatraz occupation, the Alcatraz Indians might demonstrate at the meeting or possibly obstruct its proceedings. He suggested that guards be posted so that only invitees could enter. Nordwall identified the main potential troublemaker as Richard McKenzie from the 1964 occupation, whom he claimed was supportive of Leach's leadership. Nordwall told Robertson to expect trouble from Brightman, Spencer, and Costo and warned that the council had created a monster by including these people. Indicating where his true interests now lay, Nordwall stated that the Indian group included too many from Alcatraz and too many Sioux. Leach, Brightman, and White were all Sioux. Nordwall also warned that another leadership takeover was brewing on the island and indicated that Dennis Turner, a California Indian, was possibly at the root of it.[45]

Despite Nordwall's warnings, the occupiers caused no trouble at the meeting. But the concerns of the Alcatraz group were well founded. The focus of the government's efforts had shifted from the Indians on Alcatraz to the Indians in the larger Bay Area. A clear split now existed between the two groups.

Hannon summed up the feelings of the regional council in a letter dated January 20:

> The 50 or so American Indians on Alcatraz appear to have objectives quite different from the 17,000 or so on the mainland in this area. For that reason, the Federal Government is requesting the leaders of various Indian groups in the Bay Area to agree on their order of priorities. In this way, Federal grant and assistance programs can be oriented to meet the priorities established by the Indian people themselves. . . .
>
> In my own personal view, the required $5 million to demolish the existing hazardous structures and make the terrain safe for the 50 or so Indians on the Island does not appear justified. . . . It seems to me that sums of this kind could be much better devoted to meeting the problems of housing, education, health and employment involving large numbers of American Indians in the Bay Area.[46]

Besides the Ohlone and the representatives at the council meeting, other Indian people questioned the occupation. Vine Deloria Jr., Standing Rock Sioux and author of the 1969 best-selling book *Custer Died for Your Sins*, was interviewed on April 2 and issued a cautious statement. Deloria claimed that the occupation was completely irrelevant unless the occupiers had people in Washington who understood the bureaucracy and could hand-carry the documents from agency to agency. Deloria told Juanita Curry, "You can sit on the rock for the next 100 years, but if you have nobody carrying that paper through the government agencies, then how do you expect to get title to it, see?" Deloria emphasized that he was not against militancy, he was against stupidity. Although Deloria thought the Indians on Alcatraz were raising a lot of good issues, there was more to it than getting the press involved. "If they were going to raise an issue . . . they would have to have enough force to win the battle."[47]

Howard Yackitonipah, a Comanche living in Los Angeles, acknowledged that he was unsure of the occupiers' methods and why they had decided on Alcatraz Island as the focal point for their unrest. He displayed a realistic view of the situation: "It's gonna cost, if the federal government . . . can't keep Alcatraz going with all the money that the government's got, what's the Indian going to do. . . . Sure, people are donating this and donating that, but you gotta keep that thing in water, you gotta keep toilet service, you gotta keep electricity, and all they think about is just the island and land. They're not thinking about what keeps it going."[48]

John and Lois Knifechief, two Indian people living in Stanton, California, shared Yackitonipah's disapproval. Lois stated that if the Indians on Alcatraz had found a place worth having she would have supported them: "Alcatraz, pray tell me. If the government can't afford to keep it up, they're sure not going to keep it up for the Indian. What do they want out there on that stupid rock? There's nothing but junk!" John claimed that the Indian students had no reason whatsoever to be militant or be demanding of anything because they already had everything. A reservation Indian relocated to the Bay Area, John felt that the Indian students were spoiled. "They can do whatever they want to do. They can be whatever they want to be. . . . The thing is, the biggest part of them kids don't know anything about reservation life. They were born right here or lived in cities all their life. Now what do they know anything about the Indian reservation. I really don't understand what they are demanding because they have educational opportunities that we didn't have. There's grants that Indian students can get. We didn't have that when we were growing up. They can better themselves if they want to. I can't see what these young people are demanding."[49]

Even some participants questioned the occupation. Among them was Adam Nordwall, one of the most ardent logistical supporters of those on the island. Nordwall told a reporter in April 1971 that the occupation had served its purpose. He recognized that the occupation had tuned into a personality struggle and that no organized group was still active on the island. Nordwall was correct when he stated, "When we occupied this island, we caught the government, and then our occupation forces caught us."[50]

By April of 1971, even *Time* magazine concurred with Nordwall. The magazine reported that the invasion force had become a thoroughly disorganized society plagued with growing disenchantment, lack of leadership, and loss of focus. Infighting had caused most of the original invasion leaders to leave Alcatraz and be replaced by homeless, apolitical young Native Americans more concerned with finding a place where they could "get their heads together" than in sustaining any significant political statement.[51]

Of all of the negative images of the Alcatraz occupation portrayed in the press, however, none was more damaging and sensational than the controversial fire that razed three historic buildings and the celebrated Alcatraz lighthouse on the night of June 1–2, 1970. On May 28 the water barge that had supplied the island had been removed by the coast guard with the expressed intent of refilling it and returning it to the island. At the same time, the last of the GSA personnel was removed from the island and electrical power was suspended. On June 1 seventy-five Native Americans remained on the island, which was without water or electrical power. At 11:05 P.M., PMDS realty officer Thomas Scott received a telephone call advising him that the Coast Guard was dispatching a boat to investigate a glow emanating through the fog from Alcatraz Island. At 11:20 P.M., Scott received a second call indicating that the whole east end of the island appeared to be on fire. Scott suggested that the Coast Guard not go ashore unless the Indians requested assistance. Scott received a third call at 11:29 P.M. and was advised that the Coast Guard had definitely decided not to attempt a landing.[52]

At 10:00 A.M. on June 2, a government message was released by the commandant of the Twelfth Coast Guard District indicating that, upon learning of a possible fire, two Coast Guard boats were dispatched to the island and told to "be ready to effect evacuation of personnel if required." They were quickly joined by a San Francisco fire boat. When the coast guard boats approached the Indians on the dock, they were told that they did not desire to be evacuated. A major fire had apparently occurred on top of the island, with smaller fires at various locations. It was noted that no known fire-fighting equipment existed on the island. Restricted visibility severely limited any further evaluation of the situation. Later that day, Dick Laws of the GSA property division issued a statement: "Fire destroyed three buildings and damaged the light tower on Alcatraz. 'I presume the Indians started the fire themselves.'" Hannon stated that he had received numerous calls from "outraged citizens" since the fire, demanding the removal of the Native Americans.[53]

Although representatives of the GSA blamed the fire on the occupiers, the Indians flatly denied starting the fire. Joseph Morris, a Blackfoot Indian living on the island, called the reports "damned lies." Morris professed that the fires were a clear result of white backlash. "That's all it was, they are just out to make things look bad for us." Despite his previous statement, Morris later said that "Trudell and his group" started the fires to get even with the government for removing the water barge. A Native American who requested to remain anonymous stated that he was present in a meeting when the fire was planned and that John Trudell was instrumental in the planning. In that meeting Trudell and others talked about starting the fires by throwing Molotov cocktails.[54] In a *New York Times* article some occupiers charged that the fires had been started by a group of whites who slipped past their security after dark. Hannon, on the other hand, called the fires "just one more factor" in what he described as the mounting problems of Alcatraz.[55]

Trudell was on the island at the time of the fire and provided a first-hand report over "Radio Free Alcatraz" on June 3.[56] Trudell denied in a *San Francisco Chronicle* article that he had heard rumors during a large gathering on the island "that indicated Indian dissidents might 'rip off' the warden's two-story home." He spoke of unconfirmed reports given him by other Indians that "an unidentified boat" sped away from the island shortly before the fire was discovered.[57]

A KCBS news radio editorial titled "Smoke Signals" was broadcast thirteen times on June 3, calling for the removal of the Indians from Alcatraz:

> Yesterday, there were smoke signals over Alcatraz. The smoldering issue of ownership produced flames which consumed five buildings. The structures were worthless, except as historic relics. Yet, they were public property. . . .
>
> KCBS thinks the Alcatraz situation needs immediate resolution. . . . The continued occupation of the island works against the Indian cause instead of aiding it.

This station urges the Federal Government to adopt firm measures to remove the Indians from the island.[58]

The station's wishes would not be fulfilled for another year.

Tim Findley's January 1970 articles proved prophetic. A crisis in leadership did occur that would eventually lead to the end of the Alcatraz occupation. With their numbers already dwindling because university students were forced to return to classes or risk expulsion, the occupation force was barely holding onto their dream for Alcatraz. When Richard Oakes, devastated by the death of his daughter, left the island the coherent leadership dissolved. Oakes and the other early occupiers understood that their protest was larger than Alcatraz Island, that it was a symbolic statement of sovereignty and self-determination for all Indian people, everywhere. They were determined to be true to this vision and ensure that the occupation was free from distractions such as alcohol, drugs, and violence.

After their departure a brutal island security force arose that became symbolic of a new leadership more concerned with power and money than with the rights of Indians. Tim Findley blamed booze, boredom, and bickering for the dissension but could have added self-aggrandizement, domination, and greed. The occupation truly had come to resemble, just as Findley had reported, Golding's *Lord of the Flies*.

Notes

1. Hannon, "Alcatraz Incident," Jan. 6, 1970.
2. Ibid., Jan. 5, 1970.
3. Federal Bureau of Investigation case file SF 70–51261.
4. Confidential informant interview.
5. Hannon, "Alcatraz Incident," Jan. 5, 1970.
6. Ibid.
7. Ibid.
8. Tim Findley, "Alcatraz Dissension Grows," *San Francisco Chronicle*, Jan. 7, 1970.
9. Ibid.
10. Hannon, "Alcatraz Incident," Jan. 5, 1970.
11. Ibid.
12. "Alcatraz Dissension Grows."
13. Tim Findley, "Factionalism and Feuds," *San Francisco Chronicle*, Jan. 8, 1970.

14. Zimbardo, "Pathology of Imprisonment," 5–6.

15. Sklansky, "Rock, Reservation, and Prison," 44.

16. Scott, memorandum for the file, Feb. 17, 1970.

17. Ibid.

18. DeLuca, "We Hold the Rock," 62.

19. Trudell, "Radio Free Alcatraz," Jan. 10, 1970.

20. Blue Cloud, letter to Urban Indians of New York, quoted in Igler, "This Land Is My Land," 34. This statement also conveys an undercurrent of authoritarian rule rather than the hoped for consensus government.

21. Feiker transcriptions, 37.

22. Carroll statement.

23. Odier, *The Rock*, 231–32.

24. Carroll statement.

25. Scott, memorandum for the file, Feb. 26, 1970.

26. Confidential informant, letter to author, July 31, 1992.

27. LaNada Boyer interview by author.

28. Confidential informant interview.

29. Spencer interview, 1.

30. Castillo interview, 2.

31. Livermore interview.

32. McKay-Want, "The Meaning of Alcatraz," quoted in Antell, "American Indian Women Activists," 58–60.

33. Eleanor Lopez interview. Lopez was a member of the island council.

34. Indians of All Tribes memorandum, Feb. 9, 1971.

35. GSA, "Alcatraz Island." Don Carroll reported that a group of Indians on Alcatraz Island had told him that Leach had purchased a station wagon and were angry, wondering where she obtained the money.

36. American Indian Historical Society, letter to Nixon.

37. Ibid.

38. Ohlone Indians of California, petition to the President of the United States. Page two of this petition is missing, so it is impossible to determine the number of Ohlone people who signed. When Hannon visited the island in December 1969 to meet with representatives from the occupation force, he stated that "it is noted that there are no Ohlone represented here among you," indicating that this letter had been read and considered by the White House staff.

39. Ohlone Indians of California, petition to Indians of All Tribes.

40. "More Indians to Occupy Alcatraz," *San Francisco Examiner*, Dec. 4, 1969.

41. Feiker transcriptions.

42. Hannon, "Report on Alcatraz to White House."

43. Oliver, memorandum to Hannon.

44. Hannon, memorandum to Robertson.

45. Robertson, letter to Nordwall.

46. Hannon, letter to Gano.

47. Deloria interview, 3–4. Deloria stated that he had gone to Alcatraz Island about two weeks prior to this interview and "didn't get a very good reception when he stepped off the boat."

48. Yackitonipah interview, 42.

49. John and Lois Knifechief interviews, 90–91.

50. *Eugene Register Guard*, Apr. 11, 1971, quoted in Sklansky, "Rock, Reservation, and Prison," 51–52.

51. "Anomie at Alcatraz," *Time*, Apr. 12, 1971, quoted in Patterson, *Ring of Power*, 75.

52. Scott, memorandum for official file 9DR.

53. Ibid.

54. Confidential informant interview.

55. "Fires Destroy Three Buildings on Alcatraz; Indians Blame Whites," *New York Times*, June 3, 1970.

56. See chap. 6 for the full text of Trudell's statement regarding the fire.

57. "Indians Deny They Set Alcatraz Fire," *San Francisco Chronicle*, June 3, 1970.

58. KCBS news radio editorial, "Smoke Signals," June 3, 1970. Despite continuing denials of complicity by island spokespersons, Joseph Morris informed the *San Francisco Examiner* on June 2, 1970, that the Indians were responsible for the fires. "Lighthouse, Four Buildings Destroyed," *San Francisco Examiner*, June 2, 1970. Another Native American, who requested to remain anonymous, indicated that the Indians started the fire in response to the government's removal of the water barge.

8

Government Responses

/\\.\\\.\\\\

The occupation of Alcatraz Island quickly became a public relations nightmare for government officials and policy makers. Decisions had to be made that would clearly demonstrate federal control and authority over federal facilities, yet at the same time reflect the policy of the Nixon administration toward Native Americans. Significant questions arose. Who would make the decisions about handling the situation? At what level of government would these decisions be made? What were the lines of authority? As an unused federal facility the responsibility for the island lay with the General Services Administration in Washington, D.C., but other agencies soon expressed more than a passing interest in ending the occupation as quickly as possible. The Federal Bureau of Investigation began immediate surveillance of the island and prepared for insertion of undercover agents to assist in a quick removal. The U.S. Marshal Service expressed interest in the "protection of federal property" and recommended immediate, forced removal. The U.S. Coast Guard was concerned with the safety of navigation and shipping because Bay Area navigational aids were located on Alcatraz. Clearly a torturous and circuitous route lay before the island occupiers and the various officials of the U.S. government agencies as Native Americans attempted to gain title to the island and government officials attempted to negotiate their removal.

The opening salvo came on November 21, 1969, when Richard Oakes read a prepared statement demanding that, preliminary to any negotiation, the government return the title to Alcatraz Island to the Indians free of any management by any agency of government and agree to provide funding for the various educational facilities and cultural facilities that the Indians planned to develop.

Oakes spoke for the entire occupation force, since each member had a voice in the planning. This system would prove cumbersome and unwieldy for government officials, who attempted to identify a central figure with whom they could negotiate. When government ne-gotiators asked for a single person with whom to negotiate, the coun-cil informed the negotiators that there was no such person, since the Indians were practicing "pure democracy."

Negotiations on behalf of the federal government were carried out by the San Francisco regional offices of the GSA but were orchestrat-ed by White House staff members. On December 23, 1969, Leonard Garment, special consultant to President Nixon, recognized that "some Washington backstop [was] needed." Garment formed an ad hoc group "to give the needed policy direction to Regional offices in San Francisco." The group to handle the "new account of demands or proposals" included C. D. Ward of Vice President Agnew's office, Bob Robertson from the National Council on Indian Opportunity, Alan Kirk with the Department of the Interior, Joseph Maldonado in the Office of Indian Opportunity, and Bradley Patterson, Bud Krogh, Ken Cole, and Bobbie Greene from the White House staff.[1]

The memo that established this group also suggested negotiating principles for dealing with the occupiers. Forcible removal would not be considered as long as the Indians were peaceful. In fact, the admin-istration welcomed all suggestions from Native Americans regarding the ultimate use of the island. Garment also imposed his own pre-conditions for negotiating: the press would not be allowed unless both sides agreed and the Indian negotiating group must be representative of the entire Bay Area population, not just the Alcatraz occupiers. The government did not want to negotiate with different factions who might repudiate an agreement at a future date.[2]

Bradley H. Patterson Jr., executive assistant to Leonard Garment, addressed another area of concern to government negotiators—exces-sive force:

> In a word . . . our policy was restraint. Kent State had just hap-pened that Spring in 1970, and it could very easily happen again. Jackson State happened right after that. You could have the law enforcement in such a way that you could have a Kent State out there in Alcatraz, and we just didn't think people would stand for that, with killing Indians. We'd done enough killing of Indians in the last two hundred years and we weren't about to do any more. Our policy was restraint and negotiation and talk and try to work out some alternatives, and so forth.[3]

Garment too recognized the danger in using excessive force and the public relations problems that would result. In a memorandum to George Schultz and John Ehrlichman dated July 28, 1970, Garment stated: "From its beginning (last Nov. 20) this has been a situation well suited to confrontational politics. It has all the elements: an ostensibly good cause; a sympathetic public; an irresponsible, but PR-conscious group with a feeling of having "nothing to lose." . . . We have recognized all of this from the start; we have not reacted in any way which would play into their hands. Our key strategy has been restraint; we do not want a Kent State on Alcatraz, and we could get one with little effort."[4]

In a memorandum to Bud Krogh dated November 25 Brad Patterson weighed the advantages and disadvantages of forced removal: "Since the occupiers probably want a confrontation and are reportedly armed, forcible removal will probably be ugly if not bloody. Women and children are involved. Forcible removal itself, and especially if bloody, will almost certainly ignite a local and probably a national feeling of revulsion."[5]

An article in the *San Francisco Chronicle* on November 25, 1969, gave the government negotiators even more reason to exercise restraint in their handling of the Alcatraz occupation. "Ex-GI Says He Was Ordered to Kill Civilians" detailed the My Lai Massacre of mid-March 1968, when Lieutenant William Calley Jr. and soldiers under his command shot and killed 370 unarmed villagers in a Vietnamese hamlet 335 miles northeast of Saigon in Viet Cong territory. The American public was shocked at the carnage and called for a full government accounting of the incident. This reaction was not lost on the Alcatraz negotiators. Leonard Garment clarified: "We adopted a policy to let the thing 'rock-along,' maintain a balance. We did not want any more bloodshed; the war in Vietnam—Kent State—My Lai, the public and the government had had enough."[6] Patterson summed up the government restraint succinctly: "Force was never used because the White House did not want a massacre on their hands."[7]

Nixon's advisors recognized immediately that the occupation was much more than an ordinary trespass and viewed a GSA plan to utilize U.S. marshals to take the Indians off at gunpoint as an inappropriate response. Consequently, Garment and Patterson took the responsibility for negotiating and requested that the San Francisco GSA office provide up-to-date information about the occupation. Garment, representing the president and armed with his understanding of Nixon's sensitivity toward Native Americans, informed the GSA's Washington office that he would take the lead in the negotiations and keep the GSA apprised of his actions. Patterson, Garment's executive assistant, would be second in command. Robert Robertson, executive director of the National Council on Indian Opportunity, would actually carry out Garment's and Patterson's instructions, and T. E. Hannon, the San Francisco regional director of the GSA, would serve as the GSA liaison.[8]

The proclamation demanding that Secretary of the Interior Walter Hickel meet with the occupiers on Alcatraz and turn the island over to the Indians within two weeks was delivered at 1:15 P.M. on November 20, 1969. The proclamation also demanded that supply boats be allowed to land food and other necessities without harassment. Richard Urban, acting U.S. attorney in San Francisco, contacted the San Francisco office of the FBI on November 21. The San Francisco office had been providing the Washington FBI office with Alcatraz teletype updates. Urban requested that FBI agents accompany him to the island to confront the occupation force and to request them to leave. Urban apparently was acting on his own; upon learning of this request, Mr. A. Rosen in the Washington office instructed the San Francisco office that the bureau "should not get involved either in the demands or the forcible ejection of the Indians from Alcatraz."[9] An FBI teletype from the office of the director of the FBI to the San Francisco FBI office confirmed this procedure: "To reiterate previous instructions, no agent of the FBI should physically go to Alcatraz Island and under no circumstances should an agent participate in any assault on the island."[10]

In an attempt to assess the situation on the island and to get a better sense of exactly who the government was dealing with, Robertson called Norm Rambeau of the American Indian Association. Rambeau, who was Indian himself, explained that the group consisted primarily of students augmented by members of the Sioux Club and the San Francisco Indian Center. According to Rambeau the occupation resulted from the destruction of the San Francisco Indian Center. He claimed that it "came out first as a publicity stunt to raise money for a new Indian Center, and later grew and grew and grew, and now they've decided that they want the island for a cultural center." Robertson then asked Rambeau how he would approach the occupation. Rambeau responded that if the decision rested with him, he would meet with the Indians on Alcatraz and offer them land around San Francisco as an alternative. Robertson stated, "I like the benefit of your thinking. I'll give you a call back."[11]

While the government pondered the best approach, the population on the island began to increase and the attitudes of the occupiers began to take on a new dimension. On November 23 the *San Francisco Chronicle* claimed "the invaders gave the U. S. Government two weeks to surrender" as reinforcements arrived.[12] Two days later, Oakes raised concerns among federal officials that other occupations might occur when he proclaimed, "Alaska is next, yes Alaska!"[13]

The day prior to Oakes's statement Walter J. Hickel had announced that he was available at any time to meet with Indian representatives to discuss their views of what should be done with Alcatraz, but would not follow any conditions set by the Indians. Hickel said he was hopeful that the occupiers would move off the island in the interest and safety of all concerned and that discussions on the subject could be pursued in a proper manner.[14]

Although the government had not officially announced its strategy for handling the occupation, the future security of Alcatraz Island had been planned even at this early date. A GSA memorandum released on November 26, six days following the occupation, detailed the procedure:

> We believe sentry dogs with handlers would prove to be a powerful deterrent and should be used. . . . PPD reported the availability of 40 rolls of concertina wire at Norton Air Force Base. This would add much needed interference on the beach areas until and after chain link security fencing is installed. In our opinion, it will cost the Government $38,200 initially to install security devices and that the recurring costs will range from initially $3,100 to finally $1,900 per week to secure Alcatraz Island from another intrusion such as has been perpetrated by the Indians.[15]

Although the GSA and the FBI had been informed that the Alcatraz situation would be directed from the White House, both organizations continued to look to themselves for solutions. On November 24 the San Francisco FBI office informed its Washington, D.C., office that the Department of the Interior was "not out of the picture" and furthermore, the GSA had contacted the Justice Department, which was trying to work out a solution with the U.S. attorney in San Francisco. The San Francisco office reported that the GSA might "try to commandeer enough Marshals to remove the Indians, possibly tomorrow."[16]

On November 25 the San Francisco FBI office informed its Washington, D.C., office that the GSA regional director of property management, Richard Laws, reported "that there will probably be no action regarding Indians on Alcatraz for a day or two." According to Laws, the "Indians are not hippie types and are not allowing hippie types on [the] island." It was his opinion that the occupiers were policing Alcatraz well themselves.[17]

The White House reacted to the continuing government leadership confusion by calling a meeting with President Nixon's staff, the Department of the Interior, the Department of Justice, and the GSA. During the meeting, it was reiterated that for all future Alcatraz negotiations or decisions Garment had the lead and Patterson was his assistant. Robertson would actually carry out Garment's and Patterson's instructions, and Hannon would serve as the GSA liaison. Although the FBI should continue making situation reports, it was not to interfere with the occupation or go to the island. The meeting ended with a general discussion regarding recommendations "as to what action to take."[18]

On November 28 the FBI reported that Hannon characterized the situation as stable. California senator George Murphy, a member of the Senate Indian Education Subcommittee, reacted to Oakes's earlier declaration that Alaska would be next. In a *San Francisco Examiner* article Murphy remarked, "I would hope we wouldn't get a whole rash of these, because if you come down to it, somebody's liable to claim the whole United States."[19] Oakes spoke to the press on that same day and stated, "We are planning to stay on the island forever, and we won't talk to anyone except Hickel or President Nixon."[20]

The occupation force required a constant augmentation of its numbers as Native Americans began to come and go, some deciding to take up residence, some deciding to stay only a few hours or overnight, some required by school or work to leave for extended periods. To keep their numbers stable, the occupiers asked for help on November 29:

> The Indians on Alcatraz plan to issue a call this weekend to every "tribe, band or nation" across the country to meet with

them on December 23 on Alcatraz. . . . "This will be an attempt to bring about Indian unity across the country—Alcatraz can do this—so we can come to a common understanding of our goals and ideals."

Meanwhile on the island, the Indians spent a quiet day, preparing for an influx of weekend visitors from as far away as Louisiana, Washington, and New York, to join the residents—whose number is estimated at about 200 already there.[21]

Oakes announced the same day that "seven carloads of Indians from the state of Washington were expected to arrive with an unknown number of tribesmen from Los Angeles as well as other areas expected to join a big weekend powwow on Alcatraz." Oakes stressed the pan-tribal effort of the occupation, and Brightman, president of the United Native Americans in San Francisco, termed the intertribal cooperative effort to gain the island "the most important event since we actually stopped warfare with the white man in 1889."[22]

The growing number of Indian people arriving and departing from Alcatraz Island concerned government officials. Although the government had made no firm decision regarding ending the occupation, the growing support clearly would make removal from the island more difficult. December 1969 began with an FBI teletype from the San Francisco office to the FBI office in Washington, D.C., explaining that the local newspapers had exaggerated the number of Indians on Alcatraz. Despite media figures of between 300 and 600, the GSA count suggested that in fact there were less than 200 occupiers on the island.[23] A GSA news release dated December 1 further maintained that "federal officials will not hold discussions with the Indians on the future of the Island as long as they continue to occupy it."[24] Hannon added that federal officials were aware of the plight of Indian groups nationally and had held discussions with some of their leaders to seek solutions.

The GSA news release ended with concern over the well-being of the occupiers: "GSA is extremely alarmed over the health and safety hazards that face the men, women and children occupying the Island with its run down buildings, exposed conditions and grossly inadequate utilities." The GSA pointed out that the buildings "have deteriorated to the point that the broken stairs, crumbling walls and inadequate lighting make them wholly unsuitable for living."[25] This report is contrary to a report by Thomas Scott, PMDS realty officer, who claimed that at the time of the occupation, Alcatraz was "almost like paradise": "All of the buildings were in mint condition. The warden's house was absolutely spectacularly furnished. The doctor's house next door, an old Victorian, was really beautiful. All the other buildings were in mint condition."[26]

On December 1 Oakes informed Coast Guard petty officer A. D. Garrison, who had visited the island on a routine inspection, that the lighthouse and fog signal were on Indian land and that Oakes wanted the Coast Guard to remove the light and fog signals within the next thirty days. Despite Oakes's admonition to remove the signals from the island, the inspection continued without incident and the signals remained on the island.[27]

A December 2 meeting of the Interagency Regional Council, held in San Francisco, displayed the government's inability to come to grips with the significance of the occupation. Although the meeting could have been a forum for possible resolutions to the situation, its announced purpose was to explore the possibility of council action with regard to the overall problem reflected by the Alcatraz situation, "not to discuss the future of Alcatraz." Robert Pitts of the Department of Housing and Urban Development, acting in the absence of Robertson, simply stated that "since the Indians were not interfering with business, confrontation was avoided and they hoped the Indians would leave voluntarily."[28]

Barney Old Coyote of the Sacramento office of the Bureau of Indian Affairs made a brief statement in support of the Alcatraz occupiers: "What is happening on Alcatraz is in a sense a product of what we have been trying to develop, namely, the Indian's capability and desire for self-determination." Old Coyote touched on the heart of the problem: "Many relocated Indians experienced problems in the big urban cities as federal assistance ceases with respect to job placement, two weeks after they arrive at the relocation point. They are eligible for vocational development and counseling for two years." Aubrey Grossman, an attorney speaking on behalf of the occupiers, summed up the effectiveness of the council when he stated, "The council cannot solve the Indians' problem, it was a national one, and discussion [was] meaningless unless followed by some new Government policy."[29] The following day, the government advised the city of San Francisco that Alcatraz Island "as of this date is no longer available for disposal to the City and County of San Francisco." While not spelled out in this letter, this was, in fact, a preliminary move to transfer the island to the national park system.[30]

Dean Chavers, an Indian representative, raised hopes for the future of Alcatraz Island when he reported on December 7 that he had had conversations with three members of Congress who raised the possibility of a nonpartisan bill on behalf of the Indian occupiers. According to Chavers, the bill would authorize transfer of the property to a nonprofit corporation controlled by Indians. The corporation could then develop the desired cultural center and other facilities. Chavers identified Representatives George E. Brown Jr. and Phillip Burton, both Democrats from California, and Ogden Reid, Republican from New York, as the three seeking cosponsors for such a bill.[31]

As plans for the bill continued the Alcatraz occupation moved along two separate tracks: one where the Indian occupiers refused to leave the island as they attempted to consolidate national Indian support and the other where the federal government attempted to determine the needs of the Indian people of the Bay Area, and at least to some extent the needs of the Indian occupiers, as they demanded that the occupiers leave the island.

The Indians on Alcatraz were encouraged by the support of Brown, Burton, and Reid and further hopes were raised by the prospect of a national conference on December 11 intended to unify Indians of all tribes and groups. Shirley Keith affirmed, "It will be as open as possible." "We want our elders here to provide guidance and leadership." One purpose of the gathering was to form a new organization, the Confederation of American Indian Nations. Invitations were mailed to 5,000 tribes, bands, reservations, and urban centers.[32] The turnout for this proposed national conference was much smaller than anticipated, however, and no new national organization materialized.

While plans were underway for the international conference, the government called the second meeting of the Interagency Regional Council. Five federal officials met with some fifty of the island occupiers on Alcatraz and covered "about everything from Indian employment problems to the chilling breezes sweeping over San Francisco Bay." The San Francisco Chronicle reported that despite Indian prodding, the officials shied away from any discussion of the island itself "as if the topic were a time bomb."[33] The five federal officials heard "a story of physical neglect toward the first Americans—of health cards" that are virtually worthless, and of Indians being refused medical care by doctors and medicines by pharmacists.[34] The regional council chair Kenneth Robertson said that the unusual meeting provided an opportunity for high-level officials to discuss one area of concern, while the *Chronicle* stated that the only immediate result of the meeting was the scheduling of yet another meeting and the possibility of inviting still more bureaucrats from still more federal agencies to produce some sort of urban Indian program. Meanwhile, the San Francisco GSA regional office issued a press release pronouncing that "no significant progress has been made in inducing the American Indians on Alcatraz Island to end their illegal occupancy." The GSA had taken the position that unless the Native Americans could acquire the island through legislation or proposals through the standard GSA channels, to be considered along with other proposals for use of the island, they could not be effective in acquiring use of the property. In any event, if they chose to pursue any of these alternatives, they must properly do so by ending their illegal occupation.[35]

The frustration level on Alcatraz Island rose after government representatives refused to address the Alcatraz occupation at either the December 2 or December 10 meetings. Browning Pipestem, an attorney for the Washington, D.C., law firm of Arnold and Porter, "feared the resolve of the Indian people to stay on the island [was] fading." Arnold and Porter had agreed to represent the Indians pro bono in their attempt to obtain legal title to the island. Pipestem requested that a representative of the National Council on Indian Opportunity (NCIO) accompany him to bolster the spirits of those on the island.[36] Livermore phoned the NCIO on December 11 and stated that "he was really frustrated" with the government since "nothing was being done to meet [their] needs—talk, no action."[37]

Unknown to the occupiers, the government's internal position and approach toward those on the island was beginning to solidify. On December 11 Robert Robertson, who reported directly to Garment and Patterson, phoned Patterson and informed him he thought that the occupation could be handled "by quietly taking care of whatever immediate problems they had in the San Francisco Bay Area." Patterson stressed that Garment was calling the shots *for the president*, that nothing would happen until the Indians got off the island, and that government agencies in San Francisco were not to make any promises of any kind. Robertson wrote a memorandum for the file regarding the phone conversation and mentioned that he talked about "the possibility of ignoring the protesters on the island and proceeding with what we had intended to pursue all along: the possibility of helping the Indian people in the Bay Area create an omnibus Indian center." Robertson wrote that he believed there was a need for the government to deal with responsible Native American leaders such as Earl Livermore and to "let the occupation run its course." Robertson recorded that "Morris Thompson (Eskimo), special assistant to Secretary of the Interior Hickel, recommended that a move be made to circumvent the island dissidents without making it appear that we were bowing to their demands." Robertson felt the government could "get around the occupiers" by talking to responsible urban Indian leaders and by creating a model Indian center. Even if this was not completely successful, they "will have taken the wind out of their sails and will have started constructive work in the democratic tradition which will lessen the empathy felt for those on the island." In conclusion, Robertson stated, the longer the situation continued, the worse it would be for the government.[38]

On December 12 Pipestem laid out the position of those on the island to Robertson. Speaking of the problems faced by Indians, both on reservations and in the urban areas, Pipestem emphasized that the occupation of Alcatraz Island "points up the desperate nature of the situation." Pipestem explained that he and those on the island recognized that the island was "the only negotiating instrument they had and that if they left Alcatraz they would be in the same negotiating position as they had been prior to the occupation." Pipestem urged Robertson to pull together a "full cast of characters" in an attempt to negotiate a settlement.[39]

On December 13 the National Park Service submitted a sixteen-page report to the secretary of the interior, recommending that Alcatraz Island be included in a proposed Golden Gate national recreation area. The report did not mention the Native Americans occupying the island.[40]

The Interagency Regional Council met again on December 16 and began plans for creating an "omnibus Indian center." No Indian people were invited to this meeting, and the council decided to hold the next meeting only after Native Americans had selected a representative group, consisting of both mainland and island Indians, to negotiate with the federal government. Hannon agreed to meet with Livermore to tentatively identify specific locations that might be suitable for a mainland cultural center. It was then announced that the Office of Economic Opportunity had $50,000 in planning grant funds that could be utilized *if an appropriate Indian group was formed.* The meeting adjourned with the recommendation that the council should not commit to going back to Alcatraz Island, nor should the press be present at the next meeting. The attitude of the government negotiators was beginning to focus on circumventing the island movement by funneling money into the establishment of a mainland cultural center, refusing to meet on the occupiers' chosen site, and including mainland Indian people in any recognized representative group.[41]

As 1969 and the first month of the occupation came to a close, it became apparent that the government had no intention of granting title to the island to the occupiers. On December 18 Senator George Murphy made the government's position clear when he proposed to the White House that Alcatraz be designated as a national park honoring all Native Americans. Although the proposed park would be named the Indian National Park and would be available for use by all persons, ownership would still rest with the federal park system.[42] On December 23 Garment wrote a memorandum to the Washington, D.C., Alcatraz working group that set an agenda for a January 6, 1970, meeting that would co-opt the occupiers by shifting attention to the support of a representative group of Bay Area Indians, funding such a group, and establishing a national park that would include Alcatraz Island. Agenda items included a discussion of the extent to which an Indian national park on Alcatraz could be feasible and could be made a part of the Department of the Interior's long-range plans for federal parks in the Bay Area.[43]

On December 24 the *San Francisco Examiner* reported that a portion of Fort Miley had been offered to the island occupiers as an alternate site for the establishment of their planned facilities. The offer was made to the Indians by Garment through Pipestem.[44] Although White House press secretary Ron Ziegler denied that any such offer had been made, he did, however, point out that such an offer was a possibility. Despite Ziegler's denial Fort Miley was, in fact, available and was on a list of surplus government property that was being considered as alternative sites for the Alcatraz Indians by Garment. On December 31 Hannon told the commissioner of the GSA that the Alcatraz Indians would consider the government's "offers of other federal properties, but only in addition to Alcatraz."[45]

January 1970 began more optimistically for the occupiers of Alcatraz. Livermore, who had been officially appointed to the position of coordinator of Indians of All Tribes, announced that the Native Americans had begun the second phase of their occupation. Phase two included the "development of facilities and curriculum for an Indian cultural and educational center." The occupiers were acting on the assumption that the island would be ceded to them eventually and were developing plans for tearing down the main cellblock and replacing it with a large circular building that would serve as administration headquarters of the center. Some island buildings would be destroyed and some buildings designed as housing would remain, together with the island's historic lighthouse. Livermore said that the Indians were considering "applying a totem pole facade to the lighthouse."[46] The optimism dissipated quickly as Yvonne Oakes fell to her death. The rest of the Oakes family left the island, and the struggle for leadership ensued in Richard Oakes's absence.

On the mainland other concerns were also surfacing. In a *San Francisco Examiner* article dated January 4, Don Patterson, president of the American Indian Center, expressed his frustration at trying to rebuild the center following the October 1969 fire: "It will not be easy and . . . Alcatraz, unfortunately, has been of little help to its older, mainland counterpart. Since the Center burned down . . . additional funds had to be sought; but, since they began seeking funds, the Indians had occupied Alcatraz. The result is a division of labor and money. . . . There is plenty of unity and energy among Bay Area Indians, but that contributions are split between the Center and Alcatraz." The Bank of California began an Indian Center building fund, but also set up a similar fund for Alcatraz. Although people could contribute to either fund, unearmarked donations were divided evenly between the two.[47]

The San Francisco Regional Council met on January 7 to discuss various issues impacting on the Bay Area Indian community. Stan Doremus of the Office of Equal Employment Opportunity reported on a January 6 meeting with Robert Robertson and Indian legal counsel Bruce Montgomery and Pipestem. The attorneys emphasized that, symbolically, Alcatraz was extremely important to the Indian group on the island. They were positive that no negotiations would take place unless they were convened on the island, at least at the beginning. Despite this recommendation, it was agreed that the regional council should meet with the Native Americans to attempt to open some type of dialogue, that the meeting should be private, and that it should be held on the mainland.

In the meantime the government moved to simplify its cumbersome lines of federal communications. A January 8 memorandum established a clear chain of command from Garment, representing the president, to Patterson, from Patterson to Robertson, and from Robertson to the various departments and agencies, while Hannon and the GSA would retain statutory responsibility for the security of the island.[48]

On January 10 Robertson arrived in San Francisco to begin his job as government representative. Accompanied by Hannon and GSA representative Sidney Smith, Robertson toured the island and prepared to meet with the occupiers on January 11 and 12. Robertson opened the January 11 meeting on Alcatraz by stating that the group had come to the island "to discuss the health and safety hazards." His tour the previous day led him to determine that Alcatraz was "a menace to the health and safety of any human being on it." Robertson believed that it was only "a matter of time before someone else died there."[49] Dr. Tepper, one of the volunteers serving in the island health clinic, presented a list of health needs, including standard clinic supplies, emergency hospital equipment, portable laboratories, bathing and laundry facilities, portable heaters, sterilizers, Coleman stoves and lanterns, and telephones in case of emergencies. Stella Leach attempted to disrupt the meeting by alleging that it had been called illegally by Earl Livermore, who had no right to make such an invitation.

As other issues were raised, Robertson attempted to retain control of the meeting by insisting that the conversation was ranging far afield from the safety and health topics he had come to discuss and that, while he had come with an open mind, the group would have to restrict itself to those items.

Aubrey Grossman and Donald Jelinek, two attorneys for the Native Americans, refused to restrict their comments and attempted to draw Robertson into a discussion of the title to Alcatraz. Hannon did provide a brief explanation of the federal law governing disposal of excess property: "In order of right it must first be offered to another federal agency or department, secondly to public bodies such as state, county, cities, etc., thirdly, for public sale to competitive bidders. The current state of Alcatraz Island was that the secretary of the interior had requested a study for consideration for disposal of the island."[50]

The Indians responded that "the government could do whatever it wanted in spite of the law." Hannon attempted to highlight the problems that had caused the federal government to abandon the prison in 1963. He noted the "advanced deterioration" of the buildings and that the "water barge could sink any time now." Hannon estimated it would take $8 million dollars to restore water, electricity, sanitation, and acceptable safety standards on the island. The Indians responded that "if [the government] can render foreign aid, fight a war, etc., etc., [the government] can give them everything they want."[51]

Robertson proposed that all women and children leave Alcatraz immediately and that only a small, symbolic force of five to fifteen men remain. When Robertson proposed paying the remaining men to be caretakers, he was accused of "trying to buy [them] off." Fear also was expressed that the government would "plan to arrest a reduced force." Robertson "assured them that [the government] would do no such thing."[52]

The meeting the following day opened with Stella Leach reading a list of health and safety items needed on the island, including health clinic supplies, telephone services for emergency use, boat transportation for personnel and supplies, docking privileges on the San Francisco mainland, fire-fighting equipment, and maintenance workers to repair and install plumbing, heating, and water pumps for toilets. Hannon ignored her demands and instead read a prepared statement asserting that the Native Americans were trespassers and that the government assumed no responsibility for their safety while on Alcatraz.

Following the meeting, Robertson informed the vice president and Garment that "reason is a commodity they want nothing to do with—they are emotionally charged, naive and not used to responsibility. All they want is the island and an unending flow of money to do what they want, whether what they want has any chance of success or not. Their attorneys are good only for throwing fuel on the fire of unreasonableness." He further contended that there was no real leadership on Alcatraz because of the pure democracy of the island group and the constant jockeying for power among individuals.[53] The *San Francisco Examiner* summed up the two-day meeting in a one-line headline: "Alcatraz Talks Make Little Headway."[54]

On January 15 the Indians of All Tribes filed articles of incorporation and by-laws with the secretary of state, thus becoming a legally incorporated entity. On the same day, the third meeting of the regional council and Indian representatives took place, with much the same results as in previous meetings. Robertson remarked that the purpose of the meeting was to find an "accepted representation of Bay Area Indians" so that a planning grant could be provided in order to "formulate their needs."[55] Hannon observed that "The 50 or so American Indians on Alcatraz appear to have objectives quite different from the 17,000 or so on the mainland in this area. . . . It seems to me that sums of this kind [$3 to $5 million] could be much better devoted to meeting the problems of housing, education, health and employment involving large numbers of American Indians in the Bay Area."[56] Before any representative group could be identified, however, some of the invited Indians and observers became upset and walked out of the meeting. The occupiers did not believe that the proposed group was representative of all Bay Area Indians. Robertson remained optimistic regarding the ultimate formation of a representative group and promised to "meet with them as soon as they [got] their new group and presented concrete proposals."[57]

No further progress was made during the month of January, however. Patterson, displaying a sense of frustration with the lack of Native American response to government overtures of financial support, summed up the occupation in a memorandum to his personal file titled "Notes Concerning Alcatraz":

> The Alcatraz episode is symbolic—to the Indians and to us it is a symbol of the lack of attention to the unmet needs of the Indian in America—especially the needs of urban Indians who get practically no BIA services and of whom there may be some 30,000 in the San Francisco Bay Area. Therefore our response to the Alcatraz situation has been one of restraint and willingness to remedy this lack of attention and to look at these unmet needs. . . . We are disappointed at the lack of leadership among the Island Indians; we want to talk—about health and safety and other things, but all they have constituted so far is a "pure democracy" of some 62 people all of whom must be met with at once.[58]

As January ended, Robertson considered the various options open to the government and arrived at several alternatives. The first was to let the situation continue on its present course. This did not appear to be realistic because of the difficulty in negotiating with the occupiers, the fact that the occupiers would probably not accept any-thing less than all their demands, and the fact that the island group was unwilling to recognize any other Indian group as representative of the Bay Area Indian community. The second alternative was to do something "positive" about the Alcatraz situation.[59]

The third alternative, and the one Robertson believed should be pursued, was the creation of a park on Alcatraz with Indian involve-ment, the formation of a national organization of Indians, the renam-ing of the island, the construction of an Indian cultural center on the mainland, and the development of Indian training programs on the island for Indian people as well as tourists. Although this plan did not address all the demands of the Alcatraz force, Robertson felt that this "piece of pie was better than none at all." In supporting this alterna-tive, Robertson insisted that "even though it is true that ignoring the island situation will eventually cause its demise," the government could "do something positive, imagewise, for Indian people."[60] Ne-gotiations, however, would be necessary to include the Native Amer-icans on Alcatraz in any decision-making process.

On February 9 the Indians of Alcatraz issued a press release an-nouncing the formation of a new group that would meet with gov-ernment negotiators. The Bay Area Native American Council (BANAC) represented twenty-six organizations in the Bay Area, which in turn represented some 40,000 Indians from more than seventy-eight different tribes from throughout the United States and Canada. Much to the disappointment of the government negotiators, however, the new organization's first move was to cease talks: "BANAC will go on record as supporting the Alcatraz movement by suspending any ne-gotiations with other Indian organizations in the Bay Area now in progress with the federal government until the government recognizes the Alcatraz budget and their program proposal is funded."[61]

The government had high hopes for the national organization and had "encouraged the BANAC group to organize itself and held out the prospect of real financial and other assistance if they could get their act together."[62] At the heart of this assistance was a $50,000 grant to design solutions to the needs of the Bay Area urban Indians, includ-ing the replacement of the San Francisco Indian Center. Garment was aware that BANAC members would not publicly repudiate the Al-catraz occupation but privately was told "that the Alcatraz situation will die on the vine if they are given some more time."[63] Although the White House rejected some of the Alcatraz methods, the purpose of recommending approval of the $50,000 was to "demonstrate the government's reasonableness and willingness to work with a group dedicated to improvement of Indian conditions in lawful ways."[64]

The Indian people, particularly those on Alcatraz Island, considered the $50,000 grant an attempt to drive a wedge between the urban Indian population and the Alcatraz occupiers. By funding the cultural center on the mainland the government could lead the public to believe that Indian issues had been addressed and ignore the occupiers. To further impress upon the government BANAC's commitment to the occupation the vice president spoke on "Radio Free Alcatraz," urging governmental agencies to sit down with the occupiers to discuss title to the island.

The remainder of February 1970 brought even more frustration for government negotiators. At the Oakland Intertribal Friendship House on February 11 Robertson met with BANAC representatives and called Alcatraz "a symbol to make visible throughout the country the problems of the urban Indian, and this is a good thing."[65] At that time Robertson was prepared to offer planning grant money to BANAC, but Norman Rambeau, Stella Leach, and Lehman Brightman, who spoke for BANAC, were adamant that the group would not accept any government grants until the demands of the Native Americans on Alcatraz were met. Robertson was told "the Federal government was afraid to directly face the hot issue of Alcatraz."[66] Robertson sent a telegram the following day informing BANAC that the government would "be happy to sit down with you to receive your proposal in regards to Alcatraz . . . and it [is] hoped that your proposal is reasonable and can result in a program that is in the best interest of all people concerned."[67]

In keeping with the previous statement, Robertson traveled to Alcatraz Island on February 23 for negotiations. No lessening of demands was in the offing, however. John Trudell and LaNada Boyer presented Robertson with a nineteen-page planning grant for the development of the island. The document stated that the Indians were "still holding the island of Alcatraz in the true names of freedom, justice, and equality" and that they "felt that the island is the only bargaining power that [they had] with the Federal government." They emphasized that the island was the only way to get the federal government to notice Native Americans "or even want to deal with us."[68] The proposal called for $300,000 to develop a university and cultural complex consisting of a museum, library, archives, and ecology center. Demands for electricity, water, a government surplus boat, and new docking facilities were reiterated. The proposal also included requests that the occupiers be trained to operate the island's lighthouse and foghorn, that the non-Indian caretaker be removed from the island, and that officials promise that Alcatraz would not be run by the BIA.[69] In addition to the $300,000 the occupiers requested $130,000 for salaries, $25 per week for each island occupier for one year, and another $42,000 for consultant fees.[70]

The meeting that had begun with an opening prayer and pipe ceremony by Chief Eagle Feather, a Rosebud Sioux, ended with the smoking of the pipe but no agreement. Following the meeting, Robertson advised T. E. Hannon that he intended to advocate the refusal of the proposal in Washington and recommend that some other government property be located for the erection of the cultural center. Robertson also planned "to recommend the Department of Interior assume the island and open it as a part of the national park system."[71]

On February 24 Secretary of the Interior Hickel wrote a letter to Secretary of Defense Melvin Laird stating that his department had completed its study in conjunction with Laird's "Parks to the People Program" and recommended that Alcatraz be transferred to the National Park Service. Hickel stated that public announcement of this recommendation had been postponed pending resolution of the "Indian problem at Alcatraz."[72]

Proposals and counterproposals between government negotiators and the occupiers during the months of March, April, and May 1970 effectively brought an end to the possibility of an early and amicable resolution of the occupation.

On March 31 Robertson met with the occupiers on Alcatraz and presented the government's formal response to their demands. The six-page, single-spaced counterproposal fell short of the occupiers' demands for title to the island but did address some of the concerns that had been expressed. Robertson introduced Hickel's study on the use of Alcatraz, which had been ordered on October 27 and completed on November 25. Hickel recommended that Alcatraz be turned over to the National Park Service. The proposal suggested a federal park that would emphasize Indian culture, maintain an Indian museum and cultural center, house monuments to famous Indians, and possibly carry an Indian name taken from the Ohlone language. At a cost of $1.3 million dollars, the plan would "obliterate every last reminder of its [the island's] history as a Devil's island . . . and . . . create in its place, optimum open area." "To protect the symbolic value which has been effected on Alcatraz over the past months and to insure that the ultimate park plan will have a maximal Indian quality," Robertson proposed that an Indian joint planning committee, composed of writers, historians, and artists, would report to the Department of the Interior and that Indians would be hired as park rangers.[73]

Addressing the creation of an Indian university on the island, Robertson pointed out that accessibility, lack of water, sewage facilities, heating, and lighting, which had eventually led to the island's abandonment by the Department of Justice, were still problems and made the island unsuitable as a site for a university. Robertson further observed that the first Indian-run college was already operating in Many Farms, Arizona, and thus Alcatraz would be more appropriate as a recreational resource for all people.[74]

Although there was no immediate response to the proposal, the meeting itself was not without incident. On April 3 the GSA launched an investigation into an alleged attempt to drug Robertson's coffee during the meeting. Lieutenant Gilbert Shaw of the U.S. Coast Guard, who was assigned as a public affairs officer to Robertson, witnessed David Leach appear to drop something into a cup distinctly marked with blue stripes. Lieutenant Shaw later saw the same cup, full of coffee, in front of Robertson. Robertson was advised not to drink the coffee and he did not. The caretaker, Don Carroll, reported that he had overheard and identified five Native American men and women discussing the incident in his office. Carroll professed that David Leach had put mescaline in the cup. The Indians claimed Robertson was "part of the bureaucratic system, that he was now lying to them, and that this whole thing was going to be another long, drawn out hassle." They also warned that if Robertson returned, they "ought to do a lot different or worse to him than they tried to do to him last time." The GSA investigation also alleged "that around 90 percent of the resident, Indian population of Alcatraz Island use either marijuana or some other type of drugs," that "drugs and/or marijuana were openly being sold in the Leach's apartment on the island," and "that drugs, etc., are being brought to the island on the fishing boat *Bass Tub*."[75] Although LaNada Boyer stated that the substance put in the coffee cup was a saccharin tablet, there is no evidence that the contents of the cup were analyzed.

On the same day the GSA launched its investigation, Indians of All Tribes, Inc. issued a three-page rebuke and stated that the government had not even considered the proposal of the occupiers:

> If they had considered our proposal as they say they did, they would have worked with our proposal and made adjustments to it. The government's proposal is nothing more than the formation of another park, whether it be state or federally owned; unneeded, undesired, and actually an attempt to end the Alcatraz movement. . . . The public thinks this is really going to be a tribute to the American Indians, but this proposal of the government's provides for a park which will have some supervision by handpicked Indians subjected to government control and then, from then on, Alcatraz will become just another government park. . . . Our answer to the U. S. government that this island be turned into a park and that the Indian people be appointed by Walter J. Hickel to run this park, our answer at this time, and at any other time, is an emphatic NO.[76]

Indians of All Tribes, Inc. called for the government to respond to the occupiers' original proposal on or before May 31 and proclaimed that the Indians were willing to negotiate only on "money and the time and the day that they will turnover the deed to this island. That is all that is negotiable."[77]

The government reaffirmed its position on May 27 when Hannon announced that the government would transfer title to the island to the Department of the Interior. In a GSA news release Hannon stated that a national park was deemed "the most appropriate future for this unique island." Hannon indicated that the government had held six formal negotiation sessions with the island occupiers, as well as three meetings with the newly formed BANAC organization, and called on the Native Americans to accept the government's assistance so "plans for the Golden Gate National Recreation Area could move ahead."[78]

The Indians on Alcatraz and GSA officials had reached an impasse. The occupiers were unwilling to negotiate on any of their demands and the government was unwilling to meet them. The leaders of the Alcatraz council believed that the approaching summer would bring a new influx of Native Americans to the island as well as more do-nations. They had survived a harsh winter and looked forward to a summer free from any control other than their own. They refused to negotiate away their position of strength. The FBI, the U.S. Marshal Service, and the U.S. Coast Guard, all of whom expressed interest in removing the occupiers, were denied the authority to do so. The Nix-on White House, represented by Bradley Patterson and Leonard Gar-ment, took any such authority from these agencies and orchestrated the government negotiations directly. But GSA officials, appointed by Patterson and Garment, became frustrated because they could not deal effectively with consensus leadership. On Wednesday, May 26, 1970, with negotiations at a standstill, Don Carroll, the GSA caretak-er, departed Alcatraz Island. Two days later the government cut off the remaining electrical power and telephone service to the island.

Notes

1. Garment, memorandum to National Council on Indian Opportunity.
2. Ibid.
3. Patterson interview by Good.
4. Garment, memorandum to Schultz and Ehrlichman.
5. Patterson, memorandum to Krogh, Nov. 25, 1970.
6. Garment telephone interview.
7. Patterson telephone interview.
8. Garment telephone interview.
9. Federal Bureau of Investigation case file SF 70–51261.
10. Office of the Director of the Federal Bureau of Investigation, "Indian Occupation of Alcatraz Island."
11. National Council on Indian Opportunity, "Alcatraz Indian Matter."
12. "Indian Reinforced: U.S. Delays Action," *San Francisco Chronicle,* Nov. 23, 1969.
13. "Occupation of Alaska Next, Indians on Alcatraz Say," *Los Angeles Times,* Nov. 25, 1969.
14. Hickel, statement for immediate release.
15. GSA, "Preliminary Estimates on the Security of Alcatraz Island."
16. Federal Bureau of Investigation case file SF 70–51261.
17. Ibid.
18. Ibid.
19. "Alcatraz Indians Get More Water," *San Francisco Examiner,* Nov. 28, 1969.

20. "Indians Call for Parley," *Oakland Tribune*, Nov. 28, 1969.

21. "Call Goes Out to Nation's Indians," *San Francisco Chronicle*, Nov. 29, 1969.

22. "More Indians in Trek to Alcatraz," *San Francisco Chronicle*, Nov. 19, 1969.

23. Federal Bureau of Investigation Case File SF 70–51261.

24. GSA, "Indian Occupation and GSA Response," Dec. 1, 1969.

25. Ibid. The GSA news release does not identify any of the Indian leaders with whom they had met, nor the location of the meetings.

26. Scott interview.

27. Garrison, "Alcatraz Island."

28. San Francisco Regional Council, minutes, Dec. 2, 1969.

29. Ibid.

30. Laws, letter to Mellon.

31. "Alcatraz Indians Hopeful," *San Francisco Chronicle*, Dec. 7, 1969.

32. "U.S. Indian Unity Meet on Alcatraz," *San Francisco Chronicle*, Dec. 10, 1969.

33. "U.S. 'Crisis' Aides Talk to Indians," *San Francisco Chronicle*, Dec. 11, 1969.

34. "Indians Tell of Physical Neglect," *San Francisco Examiner*, Dec. 10, 1969. This article also states that the federal officials refused to discuss the occupation.

35. GSA, press release, Dec. 11, 1969.

36. Montgomery interview.

37. Robertson, memorandum, Dec. 10, 1969.

38. Robertson memorandum for the file, Dec. 11, 1969.

39. Pipestem, "Off Record Conversation."

40. National Park Service, "The Golden Gate."

41. San Francisco Regional Council, minutes, Dec. 16, 1969.

42. Murphy statement.

43. Garment, "Indians on Alcatraz."

44. "Nixon Offer to Indians: Portion of Fort Miley," *San Francisco Examiner*, Dec. 24, 1969.

45. Hannon, "Alcatraz Incident," Dec. 31, 1969.

46. "Indian Leaders Plan Step Two for Alcatraz," *San Francisco Examiner*, Dec. 26, 1969.

47. "Indian Center Seeks Funds for New Home," *San Francisco Examiner*, Jan. 4, 1970.

48. Hannon, "Alcatraz."

49. Robertson, "Alcatraz Negotiations."

50. Ibid.

51. Ibid.

52. Ibid.

53. Ibid.

54. "Alcatraz Talks Make Little Headway," *San Francisco Examiner*, Jan. 12, 1970.

55. Robertson, "Bay Indians Meet on Alcatraz Issue."

56. Hannon, letter to Gano.

57. Robertson, "Consensus of Ad Hoc Interagency Group."

58. Patterson, "Notes concerning Alcatraz."

59. Robertson, "Consensus of Ad Hoc Interagency Group."

60. Ibid.

61. Miracle, "Bay Area," 55.

62. Patterson, letter to Waggoner.

63. Garment, memorandum to Schultz and Ehrlichman, July 28, 1970.

64. Krogh, memorandum to Ehrlichman, Aug. 13, 1970.

65. "Indian Council Won't Budge on Alcatraz Issue," *San Francisco Examiner*, Feb. 12, 1970.

66. Garment, memorandum to Agnew.

67. Robertson, telegram to Indians of All Tribes.

68. Trudell and Boyer, "Planning Grant."

69. Ibid.

70. Meeting with Federal Officials, minutes.

71. Ibid.

72. Hickel, letter to Laird.

73. "'Indianized' Alcatraz Park," *San Francisco Chronicle*, Apr. 1, 1970.

74. Robertson, "Alternate Alcatraz Plan."

75. GSA, "Attempt to Drug Coffee for Mr. Robertson." This report was based on sworn statements by Lieutenant Gilbert Shaw, Howard Ours, and Don Carroll.

76. Indians of All Tribes, "Reply to Counter-Proposal."

77. Ibid. See also "Indians Set Alcatraz Deadline: Demand Plan by May 31," *San Francisco Examiner*, Apr. 8, 1970.

78. GSA, press release, May 27, 1970.

9

Removal from Alcatraz

/\.\\/.\\/\

Despite overwhelming public support for the occupiers and despite what Nixon himself may have felt, congressional action was required to transfer excess federal property over to private ownership and that action was not forthcoming. In addition, the GSA, the Coast Guard, and federal marshals all pushed for an armed removal of the occupiers. Even though weeks and months had passed with no attempt at removal, the occupiers were constantly on guard. After all, removal and relocation, epitomized by the 1838 Cherokee Trail Where They Cried and the 1863 March of Tears made by 8,000 Navajo and Mescalero Apache, had been the government's natural solution to Native American problems for more than a century. Security guards posted around the island watched for troop deployment by water and every helicopter was scrutinized for military forces. Metal fuel drums were placed strategically in open spaces on the island to prevent surprise helicopter assaults.

In a pretext of appeasement, the government held six formal negotiation sessions with the island occupiers as well as three meetings with BANAC. Still, from the very beginning of the occupation the federal government intended to remove the Indians from Alcatraz. The only questions were which government agency would orchestrate the removal, when it would be carried out, and how it would take place. President Nixon was adamant that the removal not be forceful. He wanted no reports of violence on Alcatraz sharing television time with the already violent news of the ongoing war in Vietnam. Nixon and his advisors opted to wait to act until public support of the occupation had decreased. News reports of struggles for leadership on the island as well as alleged abuse of alcohol and drugs, they felt, would eventually turn the American people against the occupation force.

As early as May 18, 1970, T. E. Hannon had requested that the Department of Justice take steps to remove the Native Americans from Alcatraz Island. He cited the lack of leadership and discipline, the reported widespread use of narcotics and intoxicants, and the potential health problems as too serious to ignore.[1] On June 4 Hannon prepared a press release indicating that "although the government could clear the island of all Indians in half an hour," federal officials planned no use of force but preferred to play a waiting game.[2] Nevertheless, on June 9 the GSA in San Francisco met to discuss plans for the removal of the Indians. While options and logistical requirements were discussed, plans for an immediate removal were vetoed. According to PMDS realty officer Scott, however, the GSA was "prepared to initiate [its removal] plan if asked to do so by the regional administrator."[3] While waiting, however, the government planned for the future security of Alcatraz Island. In a "For Official Use Only" memorandum dated June 19, the public buildings service section of the GSA stated that any preplanning would have to be done without compromising the operation, that the date and time of the operation was at present unknown, that a state of readiness must be maintained, and that action would have to be taken to prevent any reinvasion of the island after removal of the occupiers. Falling just short of identifying an actual removal date, the memorandum listed in exacting detail the equipment, support, protection, and operation for securing Alcatraz Island "upon completion of the removal of personnel from the island."[4] To cap off the month, on June 29 H.R. Bill 18071, which transferred title of Alcatraz Island to the Department of the Interior, was approved.

July 1970, however, brought welcome news to most Native Americans. On July 8 President Nixon began his address to Congress by repudiating the government policy of termination of Indian tribes. Nixon acknowledged the unconscionable plight of American Indians when he stated, "The first Americans—the Indians—are the most deprived and most isolated minority group in our nation. On virtually every scale of measurement—employment, income, education, health—the conditions of the Indian people ranks at the bottom."[5]

In announcing a new policy of "self-determination without termination," Nixon declared, "It is long past time that the Indian policies of the Federal government began to recognize and build upon the capacities and insights of the Indian people."[6] Nixon also announced the return of Taos Blue Lake to the Taos Indians as his pledge of good faith on self-determination and thus, by extension, expressed his support for the preservation of American Indian culture and religion throughout the nation. In a memorandum from Garment to Patterson, Garment stated that he hoped that the meaning of the return of Taos Blue Lake to the Taos Indians would not be lost on the Alcatraz occupiers. Garment called the return of Blue Lake a "down payment" on Nixon's promise to Native Americans.[7] Garment and Patterson hoped that the announcement of the formal end of the termination policy and the return of Taos Blue Lake would prove to the occupiers that their voices had been heard and that the Nixon administration was sincere about addressing Indian issues.

Hard on the heels of this show of support for Indian issues, it seemed unwise to force the occupiers to leave. The actual removal would not be carried out until after public opinion had shifted to the side of the government. On July 15 Robertson recommended that even though "there will probably never be a better time than right now" to remove the Indians from Alcatraz, no confrontation should be ordered by the White House. Robertson suggested that the government set a deadline for the Indians so that the Department of the Interior could begin park construction. He acknowledged, however, that the occupiers would fail to comply with any new deadline and that "getting them to take the final step—actually deciding that they will give up the island—will be most difficult." In view of the "waning" public support and President Nixon's recent message, which had "created a font of good will nationally for him," the government's only other choice was to "isolate the Indians and simply leave them alone on Alcatraz, to make their lives there more difficult than it is now" and thereby further increase the high attrition rate among the island Indians.[8]

Unfortunately for the occupiers July ended with growing concern over increasingly hazardous navigation in San Francisco Bay waters. Admiral Chester Bender, commandant of the U.S. Coast Guard, phoned Robertson and requested that the Coast Guard be given permission to go onto Alcatraz Island and restore the lighthouse and fog signals, which had been rendered inoperable when electrical power to the island had been terminated. Bender had received numerous calls of concern and complaint from Senator Alan Cranston of California, the San Francisco Board of Supervisors, and from John Tunney, Laurence Burton, and William Mailliard, members of Congress representing the San Francisco Bar Pilots Association. Although the government had placed temporary buoys around Alcatraz, this group feared that it was only a matter of time before a major maritime accident occurred. Bender followed his telephone conversation with a memorandum in which he reminded Robertson that the Coast Guard's "paramount responsibility" was to ensure the safety of shipping. Bender wrote that "should a vessel suffer a casualty by grounding or collision in the vicinity of Alcatraz, the effectiveness of the aids . . . would most likely be challenged in an ensuing lawsuit."[9]

The attention of the federal government quickly shifted from attempts at negotiating with the occupiers to the restoration of the Alcatraz light and fog signal. On August 6 the Coast Guard issued a press release reporting on the results of an August 5 attempt to restore the navigational aids. The Coast Guard had been met by island occupants wielding what appeared to be Molotov cocktails. In keeping with the government's policy of avoiding violence, the Coast Guard did not challenge those on the island.[10]

Rear Admiral Mark Whalen expressed the frustration and anger felt at not being allowed to restore the navigational aids: "The Coast Guard had its 108th birthday just this past Tuesday, and in our long history I can find no parallel to what has happened. We have not now, nor have we ever had, a public relations staff, yet we have always enjoyed a special, close rapport with the American public. . . . Now in this Alcatraz situation, we have been painted to look like inhumane creatures who have no regard for the safety of the mariner. This we are not!"[11]

Unknown to the Indian occupiers holding the Coast Guard at bay in San Francisco, a showdown was rapidly approaching. On August 7 Garment, Patterson, and U.S. Attorney James Browning discussed the worsening situation in a conference call. They concluded that the first objective of the federal government should be to reactivate the lighthouse and fog signals. It was agreed that following another news release, the Coast Guard would make another attempt. If the Indians did not allow the Coast Guard to land, the occupiers would be removed and Coast Guard personnel would secure the island. U.S. marshals were to be on the mainland, ready to move in upon request to assist in the removal. While a removal appeared a definite possibility, the Coast Guard would not make an attempt until after August 13, at which time BANAC was expected to submit a grant proposal for the establishment of a mainland Indian cultural center to the GSA regional council. The Coast Guard would provide sufficient forces with the appropriate protective devices and have uniformed Coast Guard photographers on hand to capture events by color, motion, and still cameras as well as tape recorders.[12]

The news release discussed by Garment, Patterson, and Browning was issued by T. E. Hannon on August 8: "The Coast Guard, in response to the genuine need to provide effective and completely reliable aids to navigation in the San Francisco Bay Area, is reactivating the Alcatraz Lighthouse and the fog horns on the Island." In addition, Hannon asserted that the reactivation of the light and fog horns, as well as government access to the island, were not subject to qualification or negotiation of any kind. Although Hannon claimed he felt confident that the Indian group on the island would not wish to endanger maritime safety and would cooperate with the Coast Guard, he also commented, "When the Coast Guard is ready, the light is going to go on, and if you take what everyone says, there is a crisis in the making."[13]

The island occupiers issued their own ultimatum on August 13: "No water, no Coast Guard repair crew."[14] On August 15 John Trudell affirmed, "We will not bow down or cater to them, we don't want another My Lai or Kent State here but we will not back down when we are right."[15]

The already eroding support for the island occupiers during the discussion of maritime safety took a blow when a two-and-one-half-foot arrow with a metal tip was fired from the island and struck the crowded harbor excursion boat *The Harbor Queen.* The arrow landed approximately six feet from the nearest person and caused no damage to the boat. Three days later on August 11 a Molotov cocktail was hurled from the island in the direction of a Coast Guard boat that was servicing temporary buoy fog signals on the west and east sides of Alcatraz. The vessel withdrew and no damage was sustained.

While there had been some reports prior to this time that Native Americans had thrown rocks at passing boats, this escalation called for a government reaction. Rather than simply occupying an isolated, vacant, government facility, the occupiers had begun to endanger passengers on Bay Area boats as well as military personnel carrying out their duty. Hannon warned, "The government does not intend to tolerate the firing of one more arrow or stone at boats from Alcatraz."[16]

In response the government began to formulate plans to restore the lighthouse beacon and foghorns on Alcatraz and, under the code name "Operation Parks," to remove the occupiers. The "top secret" operation would begin by having the Coast Guard make another attempt to reactivate the aids to navigation. If they were not allowed on the island, U.S. marshals would take over and evict the Indians. After the removal, the GSA public building service guards would secure the island.[17]

In anticipation of a confrontation, the government used the rest of August to chip away at the remaining public support base for the occupiers. On August 21 California governor Ronald Reagan announced the approval of a $50,000 planning grant to BANAC for programs that would address the needs of urban Indians in the Bay Area, not to support the people on Alcatraz Island. On August 27 White House correspondent Jeb Magruder wrote a confidential memorandum to Bud Krogh outlining proposals that could be used by the government to undermine the Indians' support. Magruder suggested that "extreme care" be taken "to avoid any possible indication of a unified attack on the Indians." Magruder's suggestions included having the Coast Guard make speeches and appear on television and radio talk shows to emphasize the navigational peril in the bay. He also recommended that the Department of the Interior explain to the public that the approximately forty Native Americans left on Alcatraz Island were undermining Nixon's programs designed to assist all American Indians; that the Office of Economic Opportunity explain that Bay Area mainland programs were suffering because of the uncompromising islanders; that the Public Health Department warn the populace of a possible health epidemic; and that the Welfare Department conduct periodic health checks on children on Alcatraz. Magruder's approach was to use numerous agencies while guarding against any appearance of a unified attack on the underdog Indians.[18]

On August 28 a Coast Guard helicopter made numerous low passes over Alcatraz, taking tactical photographs for the planned removal. Additional tactical information was provided by two private citizens in high-rise apartment buildings on the mainland, who had begun surveillance of the island by high-powered telescopes in early August 1970. Referred to as "recluses," these two individuals provided daily reports of arrivals and departures as well as all observable actions on the island. These reports provided information about the island population, including what buildings were being used and for what purpose:

8/15/70, Saturday

Source A reports that there were no lights coming from the buildings on parks [code name for Alcatraz] last night. He reports that between 1325 [1:25 P.M.] and 1620 [4:20 P.M.] a black woman, with an Afro/natural hairdo, was seen standing in front of the cook house with what appeared to be a map in her hand. He said she was slender, rather attractive, and was wearing a blue coat that came over the knees. He suggested that she might be Angela Davis. He agreed to keep a watch for her but suggested that Inspector McKay, San Francisco Police Department, should be notified, which has not been done.

Source A reports no significant buildup of personnel.

Source B reports 16 adults left parks and 32 adults went to parks; net gain 16.

He said that except for 3 whites these persons were Indians. He reported no blacks to or from parks.[19]

This intense surveillance provided the government with detailed information on population numbers, which would aid agencies in formulating a removal plan.

August 1970 came to an end with an announcement in the *San Francisco Progress* that the removal of the Indians might be imminent. Hannon would not deny rumors that the Indians would be removed within the next few months, and while in the past news about Alcatraz had been easy to get from various agencies, now reporters were suddenly being told that Hannon was the sole source of information. During the previous few weeks, Hannon's office had been releasing reports of incidents on Alcatraz. The rash of reports and the way news about Alcatraz was being carefully released led some observers to speculate that the government was waging a "public opinion war" against the Native Americans to gain support for a removal action.[20]

On September 2 Herb Caen, a columnist for the *San Francisco Chronicle*, spoiled the government's confidential Operation Parks removal plan. In "Pull Cord to Stop Press" Caen reported that "the Indians are to be removed from Alcatraz, date so far unspecified. . . . Landing barges will be used, but not helicopters. Staging area for the invasion is Treasure Island." Caen quoted a message, marked confidential, which had been dispatched on August 29 and announced that the retaking of Alcatraz would appear to be within normal activities of the naval station Treasure Island and, unless otherwise directed, the commandant of the Twelfth Coast Guard District would approve the removal.[21] The government responded to the published report the following day: "The administration, which noted it has responsibility for Alcatraz, said if the Indians refrain from interfering with efforts to restore navigational aids 'there is no present intention to remove the Indians from the island by force.' Naval spokesmen flatly refused to comment on the confidential message."[22]

Caen had, in fact, uncovered the government's plan to remove the occupiers should they resist the Coast Guard attempt to reactivate the navigational aids. The removal plan included a seventeen-step operation plan that involved U.S. Special Police armed with .38 caliber revolvers, ammunition, and mace; sentry dogs and handlers; and a GSA work crew that would install concertina barbed wire as barriers on the beach at designated cliff areas and establish a security zone within 200 yards of the low-water mark for which the U.S. government would maintain exclusive criminal jurisdiction. In anticipation of a press conference following the removal, the GSA had prepared a press release with only the number of Native Americans and the actual time and date omitted: "It was announced today that _____ Indian men, women and children were removed from Alcatraz Island at _____ a.m. The move became necessary because of a series of serious incidents culminating in the refusal of the Indian group to permit access to the Island by the U. S. Coast Guard for the purpose of restoring aids on the Island."[23]

On September 4 Caen again upstaged the military by releasing part of the contents of an additional planning message. In his article "Power to the Peephole!" Caen declared, "The General Services Administration may issue denials, the Navy may stick with 'No Comment,' but from the evidence at hand it would seem that D-Day approaches for Operation Parks." An August 31 message from the commandant of the Twelfth Coast Guard District to the naval station Treasure Island called for a staging area to deploy 100–200 United States marshals, a Coast Guard buoy tender, several Coast Guard patrol craft, and an unspecified number of navy landing craft. Troop helicopters loaded with marshals would be staged from the Treasure Island landing pad. Approval for the plan was requested, and on September 1, the reply was "Concur. . . . Further developments breathlessly awaited."[24]

However breathless the Coast Guard may have been, the final orders to activate Operation Parks were never issued. Caen's article had forewarned the occupiers of the planned removal and effectively sabotaged the government's surreptitious attempt to remove the Indian people from Alcatraz Island.

Announcement of the planned removal virtually ensured that public sentiment would shift back to the Native Americans. The duplicity of the federal government had been shown in full daylight. At the same time the GSA denied plans to remove the Indian people from Alcatraz Island, it issued a formal operation plan to do just that. Additionally, with such advance notice, the Alcatraz occupiers could prepare to counter any planned removal, which increased the possibility of bloodshed. In an attempt to prevent such a confrontation, Garment wrote Ehrlichman on September 14 proposing seven steps that the government could take to change the Indians' status from trespassers to government contractors, to return approved navigational aids to the island, and to get "the island into the hands of the cabinet officer who has the best use for the island in the long run." These steps were as follows: The island would be transferred to the Department of the Interior; Hickel would designate the island as a national historic site; the National Park Service would contract with responsible Indians for maintenance and custodial services to be performed on the site; the Coast Guard would contract with responsible Indians to operate the fog horns and lighthouse on Alcatraz; the National Park Service would allow the Indians to set up and run the concession services on Alcatraz; the National Park Service would issue the Indians special use permits for Alcatraz Island; and the Department of the Interior would provide the Indian contractors with electrical power, water, and portable toilets for a monthly fee. Garment concluded by stating that these seven steps would take the "heat" off public opinion, which would certainly "be outraged by forcible removal."[25]

On September 28 the First Unitarian Church in San Francisco donated a 30–kilowatt generator to the island's occupiers, which would "solve all their lighting problems, including the Alcatraz light."[26] Despite the new generator, September ended with no Coast Guard navigational aids on Alcatraz Island.

In November the Coast Guard continued to pressure the White House to find a solution to the danger presented by the lack of permanent navigational aids in San Francisco Bay. The Pilotage Commission complained that concern was mounting as the rain and fog season neared. It was believed "that the cold winds coming across the land side of the gate [would] produce the tule fog which completely blanks out the area." The commission pressured the Coast Guard to reactivate the Alcatraz light and fog signals as well as place an amber fog piercing light on the south side of the island.[27]

Concern over the Alcatraz situation was also evident in the White House. In a November 9 memorandum, Bud Krogh queried Brad Patterson concerning the status of the Alcatraz situation because he had heard nothing of it since the decision not to mount the land-air-sea operation to extract the occupiers.[28] This occupation, which had started out, according to Grace Thorpe, as a publicity stunt, "to attract attention to Indian problems, had now turned into a headache for Uncle Sam, and a thorn in the side of the administration."[29]

Government concerns were heightened further on November 19 when Coast Guard personnel on the cutter *Red Birch* reported that eight rounds of ammunition had been fired in their direction while they were servicing a buoy approximately 150 yards from Alcatraz. The action was investigated by the FBI, but identification of the offenders was impossible. The shooting prompted Rear Admiral Mark Whalen to write a letter to the Coast Guard commandant and complain that since June 1, Coast Guard personnel had continuously been harassed. The incidents were "degrading to the Coast Guard personnel," and the image of the Coast Guard was "being splotched" to the "local public." Whalen concluded that the Coast Guard could take no further action to reactivate the navigational aids until such time as the White House resolved the dispute with the occupation force. Whalen urged that the "intolerable situation" be ended and that the navigational light and fog horns be restored, since the temporary buoys were deemed inadequate by individuals utilizing the San Francisco Bay waters.[30] It is not clear who fired the shots reported by the personnel on the *Red Birch*, at whom they were fired, or indeed if they were fired at all. The Coast Guard was frustrated after being held at bay for an entire year and may have been looking for an excuse to implicate the Indians on the island in a violent action. On the same day as the alleged assault, Hannon told the *San Jose Mercury News* that since the occupiers were not causing any trouble, there was no reason they should be removed.[31] The small contingency of Indian people on the island were somewhat amazed that the government did not move to end the occupation. Jerry Hill stated that at one point as few as five occupiers were on the island and they found it amusing that such a small handful could immobilize the entire Coast Guard.[32]

The following day the Native Americans celebrated the one-year anniversary of the occupation. Of the original occupiers, only LaNada Boyer and John Whitefox remained. John Trudell, who had come to Alcatraz ten days after the occupation began, joined with Boyer to reaffirm the Indians' goals. Boyer and Trudell unveiled plans to construct a $6 million Indian college called Thunderbird University on the island. Tuition would be free and courses would include Indian arts and crafts, laws, ecology, and languages. The San Francisco architectural firm of Donald MacDonald designed a round ceremonial lodge surrounded by ninety-six steel and glass wigwam residences that would accommodate approximately 300 students. The name for the university was suggested by Boyer and came from the Thunderbird group on the island headed by her brother Dwayne.[33]

It was thus clear that the occupiers were still adamant about the construction of a university on Alcatraz and were not going to leave voluntarily. Coupled with continued pressure from the Coast Guard for restoration of navigational aids in San Francisco Bay and the increasing number of reports of violence by the Indians on Alcatraz, this announcement forced the White House to reassess its approach to the occupation. It needed a solution that would somehow meet with the satisfaction of the island occupiers while still enforcing existing laws.

On November 27 White House aide Geoff Shepard presented alternatives to the Alcatraz occupation to Bud Krogh. These alternatives included various proposals for forcible removal including a commando operation conducted at night by navy sea, air, and land occupation forces. Other alternatives included harassment of the island occupants such as installing fog horns of such volume that sleep would be virtually impossible. He further recommended that a federal presence be established on the island to coincide with any replacement or repair of the lighthouse and fog horns. Shepard counseled caution in arriving at a decision for forcible removal. He stated that "although it is difficult to rationalize the toleration of a continued trespass by Indians on federal property and although after the election would seem to be a very appropriate time to move on this problem, we should at least consider the fact that the President's current good will with the Indian nation might be jeopardized by forcible removal of the island occupants." Shepard pointed out that the vote in Congress on the return of Blue Lake to the Native Americans would be coming up that week and that the Internal Revenue Service was reacting favorably to the administration's proposed tax exemption for Indians and Indian investments, so he thought perhaps the administration might consider waiting for the $50,000 OEO planning grant to BANAC to provide some positive alternatives for Indian development in the Bay Area. Having counseled caution and having presented all of the various alternatives, however, Shepard continued, *"I recommend we remove the Indians, forcibly if necessary, and prevent their return."* Shepard recommended that the FBI be used to gather intelligence concerning population and activities in order to ascertain the best time to affect the removal, that the Coast Guard be prepared to reactivate the navigational aids, and that precautions be taken to prevent a subsequent occupation.[34]

After having read Shepard's memorandum, Brad Patterson prepared his own memorandum to Krogh. Patterson saw four options: forcibly removing the Indians and securing the island; requesting Congress to authorize the Golden Gateway National Recreation Area that would include Alcatraz and allow the Indians to remain on the island until such time as Congress determined the future of the island; identifying other excess federal property and offering that property to the occupiers in return for their voluntary removal from Alcatraz; and transferring the island to the Golden Gateway Recreation Area except for a five-acre space that would be ceded to Indians of All Tribes, Inc. This area would allow space for a day-use-only office for an Indian-run local center for voluntary action. Despite these options, Patterson believed that the lack of Native American leadership would most likely result in the rejection of any proposal that fell short of the Indians' original demands.[35]

With Shepard's and Patterson's recommendations Krogh had sufficient input to make a decision. On December 11 he wrote a memorandum informing John Ehrlichman that the latest intelligence reports from the mainland recluses, who continued to observe the island on a daily basis, indicated that the island's population was down to twenty. Krogh recommended that the FBI gather intelligence on the island group and that the Coast Guard and GSA "confidentially prepare" to move on Alcatraz on twenty-four-hours' notice to restore the navigational aids and evict the remaining occupiers.[36] Despite the recommendations of Krogh, Patterson, and Shepard, however, no order for removal was forthcoming.

December 1970 closed with further warnings of the danger to shipping in the Bay Area. Captain Joseph W. Dickover, president of the Board of Pilot Commissioners, wrote to Admiral Bender, commandant of the Coast Guard, and stressed the lawlessness of the islanders and stated that they had created "a serious detriment to safety of life at sea and the cargoes and vessels." Dickover provided a list of ten major marine casualties that had occurred in San Francisco Bay from 1900 to 1970 and stated that the board "was extremely concerned at the continuing inoperative state of the aids." Dickover concluded his letter, "In notifying you of this hazardous condition we do so entirely in a spirit of cooperation in the cause of maritime safety."[37]

On January 18 concerns for maritime safety reached a new level of intensity when two supertankers, the *Arizona Standard* and the *Oregon Standard*, collided a quarter mile seaward of the Golden Gate Bridge. The collision provided the final impetus for removal of the occupiers. The collision, which occurred two miles west of Alcatraz Island, dumped approximately 800,000 gallons of crude oil into the ocean and caused public support for the island occupiers to decrease even further. A *San Francisco Chronicle* editorial, while acknowledging that the absence of navigational aids had nothing to do with the collision, stated that it was a "sad but incontestable fact that the Indians who have seized the island had completely inactivated its navigational aids and made it a rocky peril in the middle of the bay." The editorial called for the Indians of Alcatraz to reactivate the diaphones and the Alcatraz light in order to guard against future accidents and to save the bay and the environment.[38]

Secretary of Transportation John A. Volpe enclosed the *Chronicle* editorial as well as the December 18 letter from Dickover to Bender in a memorandum marked "Eyes Only" to Ehrlichman. Volpe outlined the brief history of the occupation and the ensuing disruption of navigational service to the maritime community. In the final paragraph of the memorandum, Volpe maintained that it was necessary to take any steps to restore these vital aids to navigation in the San Francisco Bay to full operational status and asked for Nixon's agreement.[39]

On February 5 Tod R. Hullin, assistant to John Ehrlichman, wrote a memorandum to Bud Krogh, enclosing Volpe's memorandum and asking for a response by February 12. Having received no answer from

Krogh, Hullin again queried Krogh on March 2.[40] On March 5 Krogh wrote Ehrlichman a memorandum stating that in the past he had attempted on several occasions to interest the Department of Justice in the removal of the Alcatraz Indians, but the bottom line, however, was that the Justice Department did not wish to be the lead agency in this matter. The Justice Department would act only upon a written request from the GSA or specific guidance from Krogh, Haldeman, or the president. Krogh recommended to Ehrlichman that he ask the Justice Department for help. Ehrlichman sent a memorandum to Secretary Volpe stating that the president had reviewed Volpe's memorandum and was in full agreement that the situation presented a continuing threat to safe navigation in San Francisco Bay and that Nixon would like Volpe to take the lead in securing the restoration of the navigational aids on the island. Ehrlichman recommended that Volpe work closely with Deputy Attorney General Kleindienst at the Department of Justice to assure the security of all concerned. The basic scenario was now set.[41]

In the meantime, the Native Americans on Alcatraz Island had done little to improve their bargaining position with government negotiators or to resolve the growing rift between themselves and the larger Bay Area Indian community. While rumors increased regarding the lawlessness on the island, BANAC met twice with the island council in an attempt to negotiate an amicable solution. A letter from LaNada Boyer to Indians of All Tribes, Inc., BANAC, and attorneys Aubrey Grossman and Donald Jelinek, however, dispelled any hopes regarding the intractability of the island occupiers:

> The whole action of taking the island was symbolic of telling the American Government and American people that they are not going to continue to steal our lands nor are they going to tell us what to do. We are contradicting our whole move of liberation if we just wait for the Government. We are Indians who want action and we cannot let the Government continue to ignore us. We cannot let Alcatraz die because just as it was symbolic in reawakening Indian consciousness and bringing attention to the Indian people, it will be symbolic of our death if it should die. . . . We need title to have complete and permanent victory.[42]

On March 12 U.S. Attorney James Browning, Assistant Attorney General Harlington Wood, and Chief U.S. Marshal Wayne Colburn met in San Francisco to consider the alternatives and ultimately decided that the most effective approach would be an "assault by force of U. S. Marshals, to forcefully remove the Indians." The FBI was tasked with the responsibility of furnishing intelligence data for the upcoming removal.[43]

The government spent the remainder of March observing the daily movements of the islanders and gathering intelligence. Informers continued to report on the number of Indians remaining, the alleged firing of objects from sling shots, and sightings of revolvers.[44] On March 26 Robertson complained to Patterson, "It gets more and more difficult here to continue sending out our stock letter saying that the Indians are being allowed to demonstrate on the island because their demonstration is peaceful and non-disruptive of normal governmental operations; particularly after the recent spats involving tourist boats, et al and the admission that they are destroying government property."[45]

The April 11 *San Francisco Chronicle* summed up the frustration of the Indians on the island, the Indians on the mainland, and the government negotiators:

> A band of 20 to 30 Indians still sits defiantly on Alcatraz Island, a bitter, disorganized remnant of the original invaders.
>
> What to do about them . . . is a question which equally frustrates the federal government and mainland Indian leaders. Government officials indicate some sort of unwanted show-down may be forthcoming and express hope that nobody gets hurt in the process. . . .
>
> "The purpose of occupying Alcatraz was to start an Indian movement and call attention to Indians problems," says Adam Nordwall. . . . "It has served its purpose. Look at the gains Indians have made since. I don't want to say Alcatraz is done with, but no organized Indian groups are active there. It has turned from an Indian movement to a personality thing. When we occupied the island, we caught the government, and then our occupation forces caught us."
>
> U. S. Attorney James Browning expressed similar views in different language, saying, "The leaders are all gone—Nordwall, Richard Oakes, LaNada Boyer, Grace Thorpe. John Trudell is

about the only name left. Our problem is whom to deal with. There is an increased possibility of violence by violence-prone individuals. I am hopeful of some way to avoid a confrontation, but if we have to have a showdown, we will have it."[46]

On April 13 Browning made one last attempt to negotiate by calling a meeting on the mainland with Assistant Attorney General Harlington Wood, Acting Regional Director of the GSA Bob Ireland, GSA Special Agent Larry Anderson, the island council, and A. Donald Jelinek to allow for "face-to-face discussions" without the press, tape recorders, or cameras.

John Trudell opened the session by reiterating that the occupiers wanted title to the island and inviting the government to comment on its current position. Browning replied that government access to Alcatraz was not open to discussion and reminded the council of the government's leniency toward the occupiers so far. Browning continued that he hoped the Native Americans would realize that even President Nixon was subject to the law and that title transfer must thus be conveyed according to the law. Wood then asked Trudell what the occupiers hoped to gain by having title to the island. Trudell replied that their objects were religious and educational self-determination. Trudell stated that the group was willing to make concessions regarding federal jurisdiction over the island but had been offered nothing in return. Wood asked if the Indians would settle for land on the mainland to start a school instead of title to Alcatraz. Trudell refused. That was the final straw.

Browning later wrote that it was his impression that the islanders would not settle for anything less than title to Alcatraz and that "they will not discontinue their militant stance against government access to the island in the absence of either title to the island or removal therefrom."[47] An FBI report concerning the meeting indicated that Browning believed the meeting "accomplished practically nothing" and that "he did not know if any such meetings would actually be held or if it would even be worthwhile to hold any more meetings with the Indians."[48] A subsequent meeting was scheduled for April 20, but never occurred.

Following the April 13 meeting conditions for the Indians on Alcatraz continued to worsen. On April 19 the *Clearwater*, the main link between the island and the mainland, sank at its moorings. The occupation force no longer had available funds to purchase or rent transportation. The Indians were virtually confined to the island with no fresh water, with electrical power supplied by a few overloaded, gas-powered generators, with only a small amount of donated food, and with no dedicated transportation to or from the island. The government once again opted to wait and see if the occupiers would voluntarily leave the island.

At the end of ninety days, however, the government's patience had been tried to its fullest extent. On June 7 Bud Krogh, Interior Undersecretary James Beggs, Admiral Chester Bender of the Coast Guard, Deputy Attorney General Kleindienst, Harlington Wood of the Department of Justice, and Garment and Patterson from Nixon's staff met to determine the occupation's fate. The group reviewed the latest FBI reports, the intelligence data, and the government's activities. The island population was thought to be at a low point, with between eleven and fifteen occupiers, and concern was expressed that the population and donations would once again swell as summer vacation for college students approached. Trudell and other occupiers were traveling across the United States to solicit donations and recruit other Indian people to reinforce the occupation force. Government officials concluded that the island group was trying to hold out until the anticipated summer influx and had no plans to leave the island in the near future. If the government was going to remove the Indian people from Alcatraz without a major engagement, it would have to be now.

After the meeting Krogh advised Ehrlichman that Wood and Wayne Colburn, chief U.S. marshal, were en route to San Francisco to prepare "for the forcible removal of the Alcatraz Indians by a specially trained unit of U.S. marshals." Krogh pointed out that the GSA would then secure the island with its federal protective service officers, the Coast Guard would restore all navigational aids, and the island would become a part of the Golden Gate National Recreation Area. Krogh declared that "in spite of the risk of violence, I recommend we utilize the above outlined method and procedure of removing the Alcatraz Indians." The decision had now been passed to Ehrlichman for approval or disapproval.[49]

On June 11 Tod Hullin checked "E" for Ehrlichman in the approval section of Krogh's memorandum and wrote, "Bud: E agrees with you. Go!"[50] At 1:45 P.M., the message went out to end the occupation of Alcatraz Island that had begun on November 20, 1969, an occupation of nineteen months and nine days.

U.S. marshals from the San Francisco, Sacramento, and San Diego offices, armed with hand guns, M-1 .30 caliber carbines, and shotguns;[51] federal protective officers, a group formed in April 1971 as a security arm of the GSA, equipped with radio transceivers, .38 caliber revolvers and ammunition, helmets, batons, and flashlights; and ten FBI agents landed on the island from three Coast Guard vessels and a helicopter three hours after Ehrlichman's order.[52] The removal team of between twenty and thirty federal personnel met no resistance from the fifteen remaining occupiers—six men, four women, and five children—and took less than thirty minutes to move them off the island. The fifteen were taken by Coast Guard boat to the mainland, given lunch, interrogated, and provided one night's lodging in a San Francisco hotel. In a *San Francisco Chronicle* article on June 12 Trudell accused the government of lying. Trudell claimed that he and four other Alcatraz Indians had been in negotiations with Browning and other federal officials since April 13 and "the first guarantee they made when the negotiations started was that nobody on the island would be arrested or taken off the island." Browning professed that no such promise had ever been made.[53] Oakes called the government's action "a sissy victory" and compared it with the government's failures in Vietnam.[54]

On June 13 the government allowed the media to visit Alcatraz for the first time since the removal. The *San Francisco Chronicle* reported that the tour was "more like an autopsy" and reported a vista of squalor, filth, systematic pilfering, and mindless destruction. PMDS realty officer Thomas Scott expressed the sentiments of many observers and participants when he commented that he "had a great deal of respect for Richard Oakes and some of the others who began this. They were articulate and very intelligent. . . . At first, they were so excited, charged up with a real cause. Later, they didn't seem to know what the cause was or why they were here."[55]

On Sunday, April 1, 1973, Alcatraz Island passed into the hands of the National Park Service and became part of the Golden Gate National Recreation Area. Over one million people visit Alcatraz Island each year; the Park Service makes an effort to include the Indian occupation as an important part of the history of the island.

Notes

1. GSA, press release, May 27, 1970.
2. "GSA Won't Use Force on Indians," *Oakland Tribune,* June 4, 1970.
3. Scott, "Plans for Removal of Indians."
4. Scott, "Alcatraz Island Security."
5. White House press release, "Nixon's Statement on Indians."
6. Ibid.
7. Garment, memorandum to Patterson, July 8, 1970.
8. Robertson, memorandum to Warren and Green. Robertson acknowledged that the White House had intentionally avoided forcing a confrontation because the staff members recognized that they were "dealing with a very unstable group of people" who "had developed a lifestyle, one giving them individual recognition which they otherwise would not enjoy" and "an existence requiring very little effort on their part."
9. Bender, "Alcatraz Island Aids to Navigation."
10. U.S. Coast Guard, press release.
11. Ibid.
12. Hannon, confidential memorandum for the file.
13. "U.S. Firm on Alcatraz Light Issue," *San Francisco Chronicle,* Aug. 11, 1970.
14. "Indians Dynamo Alcatraz Light Flashes Again," *San Francisco Examiner,* Aug. 13, 1970.
15. "Indians Explain Arrow Incident," *Oakland Tribune,* Aug. 15, 1970.
16. "U.S. Warns Alcatraz Indians," *Washington Post,* Aug. 12, 1970.
17. GSA, "Notes on Operation Parks."
18. Magruder, memorandum to Krogh.
19. GSA, "Alcatraz Confidential Daily Observation Reports from Source A and B."
20. "U.S. 'Attack' on Alcatraz May Be Near," *San Francisco Progress,* Aug. 26, 1970.
21. "Pull Cord to Stop Press," *San Francisco Chronicle,* Sept. 2, 1970.
22. "No Plan to Oust Indians on Alcatraz," *San Francisco Chronicle,* Sept. 3, 1970.
23. Ibid.
24. "Power to the Peephole!" *San Francisco Chronicle,* Sept. 4, 1970. The permission requested and approved was for the planning phase only, not for the actual removal.
25. Garment, "Outline of a Solution for Alcatraz."
26. "More Power—30 Kilowatts—to Alcatraz Indians," *San Francisco Chronicle,* Sept. 30, 1970.
27. Bender, memorandum to Patterson.

28. Ibid.

29. "A Year Later, What Next for Indians on Alcatraz," *San Francisco Examiner*, Nov. 8, 1970.

30. Bender, memorandum, Nov. 23, 1970.

31. "Indians Keep Firm Grip on Alcatraz," *San Jose Mercury News*, Nov. 19, 1970.

32. Hill telephone interview. Following the occupation Hill went on to earn his law degree and is a practicing attorney for the Oneida Tribe in Oneida, Wisconsin.

33. "The Indians Unveil Plan for Alcatraz," *San Francisco Chronicle*; La-Nada and Claudine Boyer interviews by author.

34. Shepard, memorandum to Krogh, emphasis in original.

35. Patterson, memorandum to Krogh.

36. Krogh, memorandum to Ehrlichman, Dec. 11, 1970.

37. Dickover, memorandum to Bender.

38. "Oil Not the Only Mess in the Bay," *San Francisco Chronicle*, Jan. 22, 1971.

39. Volpe, memorandum to Ehrlichman.

40. Hullin, memoranda to Krogh, Feb. 5, 1971, and Mar. 2, 1971.

41. Krogh, memorandum to Ehrlichman with enclosed memorandum.

42. Boyer to Indians of All Tribes, Inc., BANAC, Grossman, and Jelinek.

43. Federal Bureau of Investigation case file SF 70–51261.

44. GSA, "Confidential Reports, March 1971."

45. Robertson, memorandum to Patterson, Mar. 26, 1971. Trudell admitted that the Indians had begun tearing down two wooden cottages to use for firewood.

46. "What to Do about Indians on Alcatraz Still a Puzzle," *San Francisco Chronicle*, Apr. 11, 1971.

47. GSA, "Confidential Correspondence."

48. Federal Bureau of Investigation case file SF 70–51261.

49. Krogh, memorandum to Ehrlichman, June 10, 1971.

50. Ibid. In a phone interview by the author, Patterson did not recall the final decision-making process. Garment, however, stated in a phone interview by the author that Ehrlichman made the decision. The White House had decided to let the thing "rock-along" and to maintain a balance in an attempt to avoid any bloodshed. The final decision was a culmination of things, the theft of the copper from the island, the increasing crime on the island, the danger to navigation, the failure of the island group to align with BANAC, and the low population on the island prior to the summer break. I queried Garment if the upcoming presidential election was a factor, and Garment replied that the election was not a factor since Nixon was at that time experiencing a positive response from his return of Blue Lake to the Taos Indians

and other Indian initiatives. It is Garment's belief that Ehrlichman, not Nixon, approved the final removal, and that it was based on Ehrlichman's finely honed understanding of Nixon's general presidential policies and his policy toward the American Indians.

51. Garvey interview. Garvey interviewed Dick Billus, U.S. marshal, who was working in the Sacramento marshal's office and arrived on the island three hours after the removal. Billus and other officers spent three days on Alcatraz to guard against a possible reinvasion. In an interview LaNada Boyer informed the author that in fact another invasion was planned by Indian college students from the Bay Area. Boat transportation for the reinvasion had been secured by Al Miller, and the college students were gathering to go to the island. Unbeknownst to Boyer and the students, however, their planned reinvasion was for the same day that the government forces landed on the island to remove the few remaining occupants.

52. Contrary to official files, FBI agents were involved in the removal. Garvey interview. Garvey interviewed Thomas Sarver and Lou Lopez, both former GSA federal protective service officers. Sarver and Lopez participated in the removal of the Indians from Alcatraz. Both officers acknowledged the FBI participation in the removal.

53. "Indians Charge Double-Talk," *San Francisco Chronicle*, June 12, 1971.

54. "Indians Talk of Retaking Alcatraz," *San Francisco Chronicle*, June 12, 1971.

55. "The Dream Is Over: A Sad Visit to Alcatraz," *San Francisco Chronicle*, June 14, 1971. The remaining occupiers charged that the federal officers ransacked the island and their personal belongings after the removal, taking what they wanted as souvenirs and scattering the rest around the island, thus presenting squalor and filth for the press. Ultimately the remaining possessions that could be found were inventoried and taken to the mainland, where they could be reclaimed by the Indian owners.

Conclusion

Alcatraz: Catalyst for Change

/\.\\.\/.\

The success or failure of the Indian occupation of Alcatraz Island should not be judged by whether the overt demands for title to the island and the establishment of educational and cultural institutions on the island were realized. The underlying goals of the Indians on Alcatraz Island were to awaken the American public to the reality of the plight of the first Americans and to assert the need for Indian self-determination. In this they were indeed successful. As a result of the Alcatraz occupation, either directly or indirectly, the official government policy of termination of Indian tribes was ended and a policy of Indian self-determination was adopted.

When he took office in January 1969, Richard Nixon became the head of a troubled country uncertain about its present and fearful of its future. Chief among those with serious doubts were the Native Americans, who were distrustful of federal officials and continued to harbor a deep fear of further termination efforts. The occupation of Alcatraz at once symbolized this fear and voiced opposition to government policy. As the president, Nixon would ultimately decide the fate of the occupation and of all Native Americans.

In his address to Congress on July 8, 1970, in the midst of the occupation, Nixon admitted it was "long past time that the Indian policies of the Federal government began to recognize and build upon the capacities and insights of the Indian people. . . . The time has come to break decisively with the past and to create the conditions for a new era in which the Indian future is determined by Indian acts and Indian decisions."[1] On that same day Nixon returned Blue Lake and 48,000 acres of land to the Taos Indians. In a memorandum written just prior to this, Leonard Garment declared it was "essential that the

Blue Lake restoration be portrayed for what it is: . . . a much wider accomplishment than just the lands in New Mexico; a nation-wide symbol of this Administration's new approach toward Indian affairs."[2]

The return of Blue Lake was just the beginning of federal concession of land to Indian groups. Other grants included 40 million acres to the Navajo Indians on June 30, 1970, 21,000 acres of Mount Adams in Washington State to the Yakima tribe in July 1972, 80 acres to the Washoe tribe in California in October 1970, and some 60,000 acres to the Warm Springs tribes of Oregon in September 1972. Not merely an address to Congress, Nixon's July 1970 speech ushered in new policies and new legislation.

In 1970 the administration introduced twenty-two legislative proposals on behalf of Native Americans to support tribal self-rule, foster cultural survival as a distinct people, and encourage and support economic development on reservations. Six were passed into law. The following year forty-six pieces of Indian legislation became law. Public Law 92–22 established within the Department of the Interior the position of assistant secretary of Indian affairs, Public Law 92–265 extended the life of the Indian Claims Commission, Public Law 92–189 established the Navajo Community College, and Public Law 92–209 established the Native Alaska Claims Act. A large number of these laws returned land or awarded judgment funds as a result of decisions of the Indian Claims Commission.

In addition to the new legislation President Nixon increased the budget of the Bureau of Indian Affairs by 224 percent, doubled funds for Indian health care, established the Office of Indian Water Rights, and made special provisions for defending Indian natural resource rights in federal court. New bureaus were created in each of the government's human resource departments to help coordinate and accelerate programs for Native Americans. Education efforts were expanded, with an increase of $848,000 in scholarships for Indian college students and the establishment of the Navajo Community College, the first college in America planned, developed, and operated by and for Indians. The Office of Equal Opportunity doubled its funds for Indian economic development and tripled its expenditures for alcoholism and other recovery programs and significantly expanded programs in housing, home improvement, health care, emergency food, legal services, and education. Altogether, federal spending increased from $598 million in Fiscal Year 1970 to $626 million in Fiscal Year 1971.

The change in government policy had an effect on the court system as well. Prior to 1960 the U.S. Supreme Court seldom ruled on Indian cases. During the sixties the Court heard twelve cases and in the seventies, as the attention of the nation focused on Native American activism and civil rights, the Court ruled on thirty-two cases, supporting cultural pluralism and tribal sovereignty in areas of civil and criminal jurisdiction.

On April 27, 1994, five days after Richard Nixon's death, Tim Giago, editor and publisher of *Indian Country Today: "America's Indian Newspaper"* expressed his hope that one day Nixon might be honored and recognized for his special efforts on behalf of the Indian nations of America.[3] Mark Van Norman, attorney for the Cheyenne River Sioux, credited Nixon with formally ending the government policy of termination at a time when the Cheyenne River Sioux were third on the list to be terminated. Mario Gonzalez, former attorney for the Oglala Sioux, credited Nixon as being "one of the greatest" in making positive changes for Native Americans. Gonzalez remarked that Nixon was respected deeply by many older tribal leaders.[4] Despite the actions of Nixon's administration during the Alcatraz occupation, Nixon himself did a great deal to aid Native Americans. I hope that this book begins the process of recognition and pays the proper respect for Nixon's contributions to American Indian people.

Perhaps more important for young Indian people than Nixon's contributions is the contribution the occupation made to the spirit of Native Americans. Most scholars frequently and incorrectly credit the American Indian Movement with sparking occupations and protests, but the occupation of Alcatraz was the real catalyst because it marked the first time different Indian groups had banded together to form a multitribal organization. The takeover of BIA headquarters in 1972, the occupation of Wounded Knee in 1973, and the shoot-out between American Indian Movement members and FBI agents on the Pine Ridge reservation in South Dakota in 1975 can all be traced to Alcatraz.[5] Many planners or participants of the approximately seventy-four occupations that followed the Alcatraz occupation had been involved in the occupation or at the least gained strength from the new "Indianness" Alcatraz generated. It was to Alcatraz that members of AIM traveled just before their rise to national prominence.

It was only after visiting the Indians on Alcatraz Island and realizing the possibilities available through demonstration and seizure of federal facilities that AIM entered into the national scene.[6] AIM leaders saw firsthand, during their brief visit in June 1970, that thanks to the inherent bureaucracy of the federal government no punitive action was being taken against the occupiers. AIM recognized an opportunity for publicity and launched itself into national awareness on Thanksgiving Day 1970, when members seized the *Mayflower II* in Plymouth, Massachusetts, to protest the celebration of colonial expansion into what Europeans mistakenly called a "new world." During the protest AIM leaders acknowledged the occupation of Alcatraz Island as the symbol of their newly awakened desire for Indian unity and authority in a white world. While Indians of All Tribes, Inc. focused its attention on the Alcatraz occupation, AIM seized the historical moment and became the premier national Indian activist group, sponsoring a series of protests that would continue throughout the decade and encourage others to speak up for themselves and for their rights.

Alcatraz Island remains a strong symbol of activism and self-determination and a rallying point for unified Indian political activities. On February 11, 1978, Native Americans began the "Longest Walk" to Washington, D.C., to protest the government's continuing ill treatment of Indian people. That walk began on Alcatraz Island. On February 11, 1994, AIM leaders Dennis Banks, Clyde Bellecourt, and Mary Wilson met with other Indian people and began the nationwide "Walk for Justice" to protest Leonard Peltier's continued imprisonment as a result of the June 26, 1975, shoot-out between AIM members and FBI agents on the Pine Ridge Reservation. That walk began on Alcatraz Island. On Thanksgiving day of each year since 1969 Native Americans have gathered on Alcatraz Island to honor those who participated in the occupation and those who are engaged in the continuing struggle for Indian self-determination. On November 20, 1994, Indians returned to Alcatraz Island to commemorate the twenty-fifth anniversary of the occupation and remember everything it still stands for.

Although the leaders did not achieve their stated goals, the 1969 occupation of Alcatraz Island nevertheless stands out as the most symbolic, the most significant, and the most successful Indian protest action of the modern era. The Alcatraz occupiers served notice that they would no longer stand silently by and allow the federal government to determine their futures. The occupation of Alcatraz

Island was a major victory for the cause of Native American activism and remains one of the most noteworthy expressions of patriotism and self-determination by Indian people of this century.

Notes

1. Nixon, "Message to Congress."

2. Garment, memorandum to Patterson, July 8, 1970.

3. Tim Giago, "Nixon: His Determination to Stop Termination," *Indian Country Today: "America's Indian Newspaper,"* Apr. 27, 1994.

4. Ibid.

5. See the appendix for a chronology of Indian protests following the 1969 occupation of Alcatraz.

6. Patterson, memorandum to Hullin.

Appendix

Summary of Major Occupations

.\.\/.\

The following is a summary of the major occupations and significant activist events that grew out of the Alcatraz occupation. Wherever possible, I have identified those events in which members of Indians of All Tribes, Inc. were direct participants or motivated those involved in the events. I have also identified events that were initiated by or involved the American Indian Movement so that readers may see the approximate point at which AIM moved onto the national scene.

November 20, 1969—Indian college students occupied Alcatraz Island. The activists ultimately incorporated as an organization and became Indians of All Tribes, Inc.

March 8, 1970—A Sacramento Indian group led by Lehman Brightman marched on Sacramento to protest the fatal shooting of Hoopa Indian Michael Ferris on December 5, 1969, in Humboldt County. Ferris was a student at UCLA and was shot to death in a Will Creek bar by a white bartender. Indian people from Alcatraz Island participated in the march.

March 8, 1970—United Indians of All Tribes invaded Fort Lawton to press for the right to occupy former Indian lands about to be declared surplus based on an 1868 Sioux treaty. Seventy-seven Native Americans were arrested, beaten with clubs, and dragged to waiting vehicles after refusing to leave. The Indian people felt that the invasion was necessary because the Indians of Seattle were all but ignored when they originally requested that Fort Lawton be given to them. Senator Henry Jackson had advised Seattle mayor Wes Uhlman that Fort Lawton would be deeded to the city for use as a park once it was declared surplus property. Indians from Alcatraz Island made up the majority of the occupation force. Bernie Whitebear explained that United Indians of All Tribes was modeled after Indians of All Tribes, Inc. on Alcatraz Island. Whitebear stated, "We saw what could be achieved there and if it had not been for their determined effort on Alcatraz, there would have been no movement here. We would like to think that Alcatraz lives on in part through Ft. Lawton."[1]

March 8, 1970—Fourteen Indian activists occupied Fort Lewis, Washington, fifty miles south of Seattle, shortly after a larger group of Indians clashed with military police at Fort Lawton. The group, including Alcatraz Indians, traveled to Fort Lewis from the Fort Lawton occupation, scaled bluffs and fences, and managed to put up a teepee in a small clearing in some woods on the post. A proclamation, similar to the one prepared by the Alcatraz occupiers, was read, stating that the Native Americans intended to use the post for an ecology and cultural center. The occupiers were removed from the government facility. Jane Fonda, who also participated, was taken into custody and given a letter of expulsion banning her from the post.[2]

March 14, 1970—Indians took over the BIA office in Denver to protest discrimination and anti-Indian employment policies of the BIA. An Indian woman had applied for a job as a school counselor to Indian children in Littleton, Colorado, and although fully qualified she was refused the position. In two separate incidents at Littleton, twenty-one Native Americans were arrested, which started a countrywide chain reaction: twenty-three arrested in Chicago, twelve in Alameda, California, twenty-five in Minneapolis, and thirty in Philadelphia. BIA offices in Cleveland, Dallas, Los Angeles, and Albuquerque were also the scene of Indian protests. Those arrested in Alameda were charged with failure to leave a public building.[3]

March 15, 1970—Indian activists again entered Fort Lawton and were served eviction notices by federal authorities. The military selected sixteen Indians whom they considered to be leaders and agitators because of their participation in the previous occupation and arraigned them before a federal commissioner. A preliminary hearing was set for April 2; however, the charges were eventually dropped.[4] In their manifesto, quoted in *Alcatraz Newsletter* no. 3, the Fort Lawton group said, "The occupation of Alcatraz has seen the beginnings of a concept of unity long dreamed of by all our people." Cover stories in *Time* and *Look* magazines, covering the Alcatraz and Fort Lawton Indian occupations, referred to Alcatraz as "the symbolic act of Indian awareness."[5]

March 16, 1970—Native Americans from fourteen tribes attempted an assault on Ellis Island, but they were foiled when their sixteen-foot boat developed engine trouble. Members of Indians of All Tribes, Inc. planned to claim the abandoned federal facility for an Indian commune. The Coast Guard invoked the Espionage Act to ward off any further attempts to seize the island. The occupiers claimed that their treaties with the government permitted them to take over abandoned government land. This is similar to the claim that had been the basis of the brief 1964 occupation of Alcatraz

Island. Tina Robinson, whose husband was among those planning the occupation of Ellis Island, stated that the occupiers were affiliated with the
groups that occupied Alcatraz.[6]

March 23, 1970—Twelve Indians were arrested at the BIA office in Alameda. Approximately fifty Native Americans protested alleged job discrimination and other grievances; about thirty later went inside. Richard Oakes
and five others from Alcatraz were among the twelve who refused to leave
the BIA office and finally submitted peacefully to arrest by police three
hours later. The Indian participants were released and scheduled for a court
appearance on April 3.[7]

March 28, 1970—Over forty men, women, and children from Indians of All
Tribes, Inc. left Alcatraz to support the Paiute in protecting Pyramid Lake,
Nevada. For over a year, the Paiute had been battling to preserve the lake,
which was rapidly drying up as a result of an agreement between California and Nevada to divert the Truckee River to aid prosperous ranches and
farms in the Fallon, Nevada, area. The Department of the Interior refused
to take any action to preserve the lake, in part because it favored the rights
of white farmers to whom the department had given portions of the Paiute
tribal lands years earlier. This was precisely the nature of tribal grievances that Indians of All Tribes, Inc. hoped to publicize through the Alcatraz
occupation. The caravan to Pyramid Lake made headlines throughout
California and showed that tribal grievances would no longer be expressed
by isolated voices but would be supported by pan-Indian groups. Indians
brought water from Alcatraz in a symbolic gesture of support.[8]

April 2, 1970—Native American occupiers stormed the east gate at Fort Lawton and again entered the post. This was the day scheduled for the preliminary hearings of the Indians who had occupied Fort Lawton on March 8
and 15. Fifteen more Indians were arrested and held for arraignment, including some from the Alcatraz occupation. Charges against the group were
later dismissed. Through the continued efforts of the United Indians of All
Tribes, Fort Lawton was awarded to the Indians in 1971 to be used as an
Indian cultural center. Bernie Whitebear said in 1990, "Alcatraz was very
much a catalyst to our occupation here. We saw what could be achieved
there, and if it had not been for their determined effort on Alcatraz, there
would have been no movement here. We would like to think that Alcatraz
lives on in part through Fort Lawton."[9]

May 1, 1970—Pomo Indians moved onto Mu-Do-N (Rattlesnake Island) near
Clear Lake, California, ancient burial ground and village site of the El-Em
Pomo. The Pomo staked their ancestral claim to the island's sixty-four
acres: "Our people are buried here." When the Pomo declared their inten-
tion to stay on the island, representatives from the Boise-Cascade Lumber
Company appeared on the scene, claimed the island, and stated that they

were going to subdivide it and erect a vacation condominium complex. Indians of All Tribes, Inc. visited the Pomo and discussed the occupation. Boise-Cascade initially demanded that the Native Americans leave but later relented and allowed them to remain "for the time being."[10] Phillip White Eagle, a reservation Indian from Rosebud, South Dakota, who had participated in the Alcatraz occupation, said that "Indians have rights and are making a broadening effort to call attention to that fact."[11] The *San Francisco Chronicle* called the protest "an Alcatraz-style invasion."[12]

May 1, 1970—Pomo Indians and their supporters occupied a surplus army radio-transmitter base near Middletown, California. The occupation force, including Indians from Alcatraz Island, hoped to reclaim a 640–acre site for housing and an educational, cultural, and health center. Sheriff's deputies cut off communications and supplies to the occupiers and arrested them on May 2 and 3 on charges of trespassing and entering and occupying government property. Twelve occupiers were convicted on August 16.[13]

May 9, 1970—Approximately seventy Native Americans from the St. Regis Indian Reservation occupied Stanley Island in the St. Lawrence River. Members of the Mohawk Nation of the Six Nations Iroquois Confederacy nailed a No Trespassing sign to a tree, thus reclaiming the island complete with nine-hole golf course. The occupiers pitched tents, built a bonfire, and stated that they planed to stay indefinitely. The occupiers asserted that at no time had the title to Stanley Island been sold or leased to the U.S. government. Eight days later this occupation was extended to include Loon Island, which protestors claimed had been illegally squatted on by white recreation seekers.

June 7, 1970—Police raided the "Chicago American Indian Village," a tent city behind Wrigley Field where Indians were protesting a lack of services for Indians in Chicago and showing their solidarity with Indians of All Tribes, Inc. Following the raid, the protesters moved to and were evicted from an abandoned apartment building, a county park, the Argonne National Laboratory, and a Nike site at Belmont Harbor, Illinois.

June 1970—Pit River Indians headed for Lassen National Forest to declare the land their own. Richard Oakes brought supporters from Alcatraz Island to assist in the occupation. The caravan was met at the entrance to the forest by sheriff's deputies, local police, and U.S. marshals armed with riot equipment and shotguns. Not wishing any violence, the leaders turned the caravan around and headed for the secondary goal, the Pacific Gas and Electric Company (PG&E) camp at Big Bend, California, where the company owned 52,000 acres of land the Indians claimed were stolen from them in 1853. "We are the rightful and legal owners of the land," declared a young Indian named Mickey Gemmill. "Therefore, we reclaim all the resourceful land that has traditionally been ours with the exception of that owned by private individuals." On June 6 the Pit River Indians occupied the fully equipped and very comfortable private campground and cabins. Many of the Pit River Indians became frightened when they were tailed from Mount Lassen to Big Bend, and the ones that stuck it out were primarily supporters from Alcatraz, including Oakes, Grace Thorpe, and Buffy St. Marie. On the second day of the occupation U.S. marshals, "armed to the teeth," told the occupiers that they must leave.[14] In response, the Native Americans informed the marshals that they were trespassing on Indian land and that they, not the Indians, should leave. Eighty-two marshals responded with Black Marias and M-16s. Eighty women and twenty-six men were arrested for trespassing and willingly went to jail. Indian lawyers made motions to dismiss the charges, but the first two groups of protestors tried were convicted. When the third case was removed to Sacramento, the third group was acquitted in June 1971. Following their acquittal, Pit River Indians went back to the PG&E campgrounds and more were peacefully arrested. Later, the Pit River Indians returned to Lassen National Forest, where twenty-two were arrested on charges of building a fire without a permit. The government let the case drag on in the hope that the whole matter would cool down. The Pit River Nation was not about to let things be forgotten. Leaders announced that they would claim and occupy their ancestral lands and continue to do so until the land was returned.

Late June 1970—Prompted by the success of the Alcatraz occupation, two hundred Native American men and women seized a lighthouse in Hiawatha National Forest in Michigan.

August 1, 1970—Puyallup Indians set up a camp on the Puyallup River in Washington State and began fishing to reestablish their tribal fishing rights guaranteed under the 1854 Medicine Creek Treaty. Approximately sixty Indians and their sympathizers were arrested following a confrontation with law enforcement officers. Tacoma police used tear gas and state game officials wielded clubs to disperse the occupiers.

August 24, 1970—Members of United Native Americans, led by Lehman Brightman from the University of California at Berkeley, established a camp at Mount Rushmore to publicize Lakota claims to the Black Hills. The protesters had moved from an earlier vigil at Badlands National Monument to protest the failure of the U.S. government to return 123,000 acres of Indian land that was taken during World War II for a gunnery range. Protest powwows were held and picket lines were formed at the entrance to the Mount Rushmore memorial to advise visitors of the many injustices to American Indians, specifically the illegal taking of the Black Hills from the Lakota. Native Americans from the Minnesota National Indian Education Conference assisted in strategy and publicity for the Lakota claim. Approximately thirty protesters, including a traditional group called the Oglala Sioux Tribe, occupied the top of Mount Rushmore while an additional thirty-five, including representatives from Indians of All Tribes, Inc., occupied the lower campground. The occupiers were met by armed employees of the U.S. Park Service, but an Indian supervisor from the Badlands National Monument was brought in to negotiate a peaceful end to the occupation.

Summer 1970—More than sixty Indian nations from across North America met in Washington State where the Nisqually, Puyallup, and Muckelshoot Indians were battling the federal government and the state of Washington over fishing rights. The meeting was called the North American Indian Unity Convention.

October 7, 1970—Two Forest Service signs in Carson National Forest were blown up by plastic explosives to protest the development of a "ranger bill" for Taos Blue Lake. Days later a second bombing occurred. The proposed ranger bill was defeated, and Taos Blue Lake was returned to the Taos Indian people.

October 1970—Pit River Indians and other Indian supporters, many from Alcatraz Island, occupied a site at the Four Corners area near Burney, California. The Native Americans erected a Quonset hut and began cutting trees for building a shelter when approximately eighty federal officers, sheriff's deputies, and forestry employees appeared on the scene. Armed with mace, clubs, shotguns, and automatic rifles, the troops surrounded the camp. The Indians were building the camp as temporary housing while they were attending the trials stemming from the June 1970 occupation of PG&E lands. Peter Blue Cloud described the battle:

> As forest workers and officers moved toward the Quonset hut to tear it down, all hell broke loose, as the protectors of the law waded into the Pit River people, spraying mace, and breaking heads, swinging clubs and striking even those who already lay unconscious. . . . Rifle butts were smashed into heads and mace filled the air. Indian women shouted and cried out in anger. Arrests were made again, but officers had to fight every inch of the way, as Indian fists and wooden clubs sought to defend a people's right. A hundred-year-old woman of the tribe looked at the destruction the police had created and said, "I hope the white men are proud."[15]

Coyote, another of the young Indians who defended himself and went to jail, recalled that "the day was bloody." He remembers best the slow, painful ride from a Susanville jail to Sacramento with three other handcuffed Native Americans squashed into the back of a police car without handles on the doors.[16]

On June 14, 1971, only seven of the thirty-six Indian people arrested at the PG&E camp were convicted on 14 of 108 counts of occupying federal buildings and received probation. On March 30, 1972, five Native Americans charged with assaulting federal marshals during the Battle of Four Corners were found innocent. Charges against the remaining thirty-three were dropped because of a lack of evidence.[17]

October 1970—Sioux activists established a protest camp at Badlands National Monument in South Dakota. The land had been a traditional religious ceremonial ground before the government took over Sheep Mountain to use as a bombing area. The occupiers set up twenty-three teepees and were accompanied by representatives from Alcatraz Island.[18]

November 3, 1970—In an official ceremony Sol Elson, director of the Department of Housing, Education, and Welfare Office of Surplus Property, presented the title of a former Army communications base near Davis, California, to David Risling, a Hoopa Indian. The square mile of the Central Valley had become available for use by nonprofit organizations and the word was out that the University of California at Davis was going to get the land for primate research and rice farming despite its incomplete application. American Indian activists, including Grace Thorpe and other Alcatraz occupiers, climbed over the fence, raised a large white teepee, and claimed the land.

November 3, 1970—Two dozen activists, including Indians from Alcatraz Island, occupied a former CIA listening post used in the 1950s to monitor foreign broadcasts. The Native Americans were removed from the government property near Santa Rosa, California, on November 6 and five were arrested for trespassing. Richard Oakes participated in the strategy planning session for the occupation. Title to the land was ultimately transferred to the Pomo Indians, and the Ya-Ka-Ma "Our Land" American Indian Learning Center was established.[19]

November 4, 1970—Twelve Native Americans occupied the former Foreign Broadcast Information Service Monitoring Station at Healdsburg, California. All but four of the Indians left the property when requested by the sheriff. Indians from Alcatraz Island participated in the occupation. Aubrey Grossman, San Francisco attorney for Indians of All Tribes, Inc., appeared as the protestors' attorney.[20]

November 22, 1970—Richard Oakes was arrested after he stopped motorists driving through a Pomo Indian reservation and charged them a toll. The *San Francisco Chronicle* labeled Oakes "a leader of last year's invasion of Alcatraz" and reported that he had "allegedly posted himself, armed with a rifle, at Skagg's Springs road, after placing a fallen tree part way across the road. A sign was posted there, reading: Stop pay toll ahead—$1.00 This is Indian land." California Highway Patrol officers arrested Oakes on investigation of armed robbery but later released him from jail on his own recognizance when he agreed to a moratorium on his toll charges.[21]

November 24, 1970—Seven young Native Americans were arrested on trespassing charges in a confrontation with authorities at the federal broadcast station near the Wohler Bridge in California. The Indians, four of whom were Alcatraz occupiers, were arrested after being warned to leave the federal property, which was leased to John Gondola, a private citizen. The occupation group claimed a right to the land under an 1865 treaty.[22]

November 25, 1970—Twenty-two dollars was collected at the toll crossing on the Kashia Reservation near Stewart's Point–Skaggs Springs Road and Tin Barn Road, California. Felony robbery charges against Richard Oakes were reduced to obstructing a public roadway. Oakes was one of some twenty Indians, including his stepsons Thorn and Jon Marrufo, who barricaded the road protesting the illegal taking of Pomo land at Stewart's Point.

November 26, 1970—Members of the American Indian Movement, led by Russell Means, seized control of the *Mayflower II* in Plymouth, Massachusetts.[23] Means and members of twenty-five Indian tribes proclaimed Thanksgiving a national day of mourning to protest the taking of Native American lands by white colonists. Acknowledging the occupation of Alcatraz Island as the symbol of a newly awakened desire of the Indians for unity and authority in a white world, the demonstrators buried Plymouth Rock under several inches of sand. This occupation was the first move by AIM to extend its activism onto the national scene and soon the names Means, Banks, and Bellecourt were synonymous with AIM and Indian activism.

December 27, 1970—Approximately one hundred Indian people, including representatives from Indians of All Tribes, Inc., occupied the Southwest Museum in Los Angeles, California, for five hours to protest the sacrilegious display of sacred objects and to condemn further archaeological expeditions on Indian land. The most objectionable displays were that of a Native American burial ground containing human bones and two displays featuring a medicine bag and a Cheyenne scalp. One group of young men and women entered the museum auditorium and locked themselves inside with chains and padlocks. Twelve were arrested and convicted on misdemeanor trespassing charges. Carl Dentzel, director of the Southwest Museum, reported that no damage had been done to the facility and agreed to meet with the protesters and review the policy of the museum regarding display of Indian remains and sacred objects.

January 19, 1971—While sleeping by the riverbank near the Puyallup River in Washington State, Hank Adams, a fishing rights activist, was shot by two white vigilantes. Police implied that Adams had shot himself in an effort to gain publicity for the fishing rights cause. Witnesses at the scene stated that two white men muttering obscenities about Indians strode up to Adams, jammed a rifle into his stomach, and pulled the trigger. Adams went on to be a key player in the 1972 caravan to Washington, D.C., to take over the BIA building. Adams was also instrumental in founding the Survival of American Indians Association. He also chaired a committee that had framed a fifteen-point program for a new national policy "to remove the human needs and aspirations of Indian tribes and Indian people from the working of the general American political system and to reinstate a system of bilateral relationships between Indian tribes and the federal government."[24] These fifteen points would later become the foundation for a set of twenty demands presented during the Trail of Broken Treaties.

February 16, 1971—Fifty Native Americans marched from the University of Washington in Seattle to a BIA office to protest the withdrawal of support for Indian use of a portion of Fort Lawton as a multipurpose Indian cultural, educational, and recreational center. The group moved into the BIA office, where they met with William Murdoch, acting director of the Washington state BIA office.

April 2, 1971—The federal government formally turned the title of the former army communications base, the site of a November 3, 1970, protest, to the trustees of the planned Deganawida-Quetzalcoatl University (DQU). Trustees had initiated a court action to halt the transfer of the facility to the University of California at Davis, which did not have a complete application for use of the site. After the suit was filed, the California university withdrew its application. After the formal transfer, the Indians and Chicanos/Chicanas held a powwow and victory celebration. The White House felt that transfer of the title and subsequent establishment of DQU fulfilled the demands of the Alcatraz occupiers for an Indian university.[25]

May 16, 1971—An intertribal group occupied an abandoned naval air station near Minneapolis. Members of AIM and other Indian organizations and tribes cited the Sioux Treaty of 1868 as their authority, just as the Indian occupiers of Alcatraz Island had in 1964. The five-day occupation ended on May 21 when a force of approximately eighty-five persons, including U.S. marshals, carrying riot sticks moved onto the air base. During the occupation, the Native Americans formed a governing structure and security system similar to those on Alcatraz and issued a petition to the federal government similar to those of Indians of All Tribes, Inc.[26]

May 26, 1971—Pit River Indians and others joined a group of Wintu Indians in occupying the sixty-one-acre surplus Toyon Job Corps Center near Redding, California. They claimed that the site was suited to a number of uses by Indian people, including housing. The occupiers reached a settlement with the BIA that the center would be turned over to Native Americans in two years, during which time the Shasta Community Action Project would administer and maintain the land.[27]

May 1971—Members of AIM occupied the Twin Cities Naval Air Station near Minneapolis, citing the Sioux Treaty of 1868. Unlike earlier occupations of vacant land, this protest disrupted naval operations at the facility. A U.S. marshal special operations group attempted to evict the occupiers, who retreated to and barricaded the base theater. When the government forces broke into the theater, the protesters fought back with clubs, knives, and other weapons.[28]

June 11, 1971—The nineteen-month occupation of Alcatraz Island came to an end when government forces removed six men, four women, and five children from the island.

June 14, 1971—Approximately fifty Native Americans entered and occupied an abandoned Nike missile base in the Berkeley Hills overlooking San Francisco Bay. The occupiers settled in and announced their intention to remain on the base and called for the establishment of a liberation supply line. Early on the morning of June 17 prison buses, park rangers, marked and unmarked police cars, and army trucks loaded with some 170 members of the 30th Military Police Battalion descended. The occupiers, many belonging to Indians of All Tribes, Inc., were forcefully evicted without major incident.[29]

June 15, 1971—Approximately forty Indians demonstrated in front of the federal office building in San Francisco, protesting their eviction from Alcatraz Island. No attempt was made by any of the demonstrators to enter FBI space. No arrests were made. Many of the protesters had been participants in the Alcatraz occupation.

June 1971—A group of Native Americans including Tom Cook (Mohawk), the assistant editor of *Akwesasne Notes*, a student, and a former ironworker, threatened to hold the Statue of Liberty hostage in a protest demanding better treatment for American Indians. Speaking of the possibility of a Statue of Liberty protest Laurence Hauptman, in *The Iroquois Struggle for Survival*, states, "The Events at Alcatraz were a major turning point in the history of Indian activism. The takeover at Alcatraz became the symbol to many young, disillusioned Indians like Oakes, stimulating a rash of similar protests."[30]

July 7, 1971—Deganawida-Quetzalcoatl University officially opened with the help of Ford Foundation and federal grants totaling $300,000 that were used to convert ten military buildings. Grace Thorpe, a participant in the Alcatraz occupation, taught a seminar on surplus land and described the class as instruction in "securing surplus land for education and health purposes."

July 1971—The Pit River Nation took back a 900–acre tract near Big Bend, which PG&E claimed had been used as collateral on bank loans. The Pit River Indians constructed a round house and other structures and planted gardens on the land. PG&E filed suit against the Pit River tribe on September 22, seeking clear title. The Pit River tribe had previously filed suit in Shasta County Superior Court on June 15, 1971, seeking return of 53,000 acres of PG&E-held land and had petitioned the Federal Power Commission to refuse renewal of PG&E's licenses to operate dams on the Pit River.[31]

August 14, 1971—A group of approximately twenty-five members of AIM seized an abandoned Coast Guard lifeboat station during a predawn raid at McKinley Beach in Milwaukee, claiming a right to the property under the Sioux Treaty of 1868. AIM leaders stated that they had come in peace but would be removed only by force. The occupiers set up a community school attended by seventy students and a halfway house to serve alcoholics and former convicts. Additionally, the occupiers wanted to establish a center with programs to meet the educational, housing, employment, and health needs of their people. This was only the second attempt by AIM to expand beyond its role as an urban Indian protection organization.

August 1971—Approximately one hundred Onondaga, Oneida, Mohawk, and Tuscarora Indians went to Interstate Eighty-One in New York State, south of Onondaga Reservation lands, and sat down to protest the widening of the interstate, claiming that the initial treaty with the United States was illegal and, in any case, did not allow for additions to the roadway. The state agreed to abandon plans for the construction of an acceleration lane on Native American lands, to drop charges against those arrested, and to consult with the Council of Chiefs at all stages of the highway improvement project.

Summer 1971—A group called Indians of All Tribes traveled from San Francisco to Wounded Knee for a Sun Dance being performed by Wallace Black Elk, John Lame Deer, and Leonard Crow Dog. These young Indians had taken part in the occupation of Alcatraz Island. This was the unification of former members of Indians of All Tribes, Inc. with the American Indian Movement, now recognized as a national Indian activist organization.[32]

September 27, 1971—A group of approximately forty American Indians from the Denver chapter of AIM protested against scientific studies of Indian remains by occupying the anthropology department at Colorado State University and symbolically arresting an anthropology professor and eleven students. Led by Clyde Bellecourt, the protesters demonstrated against the disturbance of Native American remains and the committing of sacrilege upon the sacred grounds of Indian people. Bellecourt called the anthropologists "grave-robbers" and informed reporters that the Indians were determined to reclaim the bones of their ancestors, at which time other protesters entered the anthropology laboratory, grabbed the skeletal remains, and fled the scene. Bellecourt demanded that Colorado State University cease all further anthropology digs, surrender all remains, and refrain from charging the protesters.

September 1971—Twenty-four Indian youths were arrested while attempting to occupy the Washington, D.C., office of the BIA. Russell Means, an Oglala Sioux, led a delegation of approximately thirty-six men and women from AIM and the National Indian Youth Council to serve a citizen's arrest warrant on deputy BIA commissioner John O. Crow. The protesters contended that Crow was aligned with others in the Department of the Interior hostile to Indian rights and had been responsible for the demotion of several young BIA executives who were militant leaders in the Indian community. BIA commissioner Louis R. Bruce met with the occupiers and arranged for the charges against them to be dropped. Bruce stated that he wanted the BIA headquarters to be a meeting place where Native Americans could come anytime.

February 19, 1972—Pit River Indians went back to the Four Corners area and again occupied the site. No action was taken by authorities to remove them, even when tents, teepees, and round houses were erected. By mid-April the group had voluntarily moved on to more suitable sites to plant gardens.

March 8, 1972—Hundreds of American Indians demonstrated in front of the capitol steps in Sacramento, California, calling for a state investigation into the fatal shooting of a twenty-year-old Indian in December 1969. Tom Ferris, a student at UCLA, was shot to death in a Willow Creek bar by a white bartender. The grand jury did not return an indictment, and the demonstrators called for a more thorough investigation of the incident.[33]

March 11, 1972—A group of protesters occupied the three-hundred-year-old Spanish Mission in Jolon, California, claiming title to the mission and at the same time claiming title to all twenty-one missions in California under terms of a statue dating back to August 17, 1773. The church served the Indians with an eviction notice, but no plans were made for a forceful removal.

Spring 1972—At a convention of tribal leaders held at Cass Lake, Minnesota, AIM leaders openly condemned tribal councils for letting European Americans and BIA officials exploit tribal resources, especially the Chippewa Lakes. With guns ready and roads into the convention center blocked, AIM leaders demanded that the Chippewa Tribal Council take a militant stand strong enough to intimidate the surrounding non-Indians into accepting tribal control of the fishing areas.

August 2, 1972—AIM met in national conference at Pine Ridge, South Dakota. Major organizational and personnel changes were initiated to create a national unified organization. Called by AIM state coordinators, the conference resulted in a strong move to avoid the problems of factionalism that often beset Native American organizations and to keep the AIM movement relevant to current issues. George Mitchell of the Berkeley chapter and Clyde Bellecourt, the Denver chapter director, were appointed national codirectors. Dennis Banks and Rob Petite, who had been prominent in AIM leadership, were relieved of their duties. AIM took on the organizational structure that continues to the present day.

September 13, 1972—Angry Oklahoma Indians took over a federal office in Pawnee for two hours in a dispute with federal and state officials over ed-

ucational funds. John Trudell, one of the leaders of the 1969 Alcatraz occupation, stated that the Indians won a clear-cut victory when government
officials agreed to freeze all federal funds while an investigation and rene-
gotiation of disbursements of funds, requested by the occupiers, was undertaken.[34]

October–November 1972—Over five hundred protesters participated in the
"Trail of Broken Treaties." The idea for the march began at the Sioux Rosebud Reservation in 1972 as an attempt to sensitize the Republican and
Democratic parties to the problems faced by Native Americans. Although
many people supported the idea of such a march, a catalyst was needed to
spur its planning. On September 21, 1972, Richard Oakes was shot to death
by a YMCA guard in northern California. AIM leaders including Russell
Means, Hank Adams, and Sid Mills held a press conference in Seattle to
denounce the murder. One week later approximately fifty Indians gathered
at the New Albany Hotel in Denver to formalize plans for a pilgrimage to
Washington, D.C. Some would come from the West Coast; those from the
Southeast would follow the Cherokee Trail of Tears; the Sioux passed by
Wounded Knee, the sight of the massacre in 1890. When the caravan arrived in Washington and found that the accommodations promised them
were not available, the group moved to the BIA headquarters building. On
November 2, in a disagreement over housing and food provisions, members of the Trail of Broken Treaties occupied and barricaded the BIA building and presented a list of twenty civil rights demands that had been drawn
up during the march. Native Americans occupied the BIA building for seven
days. Eventually, the government promised to review the demands, refrain
from making arrests, and pay the Indians' expenses home. The occupation
was a great moral victory for the Indians, who faced white America as a
united people. The two government negotiators were Brad Patterson and
Leonard Garment, who had overseen the Alcatraz negotiations. While
many of the Alcatraz occupiers participated in the Trail of Broken Treaties, the march was directed by AIM and the National Indian Youth Council. Other sponsoring groups included the National Indian Brotherhood of
Canada, Survival of American Indians Association, National American Indian Council, Native American Rights Fund, National Council on Indian
Work, American Indian Commission of Alcohol and Drug Abuse, and
National Indian Leadership Training.

February 6, 1973—Approximately two hundred American Indian people arrived in Custer, South Dakota, to protest the murder of Wesley Bad Heart
Bull, a twenty-year-old Oglala from the Pine Ridge Reservation. Bad Heart
Bull was stabbed to death on January 21 by Darrell Schmitz, a thirty-year-
old white man. Schmitz was charged with second-degree manslaughter, the
weakest charge possible, even though there were four witnesses to the stab-

bing. Russell Means and four other AIM members led the unarmed protest. Sarah Bad Heart Bull, mother of Wesley, was grabbed, choked, beaten, and arrested by police when she attempted to identify the four witnesses to her son's slaying. Native Americans who tried to come to her assistance were attacked with clubs, tear gas, mace, and water hoses and were also arrested.

February 6, 1973—Indian demonstrators stormed the courthouse in Custer, South Dakota, to protest the charge of second-degree manslaughter filed against Darrell Schmitz for the murder of Wesley Bad Heart Bull. Insisting that the charge should have been one of murder, the protesters set the courthouse and an unoccupied chamber of commerce building on fire. Several hundred members of the National Guard were called to active duty to restore peace in the area.

February 27, 1973—A group of two hundred Native Americans, led by AIM and supported by Alcatraz occupiers, congregated at the site of the 1890 Wounded Knee Massacre to demonstrate against Richard (Dicky) Wilson, the council head of the Pine Ridge Reservation, whom they charged with corrupt practices. The Sioux traditionalists, who did not accept the government as represented by Wilson, had actually called AIM for help when Wilson and his Government of the Oglala Nation (GOON) squads began beatings and shootings to enforce Wilson's rule. Tensions between the protesters and the local authorities grew until the situation became a siege of the town that drew in two hundred Indians from around the area and lasted for seventy-one days. The occupiers were surrounded by three hundred federal marshals and FBI agents equipped with armored personnel carriers, M-16s, automatic infantry weapons, chemical weapons, steel helmets, gas masks, body armor, illuminating flares, military clothing, and almost unlimited rations. The army's 82d Airborne Division provided leadership and logistical support for the government "peace-keeping" force. On March 12 the occupiers declared Wounded Knee a sovereign territory of the new Oglala Sioux Nation according to the Laramie Treaty of 1868, which recognized the Sioux as an independent nation. The siege finally ended on the morning of May 8 when the two sides began firing on each other and two Indians, Frank Clearwater and Lawrence (Buddy) Lamont, were shot and killed, an act that called national attention to the Native American civil rights movement. Two hundred and thirty-seven arrests were made and thirty-five weapons were confiscated.

June 30–August 3, 1973—AIM held its annual convention in Whiteoak, Oklahoma, and elected new officers. Vernon Bellecourt was designated international director, Dennis Banks became national director, Clyde Bellecourt and Russell Means were selected to be members of the board of directors, and Carter Camp became the new national chair. Camp was accused of attempting to shoot Clyde Bellecourt on August 27 and was replaced by John Trudell.

June 8–16, 1974—Nearly three thousand Native Americans attended the International Treaty Council in Mobridge, South Dakota. Earlier AIM held a meeting in Cumberland, Wisconsin, to work out its new direction, identify its internal strengths, and set its priorities. John Trudell spoke of changes he felt were necessary for AIM to take its place in the lives of all Native Americans. The experience Trudell gained during the prolonged occupation of Alcatraz Island can be seen in his speech:

> Commitment is just about the number one thing to think about.
>   We've got to have commitment so strong that when we get mad at each other, we overlook it.
>   We've got to have commitment so strong that we don't take no for an answer.
>   We've got to have commitment so strong that we will not accept their rhetoric and lies for an answer.
>   We've got to have commitment so strong we will live and we will die for our people.[35]

1974—A group of Mohawk Indians occupied Eagle Bay at Moss Lake in the Adirondacks, claiming original title and founding Ganienkey, the "Land of Flintstone."

January 1–February 4, 1975—The Alexian Brothers Roman Catholic novitiate in Gresham, Wisconsin, was occupied by members of the Menominee tribe of Wisconsin. The Menominee intended to use the novitiate as a tribal hospital. Although the order offered to deed the novitiate to the Menominee, the offer was withdrawn on July 10 when representatives from the tribe stated that the acceptance of the property would impose a tremendous financial burden. Ada Deer, speaking for the Menominee, said that the buildings and land were virtually useless to the Menominee. Deer and other Menominee expressed deep concern when representatives from AIM entered into the negotiations and excluded the Menominee tribal council.

February 24–March 3, 1975—AIM members led an Indian occupation force of thirty-six to the Fairchild Camera and Instrument Company in Shiprock. The occupiers protested the company's practice of laying off underpaid Indian women for trying to protect themselves by forming a union. The occupation force declared the plant to be AIM property until a series of demands had been met that included the rehearing of 140 laid-off workers. A final agreement ending the occupation called for a tribal council pledge to seek reinstatement of the dismissed workers, a civil rights investigation for employees recently terminated, and a U.S. General Accounting Office audit of on-the-job program payments to Fairchild. AIM spokesperson John Trudell participated in the occupation, proclaimed the occupation a success, and stated that Fairchild could no longer openly and quietly exploit Native Americans.

June 26, 1975—A shoot-out occurred on the Pine Ridge reservation in South Dakota between AIM and the FBI that resulted in the death of two FBI agents, Jack Coler and Ronald Williams, and one Indian man, Joseph Stuntz. Following the incident the FBI reported that the agents had been ambushed from sophisticated bunkers as they attempted to serve arrest warrants and were riddled with bullets. An FBI representative in Washington told reporters, "We're going to make sure that the people who killed our agents don't get out of there."[36] Leonard Peltier was later charged and convicted of the murder of the FBI agents and is presently serving two life sentences in prison. The original reports that the two agents were ambushed and killed with repeated blasts of gunfire were later found to be inflammatory, distorted, and inaccurate. Officials later admitted that the initial reports were false and that exactly what had happened was unclear.

Notes

1. Blue Cloud, *Alcatraz*, 56.

2. "Army Posts Near Seattle 'Invaded,'" *San Francisco Chronicle*, Mar. 9, 1970.

3. Blue Cloud, *Alcatraz*, 57.

4. Ibid.

5. "The Angry American Indian: Starting down the Protest Trail," *Time*, Feb. 9, 1970, "America's Indians: Reawakening of a Conquered People," *Look*, June 2, 1970, quoted in Richard DeLuca "We Hold the Rock."

6. "Indian Assault of Ellis Island Foiled," *San Francisco Examiner*, Mar. 16, 1970.

7. "Twelve Indians Arrested in Alameda Protest," *Oakland Tribune*, Mar. 24, 1970.

8. Blue Cloud, *Alcatraz*, 62–63. Byron Harvey recorded on February 22, 1970, that the Indians on Alcatraz had discussed supporting Pyramid Lake. Students at the University of California at Berkeley and San Francisco State University were particularly interested in saving Pyramid Lake from being drained. According to Harvey, "Alcatraz serves as a center for other Indian concerns" (27).

9. Blue Cloud, *Alcatraz*, 56.

10. Ibid., 86–87.

11. "Indians 'Reclaim' Clear Lake Island," *San Francisco Examiner*, May 22, 1970.

12. "Indian Sit-In on Island in Clear Lake," *San Francisco Chronicle*, May 19, 1970.

13. Blue Cloud, *Alcatraz*, 86.

14. "Thirty-Four Indians Held for Trespassing," *Oakland Tribune*, June 7, 1970.

15. Ibid., 93.

16. Ibid., 89–92. See also "Thirty-four Indians Held for Trespassing," *Oakland Tribune*, June 7, 1970; "Pit Indians Keep Up Their Needling Tactics," *San Francisco Examiner*, June 29, 1970; and "Indian Flag Aloft," *San Francisco Chronicle*, June 27, 1970.

17. Blue Cloud, *Alcatraz*, 94.

18. *Indians of All Tribes Newsletter* 1, no. 4 (July 1970): 9.

19. "Culture and Carnivores Grow in These California Gardens," *Contra Costa Times*, June 13, 1992. See also "Indians Ousted, Plan New Takeover Strategy," *Press Democrat*, Nov. 8, 1970.

20. Hannon, memorandum to Patterson, Nov. 20, 1970.

21. "Oakes Freed after Jailing over Tolls," *San Francisco Chronicle*, Nov. 23, 1970.

22. "New Indian Takeover but Seven Arrested," *Press Democrat*, Nov. 25, 1970.

23. Matthiessen, *In the Spirit*, 38. Matthiessen states that "AIM had caught the imagination of young Indians in a way that the earlier activist groups had not, and soon AIM organizers and local partisans were turning up at demonstrations from coast to coast" (37).

24. Cohen, *Treaties on Trial*, 81.

25. In an April 19, 1971, letter to Robert Coop, San Francisco regional director of HEW, Patterson stated, "I would think that the comparison between Alcatraz and D-Q would start occurring to people in the Bay Area."

26. *Newsletter of the American Indian Movement*, July 15, 1971.

27. Chavers, *Indian Voice*, 30.

28. Calhoun, *Lawmen*, 298.

29. Blue Cloud, *Alcatraz*, 75.

30. Hauptman, *Iroquois Struggle*, 227.

31. Blue Cloud, *Alcatraz*, 94–96.

32. Crow Dog and Erdoes, *Lakota Woman*, 254.

33. "Indian Protest March on Sacramento," *Oakland Tribune*, Mar. 8, 1972.

34. "Indians Seize Federal Office for Two Hours," *Los Angeles Times*, Sept. 14, 1972.

35. *Akwesasne Notes* 6, no. 3 (July 1974): 10.

36. *Akwesasne Notes* 7, no. 3 (Summer 1975): 4.

Bibliography

.M.M.M

Archival Collections

Alcatraz Collection. San Francisco Public Library.

American Indian Historical Research Project. Institute of Indian Studies. University of South Dakota. Vermilion.

American Indian Studies Center Library. University of California at Los Angeles.

Doris Duke Oral History Project. American Indian Historical Research Project. Manuscript 417. Manuscripts Division. Marriott Library. University of Utah. Salt Lake City.

Doris Duke Oral History Project. American Indian Historical Research Project. Special Collections. University of New Mexico at Albuquerque.

Doris Duke Oral History Project. American Indian Historical Research Project. Western History Collections. University of Oklahoma at Norman.

Federal Bureau of Investigation Case Files. Records Section. Federal Bureau of Investigation Headquarters. Pentagon. Washington, D.C.

Golden Gate National Recreation Area Library. Alcatraz Island.

Golden Gate National Recreation Headquarters. Fort Mason. Building 201. San Francisco.

Indians of All Tribes, Inc. Archival Collection. Research Archives. San Francisco Main Library.

Leo J. Ryan Memorial Archives and Records Center. National Archives and Records Administration. Pacific Sierra Region. San Bruno, Calif.

National Archives. Washington, D.C.

Nixon Presidential Materials Project. Alexandria, Va.

Pacifica Radio Archives. North Hollywood, Calif.

Newspapers and Periodicals

Akwesasne Notes
Alameda Times Star
Buffalo Courier Express
Catholic Voice

New York Times
Oakland Press Democrat
Oakland Tribune
San Diego Union

Contra Costa Times
Eugene Register Guard
Hayward Daily Review
Indians of All Tribes Newsletter
Los Angeles Times
Minneapolis Star
Newsletter of the American
  Indian Movement

San Francisco Chronicle
San Francisco Examiner
San Francisco Progress
San Jose Mercury News
Stockton Sunday Record
Sunday Oklahoman
Washington Post

Primary and Secondary Sources

Ablon, Joan. "Cultural Conflict in Urban Indians." *Mental Hygiene* 55, no. 2 (Apr. 1971): 200–205.
———. "Relocated American Indians in the San Francisco Bay Area: Social Interaction and Indian Identity." *Human Organization* 23, no. 4 (Winter 1964): 297–99.
Aitken, Jonathan. *Nixon: A Life.* Washington, D.C.: Regnery, 1993.
Albert, Judith Clavir, and Stewart Edward Albert. *The Sixties Papers: Documents of a Rebellious Decade.* New York: Praeger, 1984.
Alcatraz Post Returns. Microcopy 617, rolls 14–16. RG 291. Leo J. Ryan Memorial Archives and Records Center. National Archives and Records Administration. Pacific Sierra Region. San Bruno, Calif.
Alcatraz Register of Prisoners at the Military Prison, 1870–1879. RG 393. Leo J. Ryan Memorial Archives and Records Center. National Archives and Records Administration. Pacific Sierra Region. San Bruno, Calif.
American Indian Historical Society. Letter to President Richard Nixon. Dec. 25, 1969. White House Central Files, Subject File IN (Oct. 1–Dec. 31, 1969), Box 4. Nixon Presidential Materials Project. Alexandria, Va.
Antell, Judith. "American Indian Women Activists." Ph.D. diss. University of California at Berkeley, 1989.
Arayando, Linda. Interview by John Trudell on "Radio Free Alcatraz." Jan. 5, 1970. Archive no. BB5457. Pacifica Radio Archives. North Hollywood, Calif.
Arquette, Mike. Interview by Michelle Vignes. Dec. 1979. San Francisco. Tape. Alcatraz Island Library. San Francisco, Calif.
Bahr, Howard M. "An End to Invisibility." In *Native Americans Today: Sociological Perspectives,* ed. Howard M. Bahr, Bruce A. Chadwick, and Robert C. Day. New York: Harper and Row, 1972. 407–8.
Bender, Chester R. "Alcatraz Island Aids to Navigation." Memorandum to Executive Director, National Council on Indian Opportunity, Washington, D.C. July 17, 1970. National Council on Indian Opportunity, Box 4, Folder 3. RG 220. National Archives, Washington, D.C.

———. Memorandum. Nov. 23, 1970. Container 15, Folder 4. RG 291. Leo J. Ryan Memorial Archives and Records Center. National Archives and Records Administration. Pacific Sierra Region. San Bruno, Calif.

———. Memorandum to Bradley H. Patterson Jr. Nov. 6, 1970. Alcatraz File Group E. Krogh (1970–71), Box 10. Nixon Presidential Materials Project. Alexandria, Va.

Bill, Joe. Interview by Dennis J. Stanford. Feb. 5, 1970. Transcript. Doris Duke Oral History Project. American Indian Historical Research Project. Special Collections. University of New Mexico at Albuquerque.

Billus, Dick. Interview by John Garvey. Apr. 14, 1987. San Francisco. Tape in the possession of John Garvey, San Francisco, Calif.

Blue Cloud, Peter, ed. *Alcatraz Is Not an Island.* Berkeley: Wingbow Press, 1972.

———. Letter to Urban Indians of New York. Undated. Alcatraz Collection. San Francisco Public Library.

Bomberry, Don. Interview by George J. Brown. Jan. 12, 1971. Doris Duke Oral History Project. American Indian Historical Research Project. Manuscript 417. Manuscripts Division. Marriott Library. University of Utah. Salt Lake City.

Bourke, John G. *On the Border with Crook.* Lincoln: University of Nebraska Press, 1971.

Boyer, Claudine. Interview by author. Dec. 5, 1992. Fort Hall Indian Reservation, Pocatello, Idaho. Tape in the possession of the author.

Boyer, LaNada. Interview by author. Dec. 5, 1992. Fort Hall Indian Reservation, Pocatello, Idaho. Tape in the possession of the author.

———. Interview by John Trudell on "Radio Free Alcatraz." Dec. 24, 1969. Archive no. BB2309. Pacifica Radio Archives. North Hollywood, Calif.

———. Memorandum to Indians of All Tribes, Inc., BANAC, Aubrey Grossman, and Donald Jelinek. Jan. 21, 1970. National Council on Indian Opportunity, Box 4, Folder 2. RG 220. National Archives, Washington, D.C.

Branch, Taylor. *Parting the Waters.* New York: Simon and Schuster, 1988.

Brant, Molly. Chronology of Alcatraz Events. Undated. RG 291. Leo J. Ryan Memorial Archives and Records Center. National Archives and Records Administration. Pacific Sierra Region. San Bruno, Calif.

Brightman, Lehman. Interview by Juanita Curry. Feb. 26, 1970. American Indian Historical Research Project. Institute of Indian Studies. University of South Dakota, Vermilion.

———. "The New Indians." *Warpath* 1, no. 2 (Winter 1968–69): 7.

Brightman, Lehman, and Earl Livermore. Press conference at the Hearings of the San Francisco Human Rights Conference. April 18, 1969. San Francisco, Calif. Transcript. National Council on Indian Opportunity, Box 5, Folder 4. RG 220. National Archives, Washington, D.C.

Brown, George E. Daily Editorial. *Congressional Record.* Dec. 23, 1969. 91st Cong., 1st sess. Vol. 115, no. 30, p. 40991.

———. Daily Editorial. *Congressional Record.* May 5, 1970. 91st Cong., 2d sess. Vol. 116, no. 11, p. 6268.

Cahn, Edgar S. *Our Brother's Keeper: The Indian in White America.* New York: New Community Press, 1969.

Calhoun, Frederick S. *The Lawmen.* Washington, D.C: Smithsonian Institution Press, 1990.

California Indian Legal Services. "How California Was Taken from the Indians: The Law as an Offensive Weapon against a Defenseless People." In *Alcatraz Is Not an Island,* ed. Peter Blue Cloud. Berkeley: Wingbow Press, 1972.

Carroll, Don. Sworn Statement to James P. Southard, GSA special agent. May 28, 1970. San Francisco, Calif. Alcatraz File, Container 12. RG 291. Leo J. Ryan Memorial Archives and Records Center. National Archives and Records Administration. Pacific Sierra Region. San Bruno, Calif.

Castillo, Edward. Interview by author. Nov. 18, 1992. Los Angeles. Transcript in the possession of the author.

———. "A Reminiscence of the Alcatraz Occupation." *American Indian Culture and Research Journal* 18, no. 4 (1994): 16–20. Special edition, edited by Troy Johnson and Joane Nagel.

Champagne, Duane, ed. *Chronology of Native North American History: From Pre-Columbian Times to the Present.* Detroit: Gale Research, 1994.

"A Characterization of the American Indian Movement." Oct. 5, 1973. White House Central Files, American Indian Movement File. Nixon Presidential Materials Project. Alexandria, Va.

Chavers, Dean, ed. *Indian Voice.* Santa Clara, Calif.: Native American Publishing, 1972.

Clark, Ramsey. Letter to the Honorable Edward V. Long, United States Senate. May 15, 1964. Subgroup Alcatraz Disposal, Series Scott 1963–71, Box 1. RG 291. Leo J. Ryan Memorial Archives and Records Center. National Archives and Records Administration. Pacific Sierra Region. San Bruno, Calif.

Cohen, Fay G. *Treaties on Trial: The Continuing Controversy over Northwest Indian Fishing Rights.* Seattle: University of Washington Press, 1986.

Confidential informant. Letter to author. Apr. 25, 1992. Original in the possession of the author.

———. Letter to author. July 31, 1992. Original in the possession of the author.

———. Telephone interview by author. Dec. 13, 1994. San Jose, Calif. Transcript in the possession of the author.

Cornell, Stephen. *The Return of the Native: American Indian Political Resurgence.* New York: Oxford University Press, 1988.

Costo, Rupert. "Alcatraz." *Indian Historian* 3 (Winter 1970): 8–15.

Crook, George. *Resumé of Operations against Apache Indians, 1882 to 1886.* London: Johnson-Tauton Military Press, 1971.

Crow Dog, Mary, and Richard Erdoes. *Lakota Woman.* New York: Harper Perennial, 1991.

Dana, Charles. Interview by Michelle Vignes. Dec. 1970. Alcatraz Island. Tape. Alcatraz Island Library. San Francisco, Calif.

Dawson, Harold K. Letter to President Nixon. Nov. 26, 1969. White House Central Files, Subject File IN (Oct. 1–Dec. 31, 1969), Box 4. Nixon Presidential Materials Project. Alexandria, Va.

Dean, John. Memorandum to Jack Caulfield. Feb. 5, 1971. White House Central Files, Staff Member and Office Files, John W. Dean III, Box 39. Nixon Presidential Materials Project. Alexandria, Va.

Deloria, Vine, Jr. *Behind the Trail of Broken Treaties: An Indian Declaration of Independence.* Austin: University of Texas Press, 1985.

———. *God Is Red.* New York: Laurel, Dell, 1983.

———. Interview by Juanita Curry. Apr. 2, 1970. Transcript. American Indian Research Project. Institute of Indian Studies. University of South Dakota, Vermilion.

DeLuca, Richard. "We Hold the Rock: The Indian Attempt to Reclaim Alcatraz Island." *California History: The Magazine of the California Historical Society* 62, no. 1 (Spring 1983): 14.

Department of Industrial Relations, Division of Fair Employment Practices, State of California. *American Indians in California.* Nov. 1965. Copy in the possession of Adam Nordwall, Shoshone/Bannock Reservation, Fallon, Nev.

Dickover, Joseph W. Memorandum to Admiral Chester R. Bender. Dec. 18, 1970. Alcatraz File Group E. Krogh (1970–71), Box 10. Nixon Presidential Materials Project. Alexandria, Va.

Dzeda, Bruce M., assistant teacher, Head Start. Letter to William H. Warren, GSA. June 18, 1971. Subgroup Alcatraz Disposal, Folder 10. RG 291. Leo J. Ryan Memorial Archives and Records Center. National Archives and Records Administration. Pacific Sierra Region. San Bruno, Calif.

Farb, Peter. *Man's Rise to Civilization as Shown by the Indians of North America from Primeval Time to the Coming of the Industrial State.* New York: Dutton, 1968.

Federal Bureau of Investigation. Case File 70–51261. Subject File "Alcatraz Indian Occupation, 1969–71." Records Section. Federal Bureau of Investigation Headquarters. Pentagon. Washington, D.C.

Feiker, Gretchen. Transcriptions of Notes Taken during GSA Telephone Conversations with the Caretaker of Alcatraz. Feb. 13, 1970. Subgroup Alcatraz Disposal, Box 6, Folder 9. RG 291. Leo J. Ryan Memorial Archives and Records Center. National Archives and Records Administration. Pacific Sierra Region. San Bruno, Calif.

Fixico, Donald. *Termination and Relocation: Federal Indian Policy, 1945–1960.* Albuquerque: University of New Mexico Press, 1986.

Forbes, Jack. "Alcatraz: Symbol and Reality." *California History: The Magazine of the California Historical Society* 62, no. 1 (Spring 1983): 24–25.

———. "Alcatraz: What Its Seizure Means." In *Alcatraz Is Not An Island,* ed. Peter Blue Cloud. Berkeley: Wingbow Press, 1972. 24–25.

———. *Native Americans and Nixon: Presidential Politics and Minority Self-Determination, 1969–1972.* Los Angeles: American Indian Studies Center, University of California, 1981.

Fortunate Eagle, Adam. *Alcatraz! Alcatraz!: The Indian Occupation of 1969–1971.* Berkeley: Heyday Books, 1992.

Garcia, Anthony. "'Home' Is Not a House: Urban Relocation among American Indians." Ph.D. diss. University of California at Berkeley, 1988.

Garment, Leonard. "Indians on Alcatraz." Memorandum to Alcatraz Working Group. Dec. 23, 1969. White House Central Files, Staff Member and Office Files, Bradley H. Patterson Jr., Box 9. Nixon Presidential Materials Project. Alexandria, Va.

———. Memorandum to Bradley H. Patterson Jr. July 8, 1970. White House Central Files, Subject File IN (May 1–July 31, 1970). Nixon Presidential Materials Project. Alexandria, Va.

———. Memorandum to Bradley H. Patterson Jr. Sept. 20, 1971. White House Central Files, Subject File IN (Jan. 1–May 31, 1971), Box 2. Nixon Presidential Materials Project. Alexandria, Va.

———. Memorandum for the File. Dec. 23, 1969. National Council on Indian Opportunity, Box 4, Folder 1. RG 220. National Archives, Washington, D.C.

———. Memorandum to George Schultz and John Ehrlichman. July 28, 1970. White House Central Files, Staff Member and Office Files, E. Krogh (1970–71), Box 10. Nixon Presidential Materials Project. Alexandria, Va.

———. Memorandum to the National Council on Indian Opportunity. Dec. 23, 1969. National Council on Indian Opportunity, Box 4, Folder 1. RG 220. National Archives, Washington, D.C.

———. Memorandum to Spiro Agnew. Feb. 16, 1970. National Council on Indian Opportunity, Box 4, Folder 2. RG 220. National Archives, Washington, D.C.

———. "Outline of a Solution for Alcatraz." Memorandum to John Ehrlichman. Sept. 14, 1970. Alcatraz File Group E. Krogh (1970–71), Box 10. Nixon Presidential Materials Project. Alexandria, Va.

———. Telephone interview by author. July 16, 1992. Transcript in the possession of the author.

Garrison, A. D. "Alcatraz Island: Light and Fog Signal." Memorandum to Commanding Office, USCG Base Yerba Buena Island, Calif. Dec. 5, 1969. Alcatraz File, Container 5. RG 291. Leo J. Ryan Memorial Archives and Records Center. National Archives and Records Administration. Pacific Sierra Region. San Bruno, Calif.

Garvey, John. Telephone interview by author. July 6, 1992. Transcript in the possession of the author.

General Services Administration. "Alcatraz Confidential Daily Observation Reports from Source A and B." General Services Administration Alcatraz Records, Region 9, Box 15. RG 291. Leo J. Ryan Memorial Archives and Records Center. National Archives and Records Administration. Pacific Sierra Region. San Bruno, Calif.

———. "Attempt to Drug Coffee for Mr. Robertson." Report. Apr. 3, 1970. National Council on Indian Opportunity, Box 4, Folder 3. RG 220. National Archives, Washington. D.C.

———. "Chronology—Alcatraz Disposal." Jan. 17, 1971. GJ-Calif-786. Subgroup Alcatraz Disposal, Series Scott 1963–71, Box 13. RG 291. Leo J. Ryan Memorial Archives and Records Center. National Archives and Records Administration. Pacific Sierra Region. San Bruno, Calif.

———. "Confidential Correspondence." General Services Administration Alcatraz Records, Region 9, Box 15, Folder 6. RG 291. Leo J. Ryan Memorial Archives and Records Center. National Archives and Records Administration. Pacific Sierra Region. San Bruno, Calif.

———. "Confidential Report." Mar. 1971. General Services Administration Alcatraz Records, Region 9, Box 15, Folder 6. RG 291. Leo J. Ryan Memorial Archives and Records Center. National Archives and Records Administration. Pacific Sierra Region. San Bruno, Calif.

———. "Indian Occupation and GSA Response." Press Release. Dec. 1, 1969. Subgroup Alcatraz Disposal, Box 15, Folder Alcatraz I. RG 291. Leo J. Ryan Memorial Archives and Records Center. National Archives and Records Administration. Pacific Sierra Region. San Bruno, Calif.

———. "Notes on Operation Parks." Undated. General Services Administration Alcatraz Records, Region 9, Box 10. RG 291. Leo J. Ryan Memorial Archives and Records Center. National Archives and Records Administration. Pacific Sierra Region. San Bruno, Calif.

———. "Preliminary Estimates on the Security of Alcatraz Island." Nov. 26, 1969. GJ-Calif-786. Subgroup Alcatraz Disposal, Box 15, Folder Alcatraz I. RG 291. Leo J. Ryan Memorial Archives and Records Center. National Archives and Records Administration. Pacific Sierra Region. San Bruno, Calif.

———. Press Release. Dec. 11, 1969. Subgroup Alcatraz Disposal, Box 15, Folder Alcatraz I. RG 291. Leo J. Ryan Memorial Archives and Records

Center. National Archives and Records Administration. Pacific Sierra Region. San Bruno, Calif.

———. Press Release. May 27, 1970. "Alcatraz (Press) March '70–August '70" Folder. National Council on Indian Opportunity, Box 5, Folder 4. RG 220. National Archives, Washington, D.C.

Getches, David H., and Charles F. Wilkinson. *Federal Indian Law: Cases and Materials.* 2d ed. American Casebook Series. St. Paul: West, 1986.

Gilbert, Madonna. Interview by Michelle Vignes. Dec. 1970. Tape. Alcatraz Island Library, San Francisco, Calif.

Gordon-McCutchan, R. C. *The Taos Indians and the Battle for Blue Lake.* Santa Fe: Red Crane Books, 1991.

Halloran (first name unknown). Interview by Michelle Vignes. Dec. 1970. Tape. Alcatraz Island Library, San Francisco, Calif.

Hannon, T. E. "Alcatraz." Memorandum for the File. Jan. 18, 1970. File Alcatraz II, Folder 2, File 9A. RG 291. Leo J. Ryan Memorial Archives and Records Center. National Archives and Records Administration. Pacific Sierra Region. San Bruno, Calif.

———. "Alcatraz Incident." Memorandum for the File. Jan. 5, 1970. Alcatraz File, Container 15, Folder 2. RG 291. Leo J. Ryan Memorial Archives and Records Center. National Archives and Records Administration. Pacific Sierra Region. San Bruno, Calif.

———. "Alcatraz Incident." Memorandum for the File. Jan. 6, 1970. Alcatraz File, Container 15, Folder 2. RG 291. Leo J. Ryan Memorial Archives and Records Center. National Archives and Records Administration. Pacific Sierra Region. San Bruno, Calif.

———. "Alcatraz Incident." Memorandum to Richard Laws. Dec. 31, 1969. Box 12, Folder—(Laws). RG 291. Leo J. Ryan Memorial Archives and Records Center. National Archives and Records Administration. Pacific Sierra Region. San Bruno, Calif.

———. "Alcatraz Island." Memorandum for the File. Mar. 23, 1970. GJ-Calif-786. RG 291. Leo J. Ryan Memorial Archives and Records Center. National Archives and Records Administration. Pacific Sierra Region. San Bruno, Calif.

———. Confidential Memorandum for the File. Aug. 8, 1970. File Alcatraz II, Container 15, Folder 2. RG 291. Leo J. Ryan Memorial Archives and Records Center. National Archives and Records Administration. Pacific Sierra Region. San Bruno, Calif.

———. "Indian Invasion of Alcatraz Island." Nov. 11, 1969. Subgroup Alcatraz Disposal, Series Scott 1963–71. RG 291. Leo J. Ryan Memorial Archives and Records Center. National Archives and Records Administration. Pacific Sierra Region. San Bruno, Calif.

———. Letter to John W. Gano, Jan. 20, 1970. National Council on Indian Opportunity, Box 5, Folder 4. RG 220. National Archives, Washington, D.C.

———. Memorandum to Bradley H. Patterson Jr. Nov. 20, 1970. White House Central Files, Bradley H. Patterson Jr., Box 4. Nixon Presidential Materials Project. Alexandria, Va.

———. Memorandum to Bradley H. Patterson Jr. Dec. 11, 1970. White House Central Files, Bradley H. Patterson Jr., Box 4. Nixon Presidential Materials Project. Alexandria, Va.

———. Memorandum to Kenneth C. Robertson. Jan. 6, 1970. File Alcatraz II, Container 15, Folder 2. RG 291. Leo J. Ryan Memorial Archives and Records Center. National Archives and Records Administration. Pacific Sierra Region. San Bruno, Calif.

———. "Report on Alcatraz to White House." Dec. 11, 1969. Container Alcatraz I, Folder 1. RG 291. Leo J. Ryan Memorial Archives and Records Center. National Archives and Records Administration. Pacific Sierra Region. San Bruno, Calif.

Harden, Ross. Interview by C. G. Crampton. July 14, 1970. Doris Duke Oral History Project. American Indian Historical Research Project. Manuscript 417. Manuscripts Division. Marriott Library. University of Utah. Salt Lake City.

Harvey, Byron. *Thoughts from Alcatraz.* Phoenix: Arequipa Press, 1970.

Hauptman, Laurence M. *The Iroquois Struggle for Survival: World War II to Red Power.* New York: Syracuse University Press, 1986.

Hertzberg, Hazel W. *The Search for an American Indian Identity: Modern Pan-Indian Movements.* New York: Syracuse University Press, 1971.

Hickel, Walter J. Letter to Melvin R. Laird. Feb. 24, 1970. National Council on Indian Opportunity, Box 4, Folder 3. RG 220. National Archives, Washington, D.C.

———. Statement for Immediate Release. Nov. 24, 1969. Subgroup Alcatraz Disposal, Box 15, Folder Alcatraz I. RG 291. Leo J. Ryan Memorial Archives and Records Center. National Archives and Records Administration. Pacific Sierra Region. San Bruno, Calif.

Hill, Jerry. Telephone interview by author. June 3, 1994. Transcript in the possession of the author.

"History in Brief—Alcatraz Island." Memorandum. June 9, 1970. RG 291. Leo J. Ryan Memorial Archives and Records Center. National Archives and Records Administration. Pacific Sierra Region. San Bruno, Calif.

Horse Capture, George P. "An American Indian Perspective." In *Seeds of Change,* ed. Herman J. Viola and Carolyn Margolis. Washington, D.C: Smithsonian Press, 1991. 188–89.

Houchins, Corbin R. Letter to anonymous Indian leader. Nov. 13, 1969. Copy in Alcatraz File. American Indian Studies Center Library. University of California at Los Angeles.

Howard, James. Memorandum to Bud Krogh. Feb. 5, 1971. Alcatraz File Group E. Krogh (1970–71), Box 10. Nixon Presidential Materials Project. Alexandria, Va.

———. Memorandum to Bud Krogh. Mar. 2, 1971. Alcatraz File Group E. Krogh (1970–71), Box 10. Nixon Presidential Materials Project. Alexandria, Va.

———. "Pan-Indian Culture of Oklahoma." *Scientific Monthly*. Nov. 1955. 215–20.

Hullin, Tod R. Memorandum to E. Krogh. Feb. 5, 1971. Alcatraz File Group E. Krogh (1970–71), Box 10. Nixon Presidential Materials Project. Alexandria, Va.

———. Memorandum to E. Krogh. Mar. 2, 1971. Alcatraz File Group E. Krogh (1970–71), Box 10. Nixon Presidential Materials Project. Alexandria, Va.

Iashi (last name unknown). Interview by Michelle Vignes. Dec. 1970. San Francisco. Tape. Alcatraz Island Library. San Francisco, Calif.

Igler, David. "This Land Is My Land: The Indian Occupation of Alcatraz, 1969–1971." Ms. History Department, University of California at Berkeley, 1990.

Indians of All Tribes. Articles of Incorporation. Jan. 15, 1970. American Indian Studies Center Library. University of California at Los Angeles.

———. Letter to Bernadine Lindy. July 25, 1970. General Services Administration Alcatraz Records, Region 9, Box 15. RG 291. Leo J. Ryan Memorial Archives and Records Center. National Archives and Records Administration. Pacific Sierra Region. San Bruno, Calif.

———. Letter to Whom It May Concern, American Indian Center, San Francisco, Calif. Nov. 20, 1969. RG 291. Leo J. Ryan Memorial Archives and Records Center. National Archives and Records Administration. Pacific Sierra Region. San Bruno, Calif.

———. Memorandum. Feb. 9, 1971. Original in the possession of Joe Morris, San Francisco, Calif.

———. Press Release. Nov. 10, 1969. Subgroup Alcatraz Disposal, Container 15. RG 291. Leo J. Ryan Memorial Archives and Records Center. National Archives and Records Administration. Pacific Sierra Region. San Bruno, Calif.

———. Press Release. Nov. 20, 1969. RG 291. Leo J. Ryan Memorial Archives and Records Center. National Archives and Records Administration. Pacific Sierra Region. San Bruno, Calif.

———. "Proclamation: To the Great White Father and All His People." Nov. 1969. Alcatraz File. American Indian Studies Center Library. University of California at Los Angeles.

———. "Reply to Counter-Proposal of Robert Robertson for the U.S.A." Apr. 3, 1970. National Council on Indian Opportunity, Box 5, Folder 4. RG 220. National Archives, Washington, D.C.

———. "Why We Are on Alcatraz." Nov. 21, 1969. RG 291. Leo J. Ryan Memorial Archives and Records Center. National Archives and Records Administration. Pacific Sierra Region. San Bruno, Calif.

Jackson, Helen Hunt. *A Century of Dishonor: A Sketch of the United States Government's Dealings with Some of the Indian Tribes.* Boston: Robert Brothers, 1885.

Josephy, Alvin, Jr. *The American Indian and the Bureau of Indian Affairs— 1969: A Study with Recommendations.* Toronto: Indian-Eskimo Association of Canada, 1969.

———. *Red Power: The American Indians' Fight for Freedom.* New York: American Heritage Press, 1971.

Kemnitzer, Luis. "Personal Memories of Alcatraz, 1969." *American Indian Culture and Research Journal* 18, no. 4 (1994): 103–9.

Knifechief, John. Interview by Clare Engles. Oct. 26, 1970. Doris Duke Oral History Project. American Indian Historical Research Project. Manuscript 417. Manuscripts Division. Marriott Library. University of Utah. Salt Lake City.

Knifechief, Lois. Interview by Clare Engles. Oct. 26, 1970. Doris Duke Oral History Project. American Indian Historical Research Project. Manuscript 417. Manuscripts Division. Marriott Library. University of Utah. Salt Lake City.

Krogh, Bud. Memorandum to John Ehrlichman. Aug. 13, 1970. Alcatraz File Group E. Krogh (1970–71), Box 10. Nixon Presidential Materials Project. Alexandria, Va.

———. Memorandum to John Ehrlichman. Sept. 14, 1970. Alcatraz File Group E. Krogh (1970–71), Box 10. Nixon Presidential Materials Project. Alexandria, Va.

———. Memorandum to John Ehrlichman. Dec. 11, 1970. Alcatraz File Group E. Krogh (1970–71), Box 10. Nixon Presidential Materials Project. Alexandria, Va.

———. Memorandum to John Ehrlichman. June 10, 1971. Alcatraz File Group E. Krogh (1970–71), Box 10. Nixon Presidential Materials Project. Alexandria, Va.

———. Memorandum to John Ehrlichman with Enclosed Memorandum from Ehrlichman to John A. Volpe. Mar. 5, 1970. Alcatraz File Group E. Krogh (1970–71), Box 10. Nixon Presidential Materials Project. Alexandria, Va.

Laws, Richard. Letter to Thomas Mellon. Dec. 3, 1969. Federal Bureau of Investigation Case File 70–51261. Subject File "Alcatraz Indian Occupation,

1969–71." Records Section. Federal Bureau of Investigation Headquarters. Pentagon. Washington, D.C.

———. Memorandum to T. E. Hannon. Nov. 19, 1969. RG 291. Leo J. Ryan Memorial Archives and Records Center. National Archives and Records Administration. Pacific Sierra Region. San Bruno, Calif.

Leach, Leo. Interview by Anna Boyd. Feb. 4, 1970. Doris Duke Oral History Project. American Indian Historical Research Project. Special Collections. University of New Mexico at Albuquerque.

Leach, Stella. Interview by Anna Boyd. Feb. 4, 1970. Doris Duke Oral History Project. American Indian Historical Research Project. Special Collections. University of New Mexico at Albuquerque.

———. Interview by John Trudell on "Radio Free Alcatraz." Undated. Archive no. BB2309. Pacifica Radio Archives. North Hollywood, Calif.

Livermore, Earl. Interview by John D. Sylvester. Apr. 8, 1970. Doris Duke Oral History Project. American Indian Historical Research Project. Manuscript 417. Manuscripts Division. Marriott Library. University of Utah. Salt Lake City.

Lopez, Eleanor. Interview by Don Carroll. May 15, 1970. Box 6. RG 291. Leo J. Ryan Memorial Archives and Records Center. National Archives and Records Administration. Pacific Sierra Region. San Bruno, Calif.

Lopez, Lou. Interview by John Garvey. June 1, 1992. San Francisco. Tape in the possession of John Garvey, San Francisco, Calif.

Magruder, Jeb. Memorandum to Bud Krogh. Aug. 27, 1970. Alcatraz File Group E. Krogh (1970–71), Box 10. Nixon Presidential Materials Project. Alexandria, Va.

Mander, Joseph E. Telegram to President Nixon. Nov. 24, 1969. White House Central Files, Subject File IN (Oct. 1–Dec. 31, 1969), Box 4. Nixon Presidential Materials Project. Alexandria, Va.

Mankiller, Wilma. Interview by author. Nov. 27, 1991. Los Angeles. Transcript in the possession of the author.

———. Letter to author. Nov. 27, 1991. Original in the possession of the author.

Mankiller, Wilma, and Michael Wallis. *Mankiller: A Chief and Her People.* New York: St. Martin's Press, 1993.

Martin, Harry W. "Correlates of Adjustment among American Indians in an Urban Environment." *Human Organization* 23, no. 4 (1964): 290–95.

Matthiessen, Peter. *In the Spirit of Crazy Horse.* New York: Viking Press, 1983.

McBeth, Sally J. *Ethnic Identity and the Boarding School Experience of West-Central Oklahoma American Indians.* Washington, D.C.: University Press of America, 1983.

McKay-Want, Rosalie. "The Meaning of Alcatraz." Quoted in Judith Antell, "American Indian Women Activists," Ph.D diss. University of California at Berkeley, 1989.

McKenzie, Richard Delaware Dion, Plaintiff, v. United States of America, Steward Lee Udall, Defendant. Complaint for Injunctive Relief, Declaratory Relief, and in the Alternative, for Money Judgment. Sept. 13, 1965. Copy in the possesion of the author.

Meeting with Federal Officials on the Island of Alcatraz. Minutes. Feb. 23, 1970. National Council on Indian Opportunity, Box 5, Folder 4. RG 220. National Archives, Washington, D.C.

Miller, Al. Interview by John Trudell on "Radio Free Alcatraz." Dec. 22, 1969. Archive no. BB5456. Pacifica Radio Archives. North Hollywood, Calif.

Miller, Dorothy Lonewolf. "Alcatraz Rain." Ms. Dec. 1969. Copy in the possession of the author.

Milliken, Randall. "An Ethnohistory of the Indian People of the San Francisco Bay Area from 1770 to 1810." Ph.D. diss. University of California at Berkeley, 1991.

Miracle, Marilyn. "Bay Area Native American Council." In *Alcatraz Is Not an Island*, ed. Peter Blue Cloud. Berkeley: Wingbow Press, 1972. 55.

———. Interview by Dennis Stanford. Feb. 5, 1970. Transcript. Doris Duke Oral History Project. American Indian Historical Research Project. Special Collections. University of New Mexico at Albuquerque.

Montgomery, Bruce. Interview by John Garvey. Washington, D.C. Nov. 21, 1984. Tape in the possession of John Garvey, San Francisco, Calif.

Montoya, Tom. Interview by Michelle Vignes. Dec. 1970. San Francisco. Tape. Alcatraz Island Library. San Francisco, Calif.

Moreland, Walter C. Memorandum to San Francisco Regional Administrator, GSA. Mar. 13, 1963. Subgroup Alcatraz Disposal, Series Scott 1963–71, Box 1. RG 291. Leo J. Ryan Memorial Archives and Records Center. National Archives and Records Administration. Pacific Sierra Region. San Bruno, Calif.

Morris, Joseph. Interview by the author. Jan. 5, 1996. Transcript in the possession of the author.

Murphy, George. Statement Regarding Future of Alcatraz Island. Dec. 18, 1969. White House Central Files, Staff Member and Office Files, Bradley H. Patterson Jr., Box 9. Nixon Presidential Materials Project. Alexandria, Va.

Nagel, Joan. *American Indian Ethnic Renewal: Red Power and the Resurgence of Identity and Culture.* Ms. University of Kansas at Lawrence, 1995.

National Council on Indian Opportunity. "Alcatraz Indian Matter." Nov. 22, 1969. National Council on Indian Opportunity, Box 4, Folder 1. RG 220. National Archives, Washington, D.C.

———. Minutes of Public Forum before the Committee of Urban Indians. Apr. 11–12, 1969. San Francisco. National Council on Indian Opportunity, Box 9, Folder 3. RG 220. National Archives, Washington, D.C.

National Park Service. *The Golden Gate—A Matchless Opportunity: A Report to the Secretary of the Interior on the Proposed Golden Gate National Recreation Area, California.* Dec. 13, 1969. Box 15, Folder Alcatraz I. RG 291. Leo J. Ryan Memorial Archives and Records Center. National Archives and Records Administration. Pacific Sierra Region. San Bruno, Calif.

Native American Research Group. *American Indian Socialization to Urban Life: Final Report.* San Francisco: Institute for Scientific Analysis, 1975.

Neils, Elaine M. *Reservation to City: Indian Migration and Federal Relocation.* University of Chicago Research Paper no. 131. Chicago: University of Chicago, 1971.

Nixon, Richard. Handwriting File. President's Office File (Sept. 1969–Sept. 1970), Box 3. Nixon Presidential Materials Project. Alexandria, Va.

———. *In the Arena: A Memoir of Victory, Defeat, and Renewal.* New York: Simon and Schuster, 1990.

———. Letter to James Frank. Sept. 30, 1970. White House Central Files, Subject File IN (Jan. 1–Mar. 31, 1970). Nixon Presidential Materials Project. Alexandria, Va.

———. "Message to Congress." *Congressional Record.* 91st Cong., 2d sess. Vol. 116, no. 17, p. 23258.

Oakes, Richard. "Alcatraz Is Not an Island." *Ramparts,* Dec. 1972, 35–40.

———. Interview by John Trudell on "Radio Free Alcatraz." Dec. 23, 1969. Archive no. BB5457. Pacifica Radio Archives. North Hollywood, Calif.

———. Telephone conversation with William T. Davorenon, Department of Interior Regional Coordinator. Nov. 21, 1969. San Francisco, Calif. National Council on Indian Opportunity, Box 4, Folder 1. RG 220. National Archives, Washington, D.C.

Odier, Pierre. *The Rock: A History of Alcatraz the Fort/the Prison.* Eagle Rock, Calif.: L'Image Odier, 1982.

Office of the Director of the Federal Bureau of Investigation. "Indian Occupation of Alcatraz Island." Memorandum to San Francisco FBI Office. Mar. 15, 1971. Alcatraz File Group E. Krogh (1970–71), Box 10. Nixon Presidential Materials Project. Alexandria, Va.

Ohlone Indians of California. Petition to Indians of All Tribes, Alcatraz Island. Jan. 6, 1970. File Alcatraz II, Container 15, Folder 2. RG 291. Leo J. Ryan Memorial Archives and Records Center. National Archives and Records Administration. Pacific Sierra Region. San Bruno, Calif.

———. Petition to the President of the United States. Jan. 22, 1970. White House Central Files, Subject File IN (Jan. 1–May 31, 1971), Box 5, File 1 of 2. Nixon Presidential Materials Project. Alexandria, Va.

Oliver, William D. Memorandum to T. E. Hannon. Dec. 31, 1969. Container

Alcatraz I, Folder 1. RG 291. Leo J. Ryan Memorial Archives and Records Center. National Archives and Records Administration. Pacific Sierra Region. San Bruno, Calif.

Orfield, Gary. *A Study of the Termination Policy.* Denver: National Congress of American Indians, 1967.

Ours, Howard W. Memorandum to T. E. Hannon. Mar. 13, 1970. GJ-Calif-786. RG 291. Leo J. Ryan Memorial Archives and Records Center. National Archives and Records Administration. Pacific Sierra Region. San Bruno, Calif.

———. Memorandum to T. E. Hannon. Apr. 27, 1970. GJ-Calif-786. RG 291. Leo J. Ryan Memorial Archives and Records Center. National Archives and Records Administration. Pacific Sierra Region. San Bruno, Calif.

Parrish, La Rayne. Interview by Anna Boyd. Feb. 5, 1970. Transcript. Doris Duke Oral History Project. American Indian Historical Research Project. Special Collections. University of New Mexico at Albuquerque.

Patterson, Bradley H., Jr. "Alcatraz—Comment on Geoff Shepard's Memorandum of November 24." Memorandum to Bud Krogh. Nov. 24, 1970. Alcatraz File Group E. Krogh (1970–71), Box 10. Nixon Presidential Materials Project. Alexandria, Va.

———. Interview by Terry W. Good. Sept. 10, 1974. Old Executive Office Building, Washington, D.C. Transcript in the possession of John Garvey, San Francisco, Calif.

———. Letter to Colleen Waggoner, University of Oklahoma Press, Norman, Okla. Oct. 1, 1993. Copy in the possession of the author.

———. Letter to Robert Coop. Apr. 19, 1971. White House Central Files, Subject File IN (Jan. 1–May 31, 1971). Nixon Presidential Materials Project. Alexandria, Va.

———. Memorandum to Bud Krogh. Nov. 25, 1970. White House Central Files, Staff Member and Office Files, E. Krogh (1970–71), Box 10. Nixon Presidential Materials Project. Alexandria, Va.

———. Memorandum to Tod Hullin. Sept. 20, 1971. White House Central Files, Staff Member and Office Files, E. Krogh (1970–71). RG 220. Nixon Presidential Materials Project. Alexandria, Va.

———. "Notes concerning Alcatraz." Jan. 26, 1970. White House Central Files, File Group E. Krogh (1970–71), Box 10. Nixon Presidential Materials Project. Alexandria, Va.

———. *The Ring of Power: The White House Staff and Its Expanding Role in Government.* New York: Basic Books, 1988.

———. Telephone interview by author. July 9, 1992. Transcript in the possession of the author.

Peters, John A. Memorandum to T. E. Hannon. Apr. 15, 1970. GJ-Calif-786. RG 291. Leo J. Ryan Memorial Archives and Records Center. National Archives and Records Administration. Pacific Sierra Region. San Bruno, Calif.

———. Memorandum to T. E. Hannon. Apr. 16, 1970. GJ-Calif-786. RG 291. Leo J. Ryan Memorial Archives and Records Center. National Archives and Records Administration. Pacific Sierra Region. San Bruno, Calif.

Petition to the President and Secretary of the Interior Signed by Forty-Six Petitioners. Dec. 1, 1969. White House Central Files, Subject File IN (Oct. 1–Dec. 31, 1969), Box 4. Nixon Presidential Materials Project. Alexandria, Va.

Pipestem, Browning. "Off Record Conversation." Undated. National Council on Indian Opportunity, Box 4, Folder 1. RG 220. National Archives, Washington, D.C.

Presidential Task Force on the American Indian. "Federal-Indian Relations." Report. 1966–67. Quoted in Alvin Josephy, Jr., *The American Indian and the Bureau of Indian Affairs—1969: A Study with Recommendations* (Toronto: Indian-Eskimo Association of Canada, 1969), 66–67.

President's Commission on the Disposition of Alcatraz Island. "Alcatraz Island Explanatory Statement, Addendum No. 1." Subgroup Alcatraz Disposal, Series Scott 1963–71, Box 1. RG 291. Leo J. Ryan Memorial Archives and Records Center. National Archives and Records Administration. Pacific Sierra Region. San Bruno, Calif.

———. Minutes. Mar. 21, 1964. Subgroup Alcatraz Disposal, Series Scott 1963–71, Box 1. RG 291. Leo J. Ryan Memorial Archives and Records Center. National Archives and Records Administration. Pacific Sierra Region. San Bruno, Calif.

———. "Report of the Commission on the Disposition of Alcatraz Island." Draft. June 15, 1964. Subgroup Alcatraz Disposal, Series Scott 1963–71, Box 1. RG 291. Leo J. Ryan Memorial Archives and Records Center. National Archives and Records Administration. Pacific Sierra Region. San Bruno, Calif.

Prucha, Francis P. *Americanizing the American Indian: Writings by the "Friends of the Indian," 1880–1900*. Lincoln: University of Nebraska Press, 1978.

Remington, Douglas. Interview by John Trudell on "Radio Free Alcatraz." Jan. 5, 1970. Archive no. BB5457. Pacific Radio Archives. North Hollywood, Calif.

Report. Jan. 6, 1970. Alcatraz File, Container 15, Folder 2. RG 291. Leo J. Ryan Memorial Archives and Records Center. National Archives and Records Administration. Pacific Sierra Region. San Bruno, Calif.

Robertson, Robert. "Alcatraz Negotiations." Minutes. Jan. 10–12, 1970. National Council of Indian Opportunity, Box 4, Folder 2. RG 220. National Archives, Washington, D.C.

———. "Alternate Alcatraz Plan: For All People." Undated. National Council on Indian Opportunity, Box 5, Folder 3. RG 220. National Archives, Washington, D.C.

———. "Bay Indians Meet on Alcatraz Issue." Jan. 15, 1970. National Council on Indian Opportunity, Box 5, Folder 4. RG 220. National Archives, Washington, D.C.

———. "Consensus of Ad Hoc Interagency Group." Jan.–Feb. 1970. File Alcatraz II, Box 4, Folder 2. RG 220. National Archives, Washington, D.C.

———. Form Letter. White House Central Files, Subject File IN (Jan. 1–Mar. 31, 1970), Box 5. RG 220. Nixon Presidential Materials Project. Alexandria, Va.

———. Letter to Adam Nordwall. Jan. 14, 1970. National Council on Indian Opportunity, Box 4, Folder 3. RG 220. National Archives, Washington, D.C.

———. Memorandum. Dec. 10, 1969. National Council on Indian Opportunity, Box 4, Folder 1. RG 220. National Archives, Washington, D.C.

———. Memorandum for the File. Dec. 11, 1969. National Council on Indian Opportunity, Box 4, Folder 1. RG 220. National Archives, Washington, D.C.

———. Memorandum to Bradley H. Patterson Jr. Mar. 26, 1971. National Council on Indian Opportunity, Box 4, Folder 3. RG 220. National Archives, Washington, D.C.

———. Memorandum to Jerry Warren and Bobbie Green. July 15, 1970. National Council on Indian Opportunity, Box 4, Folder 3. RG 220. National Archives, Washington, D.C.

———. Telegram to Indians of All Tribes, Inc. Feb. 16, 1970. National Council on Indian Opportunity, Box 4, Folder 2. RG 220. National Archives, Washington, D.C.

San Francisco Regional Council. Minutes. Dec. 2, 1969. Box 15, Folder Alcatraz I. RG 291. Leo J. Ryan Memorial Archives and Records Center. National Archives and Records Administration. Pacific Sierra Region. San Bruno, Calif.

———. Minutes. Dec. 16, 1969. Container Alcatraz I, Folder 1. RG 291. Leo J. Ryan Memorial Archives and Records Center. National Archives and Records Administration. Pacific Sierra Region. San Bruno, Calif.

———. Minutes. Jan. 7, 1970. National Council on Indian Opportunity, Box 4, Folder 2. RG 220. National Archives, Washington, D.C.

Sarver, Thomas. Interview by John Garvey. Sept. 27, 1989. San Francisco. Tape in the possession of John Garvey, San Francisco, Calif.

Scott, Thomas. "Alcatraz Island Security." June 19, 1970. National Council on Indian Opportunity, Box 5, Folder 4, RG 220. National Archives, Washington, D.C.

———. Interview by Alcatraz Rangers. July 1988. Alcatraz Island. Videorecording. Alcatraz Island Library, San Francisco, Calif.

———. Memorandum for Official File 9DR. June 2, 1970. GJ-Calif-786. Alcatraz File, Box 13, Correspondence and Documents, 12 of 14. RG 291. Leo

J. Ryan Memorial Archives and Records Center. National Archives and Records Administration. Pacific Sierra Region. San Bruno, Calif.

———. Memorandum for the File. Mar. 24, 1964. Subgroup Alcatraz Disposal, Series Scott 1963–71, Box 1. RG 291. Leo J. Ryan Memorial Archives and Records Center. National Archives and Records Administration. Pacific Sierra Region. San Bruno, Calif.

———. Memorandum for the File. Feb. 17, 1970. GJ-Calif-786. Alcatraz File, Container 12. RG 291. Leo J. Ryan Memorial Archives and Records Center. National Archives and Records Administration. Pacific Sierra Region. San Bruno, Calif.

———. Memorandum for the File. Feb. 26, 1970. Alcatraz File, Container 15. RG 291. Leo J. Ryan Memorial Archives and Records Center. National Archives and Records Administration. Pacific Sierra Region. San Bruno, Calif.

———. Memorandum for the File. June 19, 1970. National Council on Indian Opportunity, Box 5, Folder 4. RG 220. National Archives. Washington, D.C.

———. Memorandum to T. E. Hannon. Apr. 29, 1970. GJ-Calif-786. RG 291. Leo J. Ryan Memorial Archives and Records Center. National Archives and Records Administration. Pacific Sierra Region. San Bruno, Calif.

———. "Plans for Removal of Indians." Memorandum to T. E. Hannon. June 9, 1970. GJ-Calif-786. Subgroup Alcatraz Disposal. RG 291. Leo J. Ryan Memorial Archives and Records Center. National Archives and Records Administration. Pacific Sierra Region. San Bruno, Calif.

Scraper, Judy. Interview by Anna Boyd. Feb. 5, 1970. Transcript. Doris Duke Oral History Project. American Indian Historical Research Project. Special Collections. University of New Mexico at Albuquerque.

Senese, Guy. *Self-Determination and the Social Education of Native Americans.* New York: Praeger, 1991.

Shepard, Geoff. Memorandum to Bud Krogh. Nov. 27, 1970. Alcatraz File Group E. Krogh (1970–71), Box 10. Nixon Presidential Materials Project. Alexandria, Va.

Sklansky, Jeff. "Rock, Reservation, and Prison: The Native American Occupation of Alcatraz Island." *American Indian Culture and Research Journal* 13, no. 2 (1989): 44.

Smells, Sylvester. Interview by Michelle Vignes. Dec. 1970. Alcatraz Island. Tape. Alcatraz Island Library. San Francisco, Calif.

Spencer, Horace. Telephone interview by author. Oct. 19, 1992. Transcript in the possession of the author.

Steiner, Stan. *The New Indians.* New York: Harper and Row, 1968.

Talbot, Steve. "Free Alcatraz: The Culture of Native American Liberation." *Journal of Ethnic Studies* 6, no. 3 (Fall 1978): 90.

Thompson, Erwin N. *The Rock: A History of Alcatraz Island, 1847–1972.* Denver: Denver Service Center, Historic Preservation Division, 1977.

Thorpe, Grace. Interview by John Trudell on "Radio Free Alcatraz." Dec. 12, 1969. Archive no. BB5456. Pacifica Radio Archives. North Hollywood, Calif.

Trudell, John. Interview by Johnny YesNo on "Radio Free Alcatraz." Jan. 20, 1970. Archive no. BC0360. Pacifica Radio Archives. North Hollywood, Calif.

———. Interview by Ron J. Lujan. Feb. 5, 1970. Doris Duke Oral History Project. American Indian Historical Research Project. Special Collections. University of New Mexico at Albuquerque.

———. Interview by unknown interviewer on "Radio Free Alcatraz." Nov. 10, 1970. Archive no. BB5457. Pacifica Radio Archives. North Hollywood, Calif.

———. "Radio Free Alcatraz" Broadcasts. Archive no. BB5457. Pacifica Radio Archives. North Hollywood, Calif.

Trudell, John, and LaNada Boyer. "Planning Grant Proposal to Develop an All Indian University and Cultural Complex on Indian Land, Alcatraz." Feb. 1970. National Council on Indian Opportunity, Box 5, Folder 4. RG 220. National Archives, Washington, D.C.

U.S. Coast Guard. Confidential Correspondence. Undated. General Services Administration Alcatraz Records, Region 9, Box 15, Folder 8. RG 291. Leo J. Ryan Memorial Archives and Records Center. National Archives and Records Administration. Pacific Sierra Region. San Bruno, Calif.

———. Press Release. Undated. General Services Administration Alcatraz Records, Box 12, Folder 3. RG 291. Leo J. Ryan Memorial Archives and Records Center. National Archives and Records Administration. Pacific Sierra Region. San Bruno, Calif.

U.S. Congress, House of Representatives, Committee on Interior and Insular Affairs, Subcommittee on Indian Affairs. *Indian Relocation and Industrial Development Programs.* 83d Cong., 1st sess., 1957.

U.S. Department of the Interior. Press Release. Nov. 20, 1969. National Council on Indian Opportunity, Box 4, Folder 1. RG 220. National Archives, Washington, D.C.

Verdet, Paula. "Summary of Research on Indians in St. Louis and Chicago." Ms. 1959. Copy in American Indian Studies Center Library, University of California at Los Angeles.

Veterans Administration. Statistical Brief, Native American Veterans. SB 70–85–3. Oct. 1985. Veterans Administration Archives. Veterans Administration Headquarters. Washington, D.C.

Volpe, John A. Memorandum to John Ehrlichman. Undated, received Feb. 4, 1970. Alcatraz File Group E. Krogh (1970–71), Box 10. Nixon Presidential Materials Project. Alexandria, Va.

Waldie, Jerome R. "Angry American Indians." *Congressional Record.* July 15, 1970. 91st Cong., 2d sess. Vol. 116, no. 18, p. 22987.

Washburn, Wilcomb E. *Red Man's Land/White Man's Law: A Study of the Past and Present State of the American Indian.* New York: Charles Scribner's Sons, 1971.

Weibel-Orlando, Joan. *Indian Country, L.A.: Maintaining Ethnic Community in Complex Society.* Urbana: University of Illinois Press, 1991.

White House. "Nixon's Statement on Indians." Press Release. July 8, 1970. Alcatraz File Group E. Krogh (1970–71), Box 10. Nixon Presidential Materials Project. Alexandria, Va.

———. Press Release to the National Congress of American Indians in Annual Convention at Omaha, Nebraska. Sept. 27, 1968. White House Central Files, Subject File IN (Sept. 30–Dec. 31, 1969), Box 1. Nixon Presidential Materials Project. Alexandria, Va.

Whiteley, Peter. *Bacavi: Journey to Reed Springs.* Flagstaff: Northland Press, 1988.

Wilson, Darryl. "Alcatraz Is Not an Island." Paper presented at the conference American Indians in Higher Education. University of California at Davis. Oct. 27, 1991.

Yackitonipah, Howard. Interview by Marian Ryan. Nov. 20, 1970. Doris Duke Oral History Project. American Indian Historical Research Project. Manuscript 417. Manuscripts Division. Marriott Library. University of Utah. Salt Lake City.

Zimbardo, Philip G. "Pathology of Imprisonment." *Society* 9, no. 6 (Apr. 1972): 5–6.

Index

/\\.\\/\\.\\/\\.\\

Self-determination of Native
Americans, 14, 33, 34, 39, 42, 43,
45, 63, 69, 74, 90, 96, 99, 102,
103, 115, 117, 133, 179, 197, 198,
211, 217, 220
Seminole, 131
Senate Indian Education Subcom-
mittee, 177
Shasta Community Action Project,
231
Shaw, Gilbert, 191
Shelton, Fred, 61
Shepard, Geoff, 206, 207
Sherlock Indian School, 105
Sherman Institute, 7
Signs: painted by occupiers on
Alcatraz, 67, 106, 115
Simmons, Herbert, 83
Sioux, 147, 227, 228, 229
Sioux Club, 175
Sioux Treaty of 1868, 17, 18, 21, 59,
119, 231
Six Nations, 37, 226, 235
Skaggs Spring Road, 230
Skolaskin (Sanpoil prisoner), 3
Sloluck (Modoc prisoner), 3
Smith, Nolan, 20
Smith, Sidney, 185
Southwest Museum: protest at, 230
Sovereign rights, 14
Spang, Ray, 82
Spanish mission, 2, 234
Spencer, Horace, 159, 161, 164, 165
Spiritual center: proposed for
Alcatraz, 106, 120, 132
Spotted Elk, Garfield, 16
Standing Eagle, Virgil, 20
Stanley Island, 226
Stans, Maurice H., 35
Steward, Joseph, 2
Stewart Indian School, 105
Stewart Point, 230
St. John the Evangelist Episcopal
Church, 88
St. Marie, Buffy, 122, 138, 159, 227
St. Regis Reservation, 37, 52, 226

Student Non-Violent Coordinating
Committee, 28, 29, 30, 31
Students, Indian, 4, 35, 108
Students for a Democratic Society,
29
Stuntz, Joseph, 238
Sun Dance, 233
Supertankers: collision of, 208
Supratribal activity, 37
Support: from Bay Area for occupa-
tion, 79, 90, 107, 118, 122, 124,
126, 196, 198, 201, 204
Surplus Property Commission, 22,
23
Survival of American Indians, 235

Talbot, Steve, 51, 83, 86
Taos Blue Lake, 41, 42, 44, 45, 192,
198, 207, 217, 218, 228
Telephone service: on Alcatraz, 193
Tepper, Dr. (Alcatraz physician),
185
Termination era, 7, 13, 33, 34, 37,
42, 43, 143, 197, 198, 217
Textbooks: portrayal of Indians in,
35, 36
Thanksgiving 1969: on Alcatraz, 90,
91, 129
The Movement, 3
Third World Liberation Strike, 45,
52
Thom, Melvin, 33
Thomas, Robert, 32
Thompson, Morris, 182
Thorpe, Dagmar, 90
Thorpe, Grace, 45, 80, 108–9, 110,
164, 205, 210, 211, 227, 229, 232
Thorpe, Jim, 90, 120
Thunderbirds, 157
Tin Barn Road, 230
Tlingit, 147
Tlingit-Haida Club, 13
Toyon Job Corps Center, 231
Trail of Broken Treaties, 231, 234
Training school: on Alcatraz, 51,
106, 107

TROY R. JOHNSON received his Ph.D. from the University of California at Los Angeles and is currently on the faculty of the American Indian Studies Program and History Department at California State University at Long Beach. He is an internationally published author and is the editor of *You Are on Indian Land!: Alcatraz Island, 1969–1971* and *Alcatraz, Indian Land Forever: Activism Poetry and Political Statements from Alcatraz Island* and coeditor of *Alcatraz Revisited: The Twenty-Fifth Anniversary of the Occupation*, a special issue of the *American Indian and Culture Research Journal*. Johnson is associate editor of *Native America: Portrait of the Peoples, Chronology of Native North American History*, and *Native North American Almanac*.